NAPOLEON'S
MARSHALS

NAPOLEON'S MARSHALS

by R. F. Delderfield

A SCARBOROUGH BOOK

STEIN AND DAY/*Publishers*/New York

FIRST SCARBOROUGH BOOKS EDITION 1980

Napoleon's Marshals was originally published in hardcover by Chilton Book Company and is reprinted by arrangement.

Copyright © 1962, 1966 by R. F. Delderfield

Printed in the United States of America
Stein and Day/*Publishers*/Scarborough House, Briarcliff Manor, N.Y. 10510

Library of Congress Catalog Card Number 66–162–87
ISBN 0-8128–6055–1

CONTENTS

Dedicated to

GENERAL SIR BRIAN HORROCKS
K.C.B., K.B.E., D.S.O., M.C. LL.D. (HON.)

whose recent broadcasts have done so much to
present the military art to the man in the street.

R.F.D.
March 1961

PREFACE AND DRAMATIS PERSONAE

The Empire founded by Napoleon I began in December 1804 and came to an end in June 1815. During this period a total of twenty-six fighting men were awarded the baton their chief claimed was concealed in the knapsack of every private soldier in the armies of France. But Napoleon's control of France, and of a large part of Europe, was not limited to these eleven years. It had its beginning more than eight years earlier after his crop of astounding victories in Northern Italy and was finally established after his seizure of power during the *coup d'état* known as "Brumaire," in November 1799.

The men who subsequently became marshals of the Empire were already holding high rank when Napoleon became head of the state, although almost all of them did, in fact, spring from humble origins and owed their first boost to the Revolution.

This is the story of twenty-six men who held a Continent in thrall for almost twenty years. I have tried to tell a story of personalities rather than of events. Histories of the era are written for the reader who is fairly familiar with the main sequence of occurrences and the leading figures who shaped them; to write simply another history of the First Empire is not the purpose of this book. It requires a lifetime of study to understand the impact Napoleon had upon his generation and upon the political pattern of Europe that followed his eclipse at Waterloo. This story is for the average reader who may want to know something more of the brave, ambitious men who sustained the weight of Napoleon's throne—how they began, how they reacted to power, how they met their several ends, what kind of employers they seemed to the men who followed them and how they behaved to the man who had elevated them from stable boys and traveling salesmen to places in history where their names became legends in their own lifetime.

It would, of course, be quite impossible to tell the story of Napoleon's marshals without giving a brief account of the battles and campaigns in which they were engaged over two decades, but all the time I have been at work upon this book I have kept in mind the fact that most readers of biography are more interested in people than in the ebb and flow of military conquests that took place a hundred and fifty years before the explosion of Hiroshima made this kind of warfare as old-fashioned as Caesar's.

All that is necessary to follow this story is a map of Europe and the cast-list appended below. For the rest, I hope that these remarkable men will speak for themselves.

Here are the dramatis personae of the story:

Created marshals by Imperial decree, in 1804:

KELLERMAN	who began as a regular soldier with the rank of ensign.
LEFÈBVRE	who began as a hussar.
PÉRIGNON	who began as a grenadier.
SÉRURIER	who began as a sub-lieutenant.
BERTHIER	who was an engineer turned professional soldier.
MURAT	an innkeeper's son originally destined for the church.
MONCEY	who set out to become a lawyer.
JOURDAN	a doctor's son who walked the roads with a peddler's pack on his back.
MASSÉNA	who had been cabin-boy, smuggler and fruit-seller before he became an officer.
AUGEREAU	whose first wages were earned as a footman.
BERNADOTTE	a lawyer's son turned professional soldier who rose to be a sergeant major.
SOULT	who set his heart on becoming a village baker.
BRUNE	who began studying law but always wanted to be a writer.
LANNES	who began life as an apprentice dyer.
MORTIER	the half-English son of a small farmer.
NEY	who was set to work as a barrel cooper but ran away to become a hussar.
DAVOUT	who entered the Royal army as a sub-lieutenant.
BESSIÈRES	whose first job was that of a barber.

In 1807 Napoleon began adding to this imposing list, promoting several high-ranking generals on their merits. The first addition was:

VICTOR	a revolutionary sergeant in the Royal army.

In 1809 Napoleon gave three more men the baton. They were:

MACDONALD   the son of an exiled Scots clansman, who became an officer cadet at the age of twenty-two.

MARMONT   who began as an artillery cadet.

OUDINOT   who thought of following his father in the brewery trade but joined the army when the Revolution broke out.

Each year, from 1811 onwards until the fall of the Empire, Napoleon chose one more man to join the Marshalate. They were:

SUCHET   whose father was a silk manufacturer.

ST. CYR   who began life as a student of engineering and gave lessons in drawing to earn extra money.

PONIATOWSKI   who was the nephew of a Polish prince and followed the trade of arms all his life.

During the brief Waterloo campaign one more man was given a marshal's baton. He was:

GROUCHY   the son of a marquis, who enlisted as a volunteer on the side of the people when the Revolution began.

Here then are the twenty-six who were to grasp at crowns, quarrel, intrigue, fight, march, and die under the greatest captain of all time. They came from every walk of life, from the aristocracy, the middle classes and the rabble. Three things they had in common—ambition, extreme bravery, and the kind of pride that either elevates a man to the pinnacle of success or reduces him to the mental stature of an eight-year-old child.

CHAPTER ONE

DRUMBEAT

ON the afternoon of July 12, 1789, an excited but uncertain crowd of Parisians assembled in the Palais Royale. Hardly a person present knew why they were there. Each was drawn by the compulsion that often moves the individual when he sees a crowd gathering and succumbs to the curiosity that works upon city dwellers when a procession marches by. There was no procession on this occasion, simply a milling crowd of artisans, shopkeepers and shabby professional men, all apparently with nothing to do but discuss the recent decision of the States General to resolve itself into a permanent body that could not be dismissed by the King.

Outwardly there was nothing at all about this assembly to distinguish it from any other street demonstration. There were no advertised tub-thumpers and no banners, no emblems in hats or lapels, no real disorder calling for the appearance of police officers or troops of the Paris garrison. Suddenly, however, the mood of the gathering changed. Three young men, linked arm-by-arm, walked through the crowd shouting "To arms!" and almost at once another young man in threadbare clothes leaped onto a table and began to harangue the crowd. Within minutes the Palais Royale was seething with insurrection. The French Revolution, now generally recognized as by far the most important event of the eighteenth century, had begun.

Nobody knows the identities of the three young men whose cry prompted the fourth to make a speech, but the orator's name has come down to us as the man who set off the first of a series of detonations that were to continue at intervals down to this day.

This man's name was Camille Desmoulins, a twenty-eight-year-old

1

lawyer with a flair for pungent journalism. His words were not recorded but they must have had within them a power that no one, least of all himself, could recognize. Within forty-eight hours of his address the huge, lowering fortress of the Bastille, symbol of Bourbon absolutism, had been stormed and volcanoes of popular discontent, after grumbling for more than a century, erupted over the stinking, stifling city. Like a tide of lava the anger of the dispossessed rolled over the structure of church and state, carrying everything before it, kings, queens, aristocracy, priests, and centuries of privilege.

Above all, privilege! For generations now advancement in all professions, and particularly in that of the armed forces, had been regulated by birth and birth alone. No private soldier, no matter how much zeal or talent he displayed, could hope to rise beyond the rank of regimental sergeant major and only then by a great display of loyalty to the crown. The troops responsible for the King's person were not even French but Swiss mercenaries. Patriotism counted for nothing, noble lineage for everything.

All this was to change within months. All over France men saw hope of advancement opening up for them and none more surely or more joyfully than men living in barracks. Troops called out to drive the mobs back to their slums sided with the revolutionaries. Regimental deputations rode into Paris with assurances of loyalty for the new Government. One such deputation has an important place in this story and it will serve as a starting point.

.   .   .

Looking back over a period of more than a century and a half it is easy to fall into the error of supposing that the French Revolution was sustained by the power of the Paris mobs. This is not so. The mobs and their will-o'-the-wisp leaders did play an important role in the succession of riots that commenced with the attack on the Bastille in July, 1789, and ended with Napoleon's seizure of power a few weeks before the end of the century, but the real impetus of the Revolution came from two classes—disgruntled professional men, who supplied most of the politicians, and junior officers and NCO's of the armed forces. Had this latter group proved loyal to the crown the Revolution would have been stamped out in a few weeks and France might have remained a monarchy throughout the whole of the nineteenth century. As it was the presence of brave and intelligent malcontents in the army, men who hated the nepotism and inefficiency of the Bourbons, provided the fifth column which enabled the idealists and ranters of Paris to convert words into deeds that rocked every throne in Europe.

One such malcontent was a nineteen-year-old Burgundian lieutenant, quartered at Arras. His name was Louis Nicholas Davout and he came from an old aristocratic family in Auxerre. When the Paris courier came into Arras with the momentous news of the fall of the Bastille nobody questioned him with more thoroughness than Louis Davout. The subaltern was a serious young man, a keen reader of political science, and a thoughtful if somewhat pedantic student of his profession.

As far back as anyone could remember the Davouts had followed the profession of arms, but so far this youth had made no great impression upon his superiors. His sole, distinguishing characteristic was his slovenly mode of dress and his contempt for the foppery of his fellow subalterns. Gleaming brass and powdered periwigs had no attractions for Louis Davout. His conception of a perfect soldier was a man who addressed himself exclusively to the mechanics of his job and went into action after making careful provision for every eventuality—a dashing attack, a stubborn defense, and, if necessary, a fighting and orderly withdrawal. At nineteen he had already acquired a reputation for cross-grained obstinacy. His voice was never raised in laughter in the mess. He spent neither time nor money on the pursuit of women or at the card tables. He despised the outward displays of martial life and kept very much to himself, making no friends and refusing to pay lip-service to those who could have hoisted him up the military ladder.

He was probably the most unpopular cadet in the regiment but although many laughed at his unsociability and his badly tied stock, they did so behind his back. Nobody cared to mention these deficiencies to his face for there was something about Davout that commanded a grudging respect. So it was that when this unlikely young officer walked into the mess a few weeks after the fall of the Bastille and calmly suggested that a deputation of officers should ride to Paris and pledge the loyalty of the Royal Champagne regiment to the new government, nobody thought of arresting him as a traitor to the king. They heard what he had to say and then elected him their leader, an honor he accepted with a curt nod.

News of this curious mutiny soon filtered down to the sergeants' mess where it found immediate sympathy. The sergeants had their own barrack-room lawyer ready to accompany Lieutenant Davout to Paris, and the stiff, humorless officer was at once joined by a man who was a complete contrast to him in every way save in the radicalism that brought them together.

The sergeants' spokesman was a plump, rosy-faced little man who adored the sound of his own voice and cheerfully accepted the risks of mutiny in exchange for the importance that went with it. His real name was Claude Perrin but it seemed to him undistinguished and he preferred to call himself "Victor." His bristling self-importance had already carried him from drummerboy to the rank of sergeant and now, with the tide of new ideas rolling across France, he could almost see himself as a commissioned officer on terms of equality with the tightlipped Davout.

Together they trotted down the road to Paris, Davout silent and even more thoughtful than usual, Sergeant Victor-Perrin babbling away to his heart's content, speculating upon the prizes that might fall to sensible soldiers who got in on the ground floor of a successful revolution. Side by side they rode, two future marshals of France and not in their wildest dreams did they imagine what fame, riches, and alternative choices of loyalty the years had in store for them or that after more than two decades of glory one would sacrifice everything to honor and the other would make a business of hunting down old friends and handing them over to Royalists.

.   .   .

Davout was not the only serving officer who saw preferment beyond the smoke of the festive bonfires.

In at least five other garrison towns were men of good birth who openly sided with the revolutionaries and pushed themselves forward, demanding to serve France rather than its feeble king.

François Kellerman, a veteran soldier of the Seven Years war, was fifty-four when the Bastille fell. The son of a prosperous merchant he had begun soldiering as an ensign at the age of eighteen and was already close to retiring age. He was a big, hearty man and a proved giver and taker of hard knocks. He was also bilingual, speaking French and German with equal fluency, for he came from Strasbourg, on the northeastern border. Kellerman was not the kind of man to play safe and wait for the Paris cats to jump. He came roaring into the open as an out-and-out radical and from that moment he never looked back. He would have been struck dumb with amazement if somebody had whispered in his ear that the Revolution would make him a duke.

In the quarters of another professional soldier an even more startling act of partisanship was witnessed. The friends of twenty-three-years-old Emmanuel Grouchy gasped when they heard that the son of a marquis had not only espoused the cause of the Revolution but had volunteered to serve in the army as a private soldier! Young Grouchy did just this, deliberately turning his back on wealth and privilege and soon lost himself in the ranks of the patriots. He was to lose himself again twenty-six years later but this time he was carrying a marshal's baton at the head of thirty-three thousand men.

· · ·

The fires of the Revolution were burning in unexpected places that summer and the example of Grouchy was not so astonishing as it might have been. Soon it was clear to the most reactionary supporters of the established order that the mob orators had made some remarkable converts among the privileged and that not all their recruits were slum-dwellers and discontented sergeants.

Count Sérurier was forty-seven when he heard the news from Paris. He thought about it for a few weeks—he was a very slow-thinking man—and then announced that a radical change of government would be an excellent thing for his beloved country and his equally beloved profession; having said this aloud he threw in his lot with the revolutionaries. He had been a soldier since he was thirteen and it had taken him thirty-four years to reach the rank of major. Promotion was somewhat speedier now. He became a general of division in a few weeks.

Sérurier was a typical soldier of the dying eighteenth century, stolid, unimaginative, reliable, honest, and badly scarred. His decision must have made a great impression upon scores of waverers in the lower ranks of the army, and among those who heard about it was a half-Scots gentleman-cadet called Etienne Macdonald. Although born in Sedan, Macdonald had retained all the characteristics of his Scottish ancestors. He was dour, deliberate, honest, and extremely courageous. Twenty years before he was born his father had fought and marched beside Bonnie Prince Charlie, in the Young Pretender's spectacular attempt to seize the Stuart crown from the Hanoverians. Macdonald senior had fled to France after the collapse of his cause at Culloden, and had lived by following the only trade he knew. The hot blood of clansmen ran just as strongly in young Macdonald and when the people of France rose from their knees after a century and a half of absolutism he at once applauded their spirit, threw in his lot with the rebels, and was soon a lieutenant general. He was never an enthusiastic revolutionary, his inherited loyalty to a crown was too deep for that, but he was a man who wanted to make his way in the world and he had the kind of determination that carried Scotsmen to positions of authority all over the world when their clans were broken up by the brutish Butcher Cumberland after the "Forty-Five." Macdonald was to fight many battles in the years ahead but he was never sent to fight against the British. Napoleon said, half-jokingly, that he would never trust a Macdonald within sound of the bagpipes.

Not every liberal minded officer made a quick decision when the Revolution began to make progress all over the country. Here and there talented men hesitated, wanting to be sure before committing themselves one way or the other. One such man was a twenty-year-old artillery officer who had just completed the same course as that taken by a moody young Corsican, whose outlandish accent made his fellow students snigger. The more self-assured cadet was Auguste Frédéric Marmont and he was the son of a Burgundian ironmaster. The name of his gauche fellow cadet was Napoleon Bonaparte but at this period the Corsican spelled his name with a 'u.'

Marmont was an extremely shrewd young man, with dark good looks and an easy manner that won him many friends. It took those friends a long time to appreciate the true worth of Marmont's friendship but in due course they all formed an estimate, often to their cost. Not that this bothered Marmont, then or later. He outlived every single one of them, proving perhaps that in the end it was the waiting game that paid.

There was one other officer who was a long time making up his mind, but in this case the delay was due far more to a lack of self-confidence than to natural caution. His name was Louis Alexandre Berthier and he was thirty-six when the Bastille fell. Already he had shown great promise as a draftsman and staff officer. His loyalties should have been with the wretched, bewildered king, for his father was a distinguished military engineer who had been honored by the previous monarch. Berthier's first chance to distinguish himself came years before the Revolution, when the American colonists rose against the British King George III and fought a long war against the royal mercenaries. France sided with the colonists and Berthier was among the volunteers who went all the way to America to help them. He became a captain, served with distinction, and returned home to achieve steady promotion, ultimately becoming major general of the Royal Guard at Versailles.

So far his career should have given him every satisfaction but there was a single defect in his character. He was hopelessly indecisive when he was left on his own and was obliged to look around for someone more resolute in whom he could confide and to whom he could look for guidance when a decision was necessary. Throughout the early years of the Revolution we find him popping up here and there as a chief-of-staff, a post for which he was brilliantly equipped. He was in fact to become the most celebrated chief-of-staff in history and even now is still considered so, for despite his curious lack of confidence there was much to admire in Berthier's character. He was smart, loyal, steadfast, and meticulously careful in the performance of every job he undertook. He was also punctual and on hand whenever he was needed. Perhaps his lack of confidence stemmed from his appearance, for he was slightly built, almost ugly, and had a small head crowned by a shock of stiff, wiry hair. He tried very hard to offset these physical disadvantages by wearing brilliant and colorful uniforms and came to be recognized as the best-dressed man in the Imperial armies and the leader of military fashions. Even when summoned from his bed he was never caught in breeches and shirt. A night attack would find him faultlessly dressed, freshly shaved, and ready if necessary to dictate orders for twelve hours at a stretch. His memory for detail was phenomenal. At any given time he could reel off the fighting strength and positions of any formation in the army. When the news of the Revolution came to him he made no move in either direction. He was waiting for a shoulder upon which to lean and when he found one he followed it about for twenty years. The psychological shock of its removal was so great that it destroyed him.

So much for the officers, all of whom were to rise to greatness in the next decade. What of the rankers, the men who lived on hardtack and slept rough in the cheerless barracks of the Bourbon army?

.   .   .

There are eight who have a place in this story and the name of every one of them was to ring across Europe and the Near East before they were ten years older.

François Lefèbvre was a big, gruff, kind-hearted Alsatian who was thirty-four when the mob stormed the Bastille. He had just become sergeant major after fifteen years in the ranks. The son of a miller who had once been a hussar, François joined the Guards at eighteen. In character he was like the officer Kellerman, large-hearted, down-to-earth and master of a wry, drill-ground humor, the kind of sergeant major who might make an amiable joke about an awkward recruit with the object of encouraging the newcomer and getting a laugh from the ranks. NCO's like Lefèbvre are common in every army and are loved by the men they are paid to coach. He did not take very long to make up his mind what to do about events in Paris. He embraced the Revolution with large, hairy hands and was soon bellowing his way up the ladder.

Grenadier Dominique Pérignon was a similar but less picturesque regular. Aged thirty-five when the Revolution broke out he had been watching events in Paris with close attention, for he fancied his chances as a politician. Despairing of promotion in the army he flung himself wholeheartedly into politics, becoming a deputy in the legislative assembly, but he was far too unsubtle to compete with lawyers and tradesmen and was soon back in the army, working day and night to lick the enthusiastic recruits into shape for their onslaught upon the thrones of Europe.

Also studying current events with the closest attention was another sergeant major, by name Charles Bernadotte, a very different type of man from the hard-swearing Lefèbvre or the earnest Pérignon. He was a Gascon, born in Béarn and of Swiss descent. Tall, handsome, and with a large, curving nose he was physically imposing and highly intelligent. Nobody could ever quite make up their mind about Bernadotte and there are many contradictory comments on his strange, quirkish character. Most of his equals hated him and among the marshals he was to become distrusted as a climber, a fence-squatter, and a temporizer of questionable brilliance. Sometimes he was the traditional Gascon, roaring, strutting, and saber-rattling; at other times the kindest, quietest, most considerate soldier who ever buckled on a sword belt. He seemed to adjust his character and mood to every changing circumstance and whoever he happened to be with at the time, yet he was not a liar and was never wholly treacherous, for somehow he always justified actions that would have seemed outrageous had they been performed by anyone else. Perhaps he was only helping to steer his destiny. If so then he made a remarkably fine job of it, for when the mob surged up to the Bastille he was a regimental sergeant major and when all the shouting had died away he was a crown prince.

Back in France just in time to plunge into the hurly burly of the glorious Revolution was yet another professional ranker, perhaps the most colorful of them all and one who had already attained and thrown away most of the ranks in the military book. His name was Pierre Augereau and you were certain to find him in any fight that broke out in his district. He was not a Gascon but he looked and behaved like one. He was six feet in height, as strong as a bull, as tough as seasoned leather, and one of the best swordsmen in Europe. The son of a Paris mason who had married a German fruit-seller, Augereau grew up in the toughest district of the capital and earned his first wages as a footman. He was sacked for seducing a maid and took a job as a waiter but lost it for seducing a waitress. It was not that he was an incorrigible womanizer but simply that he liked to live dangerously and it soon occurred to him that he might get a better chance of doing so if he turned his back on civilian life.

At the age of about eighteen he joined the cavalry and after one false start seemed to be making headway for he became famous throughout the ranks as a swordsman and quickly disposed of two noted duellists, both of whom he killed outright. It was not long, however, before he was in serious trouble. A young officer struck him with his cane and was run through the body before he could summon his escort. Augereau fled to Switzerland and for a spell sold clocks and watches for a living. He carried his pack south-east to Constantinople and then further still, to Odessa, where, to his relief, a first-class war was in progress. He enlisted in the Russian army and became a sergeant but he did not care very much for the life of a Czarist soldier and soon drifted into Prussia, where he enlisted in the famous army of Frederick the Great. He might have done well here but there was a strong prejudice against foreigners and his promotion was blocked, so he made up his mind to desert and escape to the west.

Desertion from the Prussian army was very dangerous. Peasants were paid good money to bring in deserters, who were then shot out of hand, but this kind of risk did not deter a six-foot urchin who had already killed two famous duellists, one officer of the Royal Guards of France, and an unknown number of Turks during his Russian adventure. He made up a little army of grumblers and fought his way to the frontier. The

Prussians thus lost one of the best soldiers they were ever likely to have, together with four dozen other bright blades.

Even now Augereau's adventures were only beginning. In spite of his powerful frame he was an excellent dancer and for a time supported himself in Saxony giving dancing lessons. Presumably he had learned neat footwork as a duellist and he was a great success with the ladies until he grew bored and moved down to Athens. Here he fell deeply in love with a beautiful Greek girl and together they decided to make their way back to France. Augereau had heard there was every likelihood of a splendid fight in his native land and he did not want to miss it. He had great trouble getting there. Traveling by boat he and his wife put into Lisbon, where he at once got into trouble as a prospective revolutionary and was handed over to the dreaded Inquisition. That might have been his final adventure but his luck held. A spirited French merchant captain was talked into going to his rescue by Augereau's charming wife. Having told the Portuguese authorities that he personally would declare war on their county in the name of France unless they handed over their prisoner immediately he returned in triumph to France with the future marshal as his passenger. Rumor had been correct. There were several large and noisy fights going on and Augereau joyfully threw himself into one, rising to the rank of General of Division in no time at all.

Pierre Augereau had tried his hand at a number of civilian trades but there was another young soldier in France at that period whose mind was set on one, the trade of bakery. Nicholas Jean-de-Dieu Soult came from a respectable family in the village of St. Amand-de-Bastide, near Albi. As a youth he enlisted in the infantry and had risen to be a sergeant but immediately prior to the Revolution he suddenly expressed a burning desire to become the village baker. It is not clear whether this change of heart was due to lack of prospects in the Royal army or was the sequel to a childish desire to squash dough into interesting shapes, but the urge was real enough at the time. In the years ahead Nicholas was to have all manner of odd, urgent ambitions and was to go to extraordinary lengths to achieve them, but this time he took note of his family's protests and went back to the army. The moment the way had opened up for promising youngsters Soult shot ahead and was soon recognized as an excellent tactician. He was a calm, resourceful man, who could keep his temper in check. He had natural good taste and developed a liking for beautiful things, good furniture, good paintings, good jewelry, and particularly good crowns if there were any to be picked up for a trifle, but this was a long way ahead. In the early days of the Revolution he concentrated on acquiring the good graces of his superior officers.

Bernadotte, Augereau, Soult and even slow-witted Lefèbvre and plodding Pérignon were all to some degree spurred on by personal ambition, but one other ranker, a lawyer's son from Besançon, with the imposing name of Bon Adrien Jeannot de Moncey had no personal ambition at all beyond that of being allowed to follow the profession of arms in peace and get along with everyone, officers and men alike.

Of all Napoleon's marshals Moncey was probably the only one who had greatness thrust upon him. He was a handsome, modest, even-tempered man, who thoroughly enjoyed soldiering as an alternative to studying law. While still a lad he had run away three times to join the army. Twice they fetched him home and put him back in an office. After the third truancy they gave up the struggle and Bon Adrien, aged twenty, was allowed to remain in the Gendarmerie. When the Revolution broke out his geniality inclined him towards the Republicans and he started to rise in rank, but although the years ahead held for him wealth, honors, a dukedom and several bungled campaigns, it is not for these that he is remembered but rather for a single letter he wrote at the very end of this story. This letter alone does more than a biography to reveal what manner of man he was.

Among the men around Napoleon it is astonishing how many ran away as boys to enlist and how much time, trouble, and money their frustrated parents expended in dragging them back into civilian life. Moncey's lawyer father bought him out twice. The parents of Nicholas Oudinot approached their problem in a different way and so played upon their son's kind heart by telling him how much he was missed at home that he reluctantly resigned from the ranks of the Medoc-Infantry and came home to start a business life in Nancy. The Revolution rescued him from acute boredom. In his hometown of Bar-le-Duc, where his father was a highly respected brewer and his uncle was mayor, the news from Paris led to a declaration in favor of the Revolution by local troops. Presumably there were officers or NCO's among them who would willingly have stood for captain but they were not given the chance. On the very day that the Bastille fell Nicholas Charles Oudinot, twenty-two years old and an ex-private, was voted Captain of the Mutineers. Within thirteen days he had justified the confidence of his friends by riding alone into the middle of a

mob and stopping an outbreak of violence that followed the lynching of a
local profiteer. On this occasion he escaped unscathed, an extremely un-
common occurrence for Oudinot. During twenty-five years' active service
the brewer's son was wounded thirty-four times.

One more serving ranker demands an introduction, a man whose
name has come down to us as the most celebrated of all Napoleon's marshals, a barrel-cooper's son who was as impetuous as Augereau, as dogged
as Davout, and as brave as any soldier who ever lived.

When the Bastille fell Michel Ney was twenty years old, with two
years' service in the hussars behind him. As soon as he understood that
birth, ancestry, and influence were no longer the criteria for advancement,
he made up his mind to devote his life to the army, but he was not, as many
of them were, thinking of pay and allowances or of titles, estates and decorations. These things meant nothing to him, although he was poor and as
proud as Lucifer. He thought only of glory, the kind of glory that no
longer has a place in warfare, the glory a boy awards himself in dreams
that are hidden from his closest friends. Ney would have been content to
go through life on a private's pay if only he was acclaimed as a man who
won battles for France, and whom the public recognized as a soldier who
went into action ten paces ahead of the foremost of his men. Fearless,
hot-blooded, quick to take offence but just as quick to forgive everything
but an insult touching his honor, Michel Ney is the epitome of all that
goes to make up the Napoleonic legend. When he died with his back
to the wall on a December morning twenty-six years later the spirit of
the Empire died with him and the men who had jingled across Europe
behind the plump, indefatigable Corsican adventurer passed from fact to
saga, the kind of saga that minstrels sang in rush-strewn halls a thousand
years ago.

·   ·   ·

Of all the Republican rankers destined for high rank Ney was probably the most modest. The ninth and last ranker could lay claim to Ney's
courage but at no time in his life could his greatest admirer have called
Joachim Murat, whose career was to outdo the careers of all his comrades,
a modest or self-effacing man.

The son of an innkeeper in Cahors, Gascony, Murat possessed all
the characteristics of the Gascon and never outgrew a single one of them,
not even as a king. As a lad he was brash, impudent, vain, daring, gallant,

and utterly unreliable. As a man who was to go down in history as the most spectacular handler of cavalry since Rupert of the Rhine, he remained all these things up to the very moment of his death.

Destined for the church he wrecked his father's plans by running off at the age of twenty and enlisting in the Mounted Chasseurs. That was two years before the Revolution and when cavalry was in demand Murat was prancing and saber-flourishing with such gusto that his fellow Chasseurs decided he would either be dead or in command of the regiment before the year was out. There was something about this handsome young man that made a deep impression on everybody. His self-display was carried to such lengths that he was early recognized as a buffoon, but there was nothing ridiculous about him when it came to handling a mettlesome horse or thundering down on an unbroken square of infantry. You might laugh at him and call him a cross between a peacock and a mountebank but you had to admire him in action. Mounted on a horse that few men could manage, with his coal-black hair streaming in the wind, he looked and behaved like someone who had galloped out of fourteenth-century romance. For a long time, notwithstanding his looks and courage, his theatricality held him back, but when at last his chance presented itself he exploded like a display of fireworks. D'Artagnan may have put the word gasconade into the dictionary but Murat has kept it there ever since.

· · ·

There remain the civilians and one other. Eight future marshals of Napoleon were not even in uniform when the Paris mob surged into the inner courtyard of the Bourbon fortress. Of these eight, only two had marched to the tuck of drum. Down on the Riviera André Masséna, aged thirty-one, ex-cabin boy and ex-company-sergeant major of the Royal Italian regiment, was on the point of showing his disgust with the system when couriers rode in shouting the news from Paris. For fourteen arduous years this small, calculating man of genius had been pegging away at the trade of soldier and now he had had more than enough. The news of the Bastille did not deter him from taking his discharge and devoting himself to a calling that promised rather better financial rewards. For André Masséna loved two things and two things only—money and pretty women, in that order. As a penniless regular in the army he had been starved of both and now he thought it was time to make a change. He set up as a dried fruit seller in Antibes but his shop was only a front. His real activity was smuggling over the French-Italian border.

Dark, neatly made, good-looking by Italian standards, Masséna soon began to make a fortune handling contraband goods. His supreme qualification for the new career was his uncanny knowledge of the human race. Looking back on this period of his life friends were to say he could not only read the minds of his clients but anticipate the counter measures of the revenue officers. The customers were systematically short-changed and the officers had as much chance of laying the wily fruit-seller by the heels as a rabbit has of ambushing a fox. Here, in the heavily wooded country of Savoy, the former cabin boy spent three profitable years. Then, but still moved by motives of grain, he rejoined the army but not as a sergeant major. The days had gone when a man of brilliance could be kept standing to attention in front of an aristocratic cadet. Within three years of reenlistment Smuggler Masséna, whom some called Mannasseh the Jew, had money in the bank and was in command of a division.

There were some strange contrasts among the twenty-six men who became marshals of the First Empire but none more so than that between the two ex-servicemen tempted back into the army of the Revolution.

Jean Baptiste Jourdan was a Limoges doctor's son, who had enlisted at sixteen and served in the expeditionary force that crossed the Atlantic to help the American colonists. Major Berthier won promotion from this campaign but Jourdan saw it through as a private and when he returned home after the adventure he was given a handful of francs, a new pair of shoes, and his discharge papers. He was a philosophical young man and made no complaints. Instead he fell in love with a pretty little modiste, married her, and set up in business as a draper.

It must have been a happy and profitable marriage. Madame Jourdan looked after the shop while Jourdan himself trudged from town to town with a peddler's sample pack on his shoulders. Watching him, as he pottered from fair to fair, talking both shop and politics with his provincial customers, nobody would have dreamed that here was the man who for a short time would be regarded as the most famous soldier in France. Yet it was so; when news came from Paris that the Bastille had fallen, Jean Jourdan thought less and less about his bolts of cloth and colored ribbons and more and more about the plight of his country. Presently the itch to take part in stirring events became so intolerable that he closed his shop, kissed his little wife goodbye, and marched off carrying a different kind of pack to the depot of the volunteers of Haut-Vienne. Three years later he was a Divisional General.

Masséna had reenlisted in the armed forces from motives of gain and Jourdan from motives of pure patriotism. Masséna would have thought Jourdan a fool and Jourdan would have thought Masséna a scoundrel, yet both, without realizing it, were fulfilling a personal and national destiny. At this same moment of history six other civilians fell into step to the throb of the same drumbeat. Over on the left bank of the Seine, where street orators vied with one another in rabble rousing and there was some kind of riot every day of the week, a tall, well-built man sat at a desk, writing. He had the cut of a man who had lived a healthy, outdoor life but he was taking very little exercise nowadays. Day after day, and often far into the night, Guillaume Marie Brune, twenty-six-year-old son of a lawyer in the department of Corrèze, churned out epic verse and sonorous essays. Day after day the rain of rejected manuscripts dropped on his doormat until the young man was gnashing his teeth with rage and frustration.

In his own mind there was not the faintest doubt but that he was a literary genius but the difficulty of persuading others of this was beginning to wear him down. His friend Danton was sympathetic and suggested that perhaps Brune's themes were out-of-date. Instead of writing about love might it not be wiser and more topical to write about war? For it was now clear that the ruling families of Europe were not going to stand by and see one of their number usurped by a few hundred talkative young lawyers, who were already hammering out a ridiculous document they called "The Constitution."

Brune took Danton's advice seriously and went back to work, emerging at length with a pamphlet dealing with military tactics. Delighted with this creation he showed it to an actress, who read it through without comment. When the author asked her opinion she said, rather unfeelingly: "Ah Brune, when they fight with pens you'll be a famous general!"

The world is full of earnest writers most of whom are quite immune to this kind of discouragement but Brune had a thin skin, too thin for the literary profession. Shaking with rage he presented himself to the now famous Danton and demanded a commission in the volunteer army. Danton obliged and the poet became a major overnight. Brune's first job was to escort a batch of enthusiastic Republicans down into the southwest and the ex-poet rode out gaily enough. How could he know that he was riding both to glory and ultimate death under the feet of an enraged mob? And if he had known would it have deterred a man in his early twenties? The glory was just over the horizon. The lynching lay more than twenty years in the future.

About the time Brune despaired of producing an epic poem and turned his talents to writing military text-books another would-be artist was finding life very frustrating. His name was Gouvion St. Cyr, and at this time he was twenty-five years of age. The son of a tanner in the town of Toul he was to prove the most eccentric marshal of all. In his short life he had already been an engineering student, a drawing master, and an actor. In most respects he was to remain an actor all his life. He was very good looking, precise in whatever work he undertook, and utterly inscrutable. At eighteen he had abandoned his engineering studies and gone to Rome to study art but, like so many artistically inclined young men, he soon fell victim to the play-acting virus and abandoned his studies to go on the stage. The managements told him he would never make an actor, explaining that he was far too shy. To those who campaigned with St. Cyr in later years this estimate would have struck them as a very lame excuse for getting rid of a stage-struck youth. He drifted back to Paris in time for the Revolution, and nobody knows how he came to enlist in the army. Once there, however, his brilliant draftsmanship and his keen powers of observation singled him out for leadership, and he found in army life the outlet for creative talent that had been tormenting him throughout his youth.

A month or so out of his teens on the day the governor of the Bastille was suspended from the lanterne, a lively young Gascon was learning to be a dyer in his home town of Lectoure. Everybody told popular Jean Lannes that he would never make a dyer and should look about for something more exciting. He was a small, neat youth, with a physical toughness and stamina belied by his build. He was usually up to mischief and in and out of trouble with his parents, employers, and the local authorities, but everybody in Lectoure liked the scapegrace and was glad when he dropped in for a chat and a glass of Bordeaux wine. It took no more than a whisper of what was happening in Paris to induce young Lannes to slam the door on the dyeing sheds and march off to join the volunteer army of the Pyrenees. Inside a year his intelligence, personal gallantry, and perhaps his remarkable vocabularly of Gascon oaths had singled him out for rapid promotion, but Lannes himself would have roared with laughter if anyone had suggested that he was now laying the foundations for a reputation that gave him the *nom de guerre* of "The Roland of the French Army."

Lannes had a single sour streak in his character. He loathed everything English and all his life he was to regard the English as meddlesome, intractable people to whom it was impossible to be civil. Austrians, Prussians, Russians, and even Italians he could tolerate but to Jean Lannes the only good Englishman was a dead one.

At the time the apprentice dyer ran away to join the army a young man almost the same age slipped away from his father's farm with an identical object in view. The farmer's son was by no means ill-disposed towards the English because he was half-English himself and spoke the language as fluently as he spoke French. In many other respects, however, he favored Lannes. He had the same boisterous and amiable approach to life, the same love of laughter, wine, song and the same flair for the easy companionship of the mess. His name was Edouard Mortier and he looked like a successful publican, his big jolly face glowing with goodwill and his heavy farmboy's hands poised to slap a comrade on the shoulders and recount the latest camp-fire story about the girl who ran away from the convent.

Edouard had no intention of wasting good drinking time tilling his father's acres while a revolution was taking place just over the hill. He was a man who needed action and boon companionship as he needed food and fresh air and he found all four in the ranks of the volunteers. He was to rise to great heights in the next ten years although not so rapidly as did some of the less amiable men whom he met in billet and bivouac. He is, however, the one man among the twenty-six about whom it is impossible to find an adverse comment in the memoirs of the period. All write of Edouard Mortier with goodwill and to the end of his life he was welcome wherever he went. Even the English squires who, for the next twenty years were to sneer at everything French, voted Mortier "a thoroughgoing gentleman."

One other "thorough gentleman" emerges from the short list of volunteers, by name Louis Gabriel Suchet, of whom Napoleon was to say, "If I had two men like that I could have held Spain." Suchet came from Lyons where his father was a silk merchant and he was only nineteen when the Bastille fell. He abandoned a profitable business and joined the army. He had a long time to wait for official recognition of his remark-

able talents but when that time arrived it was seen to have been worth
waiting for; Suchet's reputation among the remarkable array of fighting-
men of the First Empire stands as high as anyone's and a great deal higher
than most.

Each of these young men was imbued to a greater or lesser degree
with enthusiasm for the new ideas, and beyond those ideas, with a love
of glory and patriotism. All of them, even the grasping Masséna, welcomed the great changes that swept across France in 1789 and each, according to his talents and luck, took full advantage of the opportunities
those changes presented. In that respect therefore they were alike but there
is one exception, last but one of the twenty-six.

Loyalty can be found in unexpected places. British tars, press-ganged
into the Navy and flogged to the guns on a diet of rancid pork and
weevil-ridden biscuits, could still hurrah for the king whose agents had
reduced them to such circumstances. The loudest cheer at any coronation
procession always comes from the man with the slender purse, who finds
in pomp and circumstance a palliative for his own deprivations. This was
so in the heart of at least one man who was to become a marshal of
France, a polite and reserved young barber of Languedoc. His behavior
at this crisis of history was as strange and quixotic as any episode in the
legend.

The barber's name was Jean Baptiste Bessières and he was the son
of a surgeon, but this does not mean, as it might today, that he came
from the prosperous professional classes. The trades of surgeon and barber
were so closely linked as to be almost one in pre-Revolutionary France.
There was, in fact, nothing at all to distinguish young Jean Bessières from
any other young man plying his trade in the provinces and no one would
have been much surprised had he downed razors and lather brush and
marched off in the wake of dyer-apprentice Lannes or ploughboy Mortier
to fight under the banners of Liberty and Equality. Jean Bessières, however, did the exact opposite, inasmuch as he marched off in the wrong
direction and enlisted in the remnant of the army still loyal to the king!
He was attached to the Royal Guard and fought all day when the Paris
mob, maddened by the false dawn of the Revolution, stormed into the
Tuilleries, massacred the Swiss Guard, and stuck a cap of liberty on the
king's round head. On this day, August 10, 1792, the young barber was
lucky to escape with his life but he had made his gesture and was satisfied
that he had done his duty. From then on he swam with the tide. We

shall hear a good deal more about this strange young man after he had staggered out of the reeking palace and disappeared into the turmoil of Paris under the Terror. His loyalty to the man who made him a marshal was never put to the test. Had it been, it is probable that it would have survived every trial.

With few exceptions the men we have met so far were born into poor or modest homes. Apart from the odd, radical aristocrats like Sérurier and Grouchy, these penniless youngsters had everything to gain and nothing to lose by identifying themselves with the Revolution. Twenty-five of the marshals have now been introduced. Only one remains and he was already a prince and the nephew of a king when the first shots were fired at the Bastille.

His name was Poniatowski and he was twenty-six when he heard what was taking place in France. It meant very little to him at that time, just one more rising of starvelings against entrenched tyranny, but his interest increased when, a year or so later, hordes of French civilians drubbed every army the autocrats sent against them. Poniatowski was a Pole with a dream and it was a favorite dream of every other patriot in Poland—namely to rise up and free their beloved country from the tyranny of the Russian Czars and reestablish the ancient kingdom of Poland.

Sixteen years were to pass before Poniatowski was able to look south and watch the armies of the Czar streaming back before the invincible cavalry of the Grand Army. Another year was to pass before the Great Liberator, Napoleon, was to ride into Warsaw and fall in love with a beautiful Polish countess. In the meantime the Prince waited and brooded, deliberating on his country's wrongs and seeing himself as the Liberator of Eastern Europe and the darling of his country.

The roll-call is done. Officers, sergeant majors, rankers, apprentices, farmer's-boy, brewer, poet, smuggler, play-actor, barber and Prince—these men followed the drumbeat that was to lead them out of France and across the length and breadth of Europe during the next twenty-five years. Eight were to die violent deaths, the majority were to betray the man who wrote their names into history, all were to acquire fortunes and high-sounding titles that made nonsense of their revolutionary principles. Only a few were to emerge from the test of the years without scars on their souls as well as their bodies but each was to add something to the most colorful period in the annals of warfare.

In the hundred and fifty years that have passed since their names were as familiar to their contemporaries as are the names of Eisenhower, Montgomery, and Patton today, they were to wear a variety of labels. They were to be called callous, greedy, treacherous, rapacious, brutal, and a hundred other things. There is only one word that no writer has ever dared to use in respect of any one of them. That word is "coward."

CHAPTER TWO

THE GAGE OF BATTLE

"THE kings of Europe advance against us. We shall throw at their feet, as a gage of battle, the head of a king!"

So roared the massive Danton when the professional armies of the reigning houses of Europe set their rusty military machines in motion against the French nation, and France, ringed by the champions of kings, had nothing but patriotism with which to oppose the steamroller of autocracy. Prussia and Austria were first in the field, and the tide of invasion came rolling over the northeastern border and across the cockpit of Europe towards the French frontier fortresses. Down in the Pyrenean area the Bourbon house of Spain was menacing, and the day after the execution of Louis in the Place de la Revolution, the English trinity of Hanoverians, country squires, and city banking houses, despatched its powerful navy to scour the seas for French shipping and maintain a blockade of the coasts. France's only friend in the world was three thousand miles away where the infant American Republic was groping for the guide rails of democracy.

Of the twenty-six marshals of the Empire every one played a part in repulsing the far-flung attack. What of the sun around which these stars were to revolve throughout the next two decades?

Napoleon Bonaparte was within a few weeks of his twentieth birthday when the Bastille fell, and the effect of this stupendous event upon the moody young man was not as stimulating as it proved to the vast majority of French nationals. When the smoke of the first cannonade rolled away he was not looking at Paris but southward to his homeland. Corsica had been ceded to France a few months before Napoleon was born, and for the last twenty years the independent islanders had been waiting for a chance to expel the foreigners and establish themselves as a free community. Their beloved leader, Paoli, was in England, but the young artillery officer who had studied at Brienne and Paris had long since made up his mind to step into Paoli's shoes and win the crown of Corsica's liberator. With the official French government overthrown and the country in a turmoil he at last saw a chance of assuming this role. When most Frenchmen were hurrying into the ranks of the volunteer battalions he applied for extended leave, turned his back on the country that had educated him, and embarked for his homeland. It is not until 1793, as a disillusioned rebel of twenty-four, that he reappears in this story as a belated defender of the French Republic.

.　　.　　.

At this time only one of the future marshals, Marmont, had met Napoleon Bonaparte but each, in his own way, was already making his way in the world. The professionals among them were learning a new style of warfare by the painful process of trial and error. The recruits, like Jean Lannes and Mortier, were taking to the trade as cheerfully as ducklings take to water.

We left Lieutenant Davout and Sergeant Victor riding into Paris with the greetings of the mutinous Royal Champagne regiment and the mission, as far as it went, was successful. Unhappily for Davout reaction set in while he was away and on his return he was clapped in the guardhouse as a mutineer. Things happened very quickly in France during the last years of the eighteenth century but Lieutenant Davout had outstripped events. The revolutionaries were aiming at the establishment of a constitutional monarchy and it must have seemed to Davout's commanding officer that this young man was setting a dangerous example to officers and men. Had his superiors been more sure of themselves he might have been shot out of hand. As it was, he was court-martialed, cashiered, and sentenced to six weeks' fortress detention. The setback did not deter him. On leaving his regiment he at once re-enlisted in the Republican army where trained officers were desperately needed. In a matter of weeks he was a lieutenant colonel and in action at the frontiers.

With luck there was now little to stop him attaining the rank of general, but Davout was to discover that Republican slogans were one thing and Republican logic another. It was an old story of theorists at home versus men in the field, and the fraternal note of letters from Paris was nothing but a source of irritation to the men in the field. Even a revolution, it seemed, was unable to throw off the dead weight of chairborne bureaucracy and as things went from bad to worse in Paris, and extremists like Murat began to gain a stranglehold on moderate revolutionaries, Lieutenant Colonel Davout found himself flung out of the army a second time, this time on account of his aristocratic origins!

Davout was not endowed with a sense of humor. Had he been, the irony of the situation might have made him laugh. For here he was, court-martialed by the Royalists on account of his Republicanism and cashiered by the Republicans because of aristocratic connections. It was enough to make a less determined man shed his uniform with disgust and look about for a more rewarding profession.

Davout never thought of doing this. Grim, uncommunicative, and mulishly obstinate, he hung about waiting for the politicians to change their minds and employ his sword against the mercenaries now striking southwest at Paris. It was a desperately tricky situation for any Frenchman who rated the welfare of his country above the popular slogans of the day. In our own time Davout's dilemma has taxed the patience and loyalty of many professional soldiers, for the new government of France anticipated by a century and a half the rule of Commissars and Gestapo agents. Every military headquarters had its political "adviser" and a swarm of informers bent upon justifying their employment to the morbid central government. Dumouriez, one of the most brilliant of the Republican generals, gave up the struggle and went over to the enemy, and in every camp the agents of scared terrorists watched and probed for potential traitors. The guillotine in Paris was already busy with such men and it seems almost a miracle that this renegade nobleman was not arrested and executed. In the end his doggedness and courage had their reward and he was grudgingly reemployed in the Army of the Moselle. For the next few years he disappears into the ebb and flow of battle along the Rhine, where he fought under the famous Moreau.

No such dangers and frustrations faced Davout's traveling companion, the plump, rosy-faced, talkative Sergeant Perrin, who insisted on calling himself "Victor." Victor had no aristocratic connections. He had forced his way through a military crust by a combination of bluff and left-wing jargon and he emerged on the far side breathless but unscathed.

The rankers laughed at him—they were already calling him *Le Beau Soleil* on account of his rosy face—but they listened to him and they followed him as they will follow any man who knows exactly what he wants. He next appears as the leader of a storming party at Toulon, where Captain Bonaparte blasted his way into history with a battery of six-pounders. Victor might have been a boaster and a buffoon but there was never any question about his physical courage. He penetrated the curtain of enemy fire with the confidence of a man absolutely convinced of the rightness of his cause. The fact that this cause was always the advancement of Sergeant Victor-Perrin did nothing to shake his confidence. After every engagement he bobbed up like a champagne cork.

The few other officers who had followed Davout's example and sided with the Revolution from the outset avoided embroilment with the extremists. Grizzled old Kellerman, who we last saw exulting over the change of government and pledging himself to support the new order, emerged from the revolutionary wars as the personification of French patriotism. His big moment came at Valmy, where he was second-in-command to the ultimate deserter, Dumouriez. Valmy was the turning point of the first invasion. It was here that the ragged, ill-equipped volunteers met and threw back the dreaded Prussian army after taking up an impossibly dangerous position in the densely wooded hills of the Argonne and inviting the invaders to dislodge them.

There was no hand-to-hand engagement and the battle was confined to a long cannonade, with old Kellerman in command of the exposed French line. Everyone, including the French commander, expected the civilian rabble of patriots to break and flee at the first discharge of Prussian guns, but instead a kind of miracle happened. The line stood as firm as a mountain range and when the Prussian infantry, urged on by the curses and canes of their drillmasters, came within striking distance it halted, wavered, and suddenly turned right-about face and left the field.

Peering through the smoke veteran Kellerman could hardly believe his eyes. In a perverse way the victory was an affront to his professionalism, an army of regulars turned back by a few thousand white-faced civilians, most of whom hardly knew how to load a musket. The astonishing victory resounded up and down the frontier, and because of its moral impact upon the autocrats it has gone down in history as one of the most decisive battles of the world. Kellerman reaped most of the credit, particularly after Dumouriez' desertion, and it established him as one of the heroes of the Republic. He was already nearing sixty but there was plenty of bite and bark in the old fellow for the great days ahead.

Ex-Count Sérurier, one of the other officers who put his country before his class, had no cause to regret his decision. He was sent to command a division in the Italian theater of war, where Austrians and Sardinians were trying to enter France by the door upon which Mussolini knocked so feebly in 1940. Here he saw plenty of fighting and held fast to the drill-book methods so dear to his slow, stubborn nature. He was due for a series of shocks in the near future but it was not the enemy who administered them. They were administered by a busy little Corsican who had somehow managed to win the confidence of the despised civilian politicians in Paris and obtain command of the half-starved Army of Italy. Perhaps this is the place to recount exactly what happened in the early spring of 1796, when the plight of France, notwithstanding its series of victories, was still desperate.

Three future marshals were among the group of four divisional commanders who answered a summons to the headquarters of the newly-arrived General Bonaparte. They were drill-book Sérurier, ex-smuggler Masséna and the swaggering, devil-may-care Augereau, all of whom had spent the last year or more holding off the Austrian threat with inadequate forces of unpaid, undernourished men.

Bonaparte, fresh from his victory over the Paris mob and a lovesick bridegroom of less than a fortnight, met the veterans in Nice, and from the outset all three were prejudiced against the undersized upstart. Sérurier was exactly twice his age. He had been in action when the sallow little Corsican was in his cradle. Augereau, with a hundred adventures behind him, could have broken the new commander-in-chief across his knee. André Masséna looked at the new general from under dark, thoughtful brows and decided that here was a lucky coxcomb unlikely to possess a nose for a quick profit. All three had been fighting in this theater long enough to be heartily sick of it and all showed their contempt for the new man by failing to doff their plumed hats when he entered the room. Thereupon Napoleon promptly removed his own and they were obliged to follow suit. He at once replaced his hat and looked them straight in the eyes. They met his glance steadily for a few seconds, then each of them dropped his eyes and studied the floor. Without a word having been spoken Napoleon had mastered them. Curtly, but not impolitely, he told them precisely what he intended to do, issued their instructions, and dismissed them with a nod. Outside they looked sheepishly at one another and it was the psychologist Masséna who summed up their feelings: "That little rascal almost frightened me!" he said quietly.

When Napoleon came to Nice to take over command of the Army of Italy he was accompanied by three other men we have already met. Each was to become a marshal of the Empire. The trio consisted of the ugly little dandy, Berthier, he of the uncertain manner and stiff shock of hair, the innkeeper's son Murat, already vying with Berthier in the splendor of his uniforms, and finally the watchful gunner-cadet, Marmont, who had taken a long time to make up his mind whether or not to support the Revolution. All three had had plenty of adventures in the last few years.

Berthier, as a man who stood well with the royal family, had walked a tightrope during the Terror. He was a kindly, sensitive man and had hated the cruelty of men like Robespierre and Carrier, the Beast of Nantes. As commander of the troops at Versailles, where the royal family had resided during the early part of the Revolution, he was under a spotlight. Soon he was suspected of helping fugitive aristocrats to escape over the border and many a man went to the scaffold for less. By this time, however, Berthier's talents as a staff-officer were generally known and the Republicans could not afford to lose him. He was chief-of-staff to a series of jack-a'-lantern generals in the west, where the stubborn peasants waged unceasing war on a government they loathed, but he escaped from this atrocious theater to serve old "Valmy" Kellerman in the Alps. Napoleon quickly recognized this man's administrative ability but thought poorly of him as a leader of storm-troops. "He isn't fit to command a battalion!" he said, but as chief-of-staff he kept Berthier by his side for nearly twenty years and the veterans were soon referring to the shock-headed little genius as "The Emperor's Wife." For his part Berthier idolized the new commander-in-chief. "It would be a fine thing to serve under him!" he said, a moment after they had met, and he did serve him, faithfully and selflessly, almost to the end.

The former innkeeper's son, Murat, had no self-doubts at all about his brilliant future. From the moment the new order had opened up the ranks of advancement in the army the handsome young hussar began to lay the foundations for a reputation as the most dashing horseman in Europe. A good mixer, an extrovert, a fearless and expert handler of horses, and chock full of Gascon impudence and braggadocio, Murat was a success from the moment he obtained his lieutenant's commission. He first met Napoleon the night before the famous "Whiff of Grapeshot," when the Directors of the tottering government lunged around for a sword to stand between them and the mob. Napoleon, as the only general available, was given command of the government troops but he was without artillery and his study of the tactics of revolutionary mobs during the last few years had convinced him that they could only be handled with grapeshot. There was a park of artillery at Sablons, just outside Paris, and Napoleon called for the guns. If they arrived at the Tuileries before the mob converged on the seat of government then the Directors had nothing to fear. If they failed to arrive there would soon be more bodies on the lanterns in the Tuileries gardens. One of the Directors knew of an enterprising young cavalryman and at once sent for him. Captain Murat, coal-black hair floating over his dazzling dolman and an expensive-looking saber clanking against his spurs, strolled into the room. Napoleon assessed his capabilities in an instant and told him to saddle up and race across the city to Sablons.

It was Murat's first noted exploit and it was carried out with the dash and élan that were to confound armies from Madrid to the plains beyond Moscow. Just as dawn was breaking over Paris the young Gascon's squadron galloped up to the artillery park seconds ahead of the force sent by the mob-leader for the very same guns. Murat had three hundred sabers. The artillery guard numbered fifteen! One "view halloo!" and the guns were Murat's. Within a few minutes they were trundling back to the Tuileries to be posted at strategic points by artilleryman Bonaparte.

The counter-revolution was crushed in two hours and the Directory was saved. That day Napoleon won command of an army. By fetching the guns so promptly Murat, ex-trooper and as yet only a captain, earned himself a crown.

The third member of Napoleon's suite, Gunner Marmont, was the first of the twenty-six to meet and become intimate with the future Emperor. Long before they accompanied one another down into Italy, they had been stationed in the adjacent garrison towns of Dijon and Auxerre. Napoleon, penniless and dispirited, spent most of his time in his room writing essays and caring for his young brother Louis. From time to time, however, Napoleon needed the sympathy and understanding of a man of his own age and he rode over to the artillery school at Dijon for an exchange of ideas. Marmont sang his new friend's praises everywhere and even took him home to meet his parents. Marmont senior was not at all impressed by this dark, brooding young man, and this is not surprising for Napoleon's parlor manners left a great deal to be desired. One evening, in Marmont's home, a pretty girl told him that she could speak Corsican and tried it out on him. "How was my accent?" she asked, smiling. "Vile!" snarled Napoleon, turning away.

Marmont, however, was a very discerning young man. In spite of everyone else's advice he stuck closely to his somber friend. He could recognize genius when he saw it and he was thus the first man in France to hitch his wagon to a star. Marmont, now a major, went with Napoleon to the famous siege of Toulon, where the latter's plan of storming the harbor and driving out the English proved so successful. From then on there was love and trust on one side, a cold calculating acceptance of those sentiments and shrewd lip-service on the other. Marmont's nature was not unlike Masséna's except that in the place of money he put power and a determination to be on the winning side at all costs. Napoleon's deep affection for his oldest friend was to cost him his dynasty. At the commander's headquarters at Nice the shrewd Marmont and the swaggering Murat represented the new conception of warfare opposed to the old, represented by Sérurier.

.   .   .

Of the future marshals who were serving soldiers at the time of the fall of the Bastille we have now caught up with Davout, Victor, Kellerman, Sérurier, Augereau, Murat, Berthier, and Marmont. What of the others? What were they doing in these strenuous days that saw the curtain rise on the drama of the Empire?

Ex-sergeant major Pérignon, disgusted with chattering lawyer-politicians who spouted Latin and came out with outrageously silly ideas about how to run wars, soon abandoned politics and returned to his old trade. He could have been found during these strenuous years giving and taking hard knocks in the Pyrenees.

Macdonald, the son of the Scots clansman, was rising very rapidly. He was a lieutenant colonel within three years of declaring for the new government and a general a year later. Ex-sergeant major Lefèbvre was also making his mark. From being a mere NCO, famous for his brisk way of handling recruits, he had become the host of a king. It was a gold-epauletted Lefèbvre who commanded the Republican guard charged with the difficult task of escorting the wretched royal family back to Paris after their dramatic flight to Varennes. The old sergeant major was an outspoken man on the parade ground but he was not a bully and there was no trace of vice in his nature. With sword swipes and oaths he kept the jeering mob at a respectable distance as the heavy coachload of fugitives entered the Paris barriers. He believed in frightening recruits but he had no stomach for frightening children. After that they gave him more congenial work and he fought through the frontier wars with the Army of the Moselle and the Army of the Rhine.

In the seven years that passed between the fall of the Bastille and the flowering of Napoleon's genius in Northern Italy, one future marshal, and one only, came within a mere fifty yards of achieving what every one of them longed to do in their more mature years—to strike a mortal blow at the heart of France's arch-enemy, Britain.

When, in the early eighteen-hundreds, Napoleon announced that he would land an army in Britain, the London cartoonists treated the subject as though it was one of awesome originality. In point of fact it was not so. An invasion of Britain had been a pipe-dream of all Britain's Continental rivals for centuries, and in Napoleon's youth there were several half-baked attempts and two actual descents on British soil. With better luck and better leadership either might have succeeded and created the kind of panic in London as that caused by the Young Pretender's march to Derby half a century earlier. In command of the first of these expeditions, the Bantry Bay invasion of December 1796, was ex-aristocrat, ex-citizen volunteer Grouchy, one of the serving officers who had thrown in his lot with the Revolution at the outset. Grouchy was the unluckiest of all Napoleon's fighting men. He has gone down in history as an idiot but he never deserved this reputation.

His command on this occasion was an accident. The descent on the Irish coast, which aimed at landing 6,000 men from seventeen warships to raise rebellion throughout Ireland, should have been led by the dashing Hoche, one of the Republic's most celebrated generals (and sometime lover of Napoleon's Creole wife, Josephine, when they were both in the Carmes prison during the Terror), but Hoche's vessel became separated from the main squadron at the very commencement of the venture. When the main force dropped anchor in Bantry Bay, in south-west Ireland, Hoche's second-in-command, Emmanuel Grouchy, found himself saddled with full responsibility.

Grouchy had made great strides in his profession since he had embraced revolutionary principles. He now held high rank but he was a man who did not relish responsibility. This fact does not, in itself, explain his blundering career, nor his undeserved reputation for bungling. He was a plodding, courageous man but a born worrier and pessimist, with just too much courage and conscientiousness to prevent him from hunting round for a pair of broad shoulders upon which he could lay his cares. He muddled along, doing what seemed right at the time, and when he became bogged down, as he almost invariably did, he fell back upon strict adherence to written orders. He was a reliable man in a fighting retreat but hopeless at anything calling for improvisation.

When the French ships dropped anchor in Bantry Bay they were still nominally in command of a cautious admiral called Bouvet. The admiral disliked the entire adventure and could see nothing but disaster ahead. He cocked an eye at the weather and declared that he could not risk his vessels long enough for Grouchy to get his men ashore.

A man like the hot-blooded Murat or the impulsive Lannes would have shouted with laughter, elbowed Bouvet aside, and ordered disembarkation but Grouchy was too formal for that kind of behavior. After a furious wrangle with the seaman he locked himself in his cabin and began a long, detailed report of the situation. By the time he had dotted his last "i" the squadron was back in France. The frustrated Hoche read the report and promptly dismissed his second-in-command as "a scribbler of no consequence." Napoleon was to express even more forthright opinions of Grouchy's talents in the years ahead and history has been agreeing with both ever since.

Poor Emmanuel, having missed the crown of glory by such a narrow margin, begged permission to try again but his request was refused. Years later, when he ran into the hopeful Irish Nationalist Wolfe Tone, in Paris, he recalled his failure at Bantry Bay with a bitterness undimmed by time. "I should have taken Bouvet by the scruff of the neck and thrown him overboard!" he growled.

After Bantry Bay Grouchy settled down as a leader of heavy cavalry and was sent to the Italian theater of war, where he met Napoleon. It might have been better for the reputations of both men if their paths had never crossed.

Moncey, fighting fit at forty plus, was enjoying himself down in the Pyrenees during these wars. After a military standstill that had lasted fifteen years he was now making rapid progress in his profession and already fancied himself a strategist of the first order. At long last he could turn to the relations who had spent so much time and money to buy him out of the army and drag him back to his legal studies, and say "I told you so!"

Bernadotte, the sergeant major fence-squatter of the Bastille period, had now decided that the Paris Republicans were on a good wicket and had promptly enlisted in the team. He was fighting brilliantly under ex-peddler Jourdan in the Army of Sambre-et-Meuse; and somewhat just over the hill, leading light cavalry charges for fun and exercise, was ex-trooper Ney, now a Captain and beginning to be noticed for dash and ingenuity in the field. Soult was there too, the suave, polite young man who had once dreamed of becoming the village baker, and so was Oudinot, who might have been a worthy brewer but who preferred to lead grenadiers in headlong rushes against the enemy batteries. Mortier, the farmer's son, and Suchet, the silk merchant's son, were in the field winning their spurs, and so was Jean Lannes, the hard-swearing dyer's apprentice. Lannes spent this period in the Pyrenees and discerning officers had already singled him out for rapid promotion. Brune, the frustrated poet of the Left Bank, was becoming known in the Swiss and Italian theaters, and St. Cyr, the former engineering student who had once dreamed of being a famous actor, was in the Vosges where his talent for draftsmanship was in great demand among generals who needed accurate maps of the fighting areas.

Every one of these men was in the field and each was making extremely rapid progress in his profession, an advance due in part to the remarkable opportunities existing in the Republican armies but accelerated by their courage in action. Their successes are the more striking when one reflects upon the kind of material the officers had at their disposal. The patriots under their command had the one advantage of enthusiam over their over-disciplined opponents but they would not have impressed a professional soldier if he had happened to take the salute from one of the French columns going up to the front. Here is a description from the graphic pen of Lenotre of what a patriotic levy looked like in the early stages of war. . . . *On their feet were sabots and they were clothed with second-hand effects from old clothes shops . . . carmagnoles, guardsmen's old uniforms, dragoon's helmets without leather or horsehair, straw hats in which pipes and spoons were stuck, buttonless waistcoats and breeches full of holes. Barebreasted, heedless, fault-finding and heroic, they marched along, ready to die without a murmur but refractory to all discipline. They drank, and sang and kept themselves warm; they stopped to rest in the shade: and they danced around camp fires.*

It was with mobs like these that Sergeant Major Lefèbvre, draper Jourdan, ex-Count Sérurier, Masséna, Augereau, and ultimately Napoleon Bonaparte, scattered the armies of kings and principalities like straw in a gale. It was with a few thousand of these zealots that Hoche and Kellerman won victories that were to echo round the world and drive despots to despair. With these men, or with the soldiers they became, the marshals of the Empire were to stable their horses in Vienna, Berlin, Madrid, Rome, Venice, Cairo, Warsaw, and Moscow and it was to require a million men in arms to force them back across their natural frontiers of the Rhine, the Alps, and the Pyrenees. "I do not win the victories," wrote Napoleon to the Directory in the late spring of 1796, "they are won by the courage and skill of my men!" This was no special plea on his part, even though it was said in an attempt to persuade the Directors to cancel their order to share the command of the triumphant Army of Italy with Kellerman. At that time he meant every word of it, for the response of the sansculottes to his first, ringing proclamation, had been instantaneous. This is understandable since it was an invitation to win as much loot as they could cram into their knapsacks. Yet, bold and tireless as these men were, their successes could never have been achieved without the officer talent of dyers and brewers, lawyers and actors, who led them. These were the men who planted Napoleon's feet on the steps of a throne and it was their blood, sweat, greed, and personal loyalty that kept him there until the Empire was overthrown by a continent in arms. Then all but one left him. Sated with riches and growing old they longed for the comfort of their firesides and the company of their families, and with their withdrawal the scaffolding supporting the Empire collapsed. Much that was splendid, as well as much that was unjust and squalid, disappeared under the wreckage.

.   .   .

Only one future marshal has not been mentioned. Prince Poniatowski, the dreaming, dark-browed Pole, took no part in the wars of the Republic. He was waiting in Warsaw until the battle cry of *"Liberté, Equalité, Fraternité"* changed to the thunderous *"Vive L'Empereur!"*

CHAPTER THREE

ITALIAN SPRING

"WHAT promise he holds out to us all?" wrote the ecstatic Marmont at the close of the first stage of the Italian drama, in the early summer, 1796.

What promise indeed? Marmont's enthusiasm is typical of the surge of confidence that swept through all ranks of the tatterdemalion army that twenty-six-year-old Napoleon Bonaparte used to stamp the seal of his genius upon history that spring. Immediately ahead lay a dazzling succession of victories, a new aristocracy based on merit rather than birth, and an Empire that was to compare in wit, elegance, and beauty to the dog days of the Sun King, a century before.

On March 26 Napoleon, fresh from his easy triumph over the mob in Paris, interviewed his divisional generals in Nice, the four men commanding the rabble of shoeless, mutinous men. By April 28, thirty-three days later, the gunner-general was famous and every man in that rabble, from the chief-of-staff Berthier down to the youngest drummer boy, shared his glory. Is it any wonder that Marmont wrote of "splendid promise" or, in reviewing the events of the summer, added: "Surely this is a fine thing to have done!"

What was so outstanding about the Italian campaigns? Why do they occupy the pinnacle of legend in Napoleonic saga? They were brilliantly conceived and dashingly executed but French Republican armies had been achieving dashing and spectacular victories for some time past and had many times demonstrated their superiority over the cumbersome tactics of their opponents. Untrained volunteers threw back the legacy of Frederick the Great at Valmy. French hussars had galloped over the ice in Holland

and captured the Dutch Fleet with sabers. Carnot, republican organizer of victory, had led the French volunteers against the professional armies of the Hapsburgs holding his civilian hat on a stick, storming into the Austrian trenches and saving the Republic in an hour. Deeds like this were commonplace in the flood tide of revolution and, at first sight, it is difficult to understand why the spotlight of publicity fell with such brilliance upon the Italian campaigns. The answer lies in the fantastic speed with which they were conducted.

Up to this time, indeed, throughout the entire history of warfare from earliest times, military campaigns had been slow, plodding affairs, almost always confined to the summer months and culminating, every now and again, in a slogging match between ineptly handled bodies of men. Eighteenth century armies were accompanied by vast trains of wagons and camp followers. The rate of march was slow and wars usually degenerated into a series of protracted sieges. By common consent commanders broke off hostilities as soon as bad weather set in and their armies went into winter quarters.

Napoleon changed this pattern in a month and the Austrian-Sardinian coalition that faced him in the spring of '96 was the first to go down under the sledge-hammer of his conception of how war should be waged. A month after the first shot the Sardinians sued for a separate peace, the French had entered Milan, and Napoleon was master of Northern Italy. Within eighteen months French armies were supreme throughout the Italian theater and when peace was made they were within striking distance of Vienna. To those who watched, the first Italian campaign was as startling and terrifying as the Nazi *blitzkreig* through the Low Countries in 1940.

· · ·

Of the twenty-six future marshals ten played an active part in this and the subsequent Italian campaigns. Four in particular made their mark upon their commander and troops but all ten distinguished themselves in one way or another.

Stiff, soldierly old Sérurier was present in the early stages but his health was unable to withstand the terrible demands of the new warfare and he soon dropped out, although not before Napoleon had written home commending his qualities to the government in Paris. He was brave and he was reliable, and Napoleon did not forget him when he was looking round for men who could typify the glories of the early days of the Republic.

Augereau, entering his fortieth year, should also have been too old for this kind of warfare but he supplied incontestable evidence to the contrary. His tough, seasoned frame responded to every demand and he was seen in the thick of every fight, bellowing oaths picked up during his service with the Russian and Prussian armies and earning the *nom de guerre* of *Le Grand Prussien* on account of his size and explosive language. The ex-valet led his men into the hottest fire time and again and his counsel, when it was asked, was always the same—"Attack! attack! attack!"

At Castiglione he saved the army. Grossly outnumbered, Napoleon's nerve faltered for a moment and he called a council of war. Most of those present urged retreat and Napoleon himself was inclined to agree. He then asked Augereau's advice and was told to advance with every musket he could summon. "If we are defeated, we can think about retreating then," he said, "and in any case, I shall be dead, so why should I worry?" Napoleon finally came down on Augereau's side, ordering an advance that culminated in a smashing victory. He never forgot the adventurer's courage. In after years Augereau shared with Lannes the distinction of being in and out of trouble most of the time and complaints about him were very frequent indeed. Napoleon would listen patiently, smile and then dismiss the complainant with: "Ah well, he's a terrible fellow it's true but just think of what he did for us at Castiglione?"

It would be a mistake, however, to imagine that Augereau's appearance and behavior as an officer matched his language and general impetuousness. He was a man of contradictions. Just as the iron Davout was invariably unkempt and ill-dressed yet was faultless as a disciplinarian, Augereau, reckless and violent, invariably went into battle well-groomed and powdered. He soon became known, moreover, for scrupulous concern for his men, particularly the wounded. The truth is, of course, that he was a soldier and nothing but a soldier, and every ounce of his dynamic nervous energy was fed into his profession. He could lead a charge, trounce the enemy, and then tackle the mass of administrative detail that falls to high command. A young officer who served six of the marshals as an aide-de-camp had no hesitation in selecting Augereau as the closest to his conception of an ideal commander and as the marshal who showed most consideration towards civilians overrun by the armies.

Writing an early report on the character and qualities of his divisional generals, Napoleon selects Masséna as the one with the highest ability. His confidence was fully justified by the nineteen years of warfare that followed the first campaign. Masséna emerges as the one marshal whose first-class ability most nearly approaches that of the commander-in-chief. In this campaign his dispositions were perfect. He applied his cool, impersonal mind to every problem that arose and emerged every time with the correct answer. At Rivoli, one of the most important engagements, he contributed more than anyone else to the French triumph by his stubborn defence of the threatened left-wing, and his work on that particular day earned him his subsequent title. But Masséna, faultless in the field, was probably thinking of other things than military glory. When Napoleon took command of the army in March one of the first things he did was to issue a proclamation that licensed looting, and the former smuggler was quick to take the hint. It was in Italy that he built the foundation to his vast fortune. How he set about it, what town, city, or terrified civilian contributed to the first deposits, was never established. Masséna did not talk much about anything and no one could coax a single word out of him about money unless it was *"Non!"* when subscriptions were solicited. When the campaigns in Italy ended, Masséna was already a rich man and despite a severe financial setback, he was destined to become even richer. He fought like a lion and as a divisional commander proved utterly reliable but saw no reason at all why his rewards should consist of glory alone. Glory, he reasoned, was all very well but it cannot be banked. Cash, not cachet, was what mattered to Masséna.

In the forefront of every infantry attack that spring was Jean Lannes, one-time apprentice dyer, whose gallantry quickly earned him the sobriquet of "Roland of the French Army." The neat, stocky little Gascon, who could swear as profoundly as Augereau and handle men as efficiently as Masséna, was already demonstrating a curious indifference to wounds that would put most men on their backs for a month or so. At Lodi he was first across the river Adda in the face of a hail of grapeshot. Berthier and Masséna were close behind but Lannes was the first to strike at the fleeing Austrian gunners.

Later on, Lannes came under the direct eye of Napoleon on another shell-swept bridge. At Arcola a wooden causeway ran across high dykes into the enemy's position. It was commanded by guns and the French tried to rush it. Three columns withered under point-blank fire. Then

Napoleon himself rushed forward, holding the tricolor flag, and the grenadiers rallied for a fourth attempt. Lannes had been twice wounded in previous actions and his wounds were unhealed, yet he insisted on leaving the field hospital to take part in the fight and was close to Napoleon when the assault columns wavered. Running forward in an attempt to shield the commander-in-chief he received a third wound. It sent him back to the hospital but it paid a handsome dividend. Napoleon mentioned his gallantry in dispatches and from that moment the Gascon's future was assured.

Another man who made his reputation in these months was Berthier, the chief-of-staff. Today, it would be unthinkable for a chief-of-staff to engage in hand-to-hand combat with the enemy but at every one of these fights Berthier was there, saber in hand, jostling with Lannes and others to be first through a curtain of fire. His true laurels, however, were not gained in the field but at the table, bending over his maps and assessing with compass and pencil the shortest distance between two points or the number of men available for risky flank attack. Napoleon watched him closely and made up his mind that here was a man who was indispensible to an ambitious general. He praised and encouraged him and because Alexandre Berthier was the kind of man to whom encouragement is essential, a strong bond of mutual respect was forged between the little staff officer and his commander-in-chief.

Berthier formed another and more romantic attachment during the halcyon days of this campaign. When the French made a triumphant entry into Milan two of the most celebrated women in Northern Italy hurried to greet them, Grassini famous for her lovely voice, and Madame de Visconti, famous for her beauty. Both tried very hard to seduce the conqueror and both failed on account of Napoleon's attachment to his absent bride, Josephine. Grassini bided her time and a disillusioned Napoleon soothed her pride three years later. Visconti took second-best. She had noticed that Chief-of-Staff Berthier had fallen deeply in love with her at first sight and she became his mistress. The affair lasted so long that it became a standing joke in the army. We shall hear a good deal more of Madame de Visconti in the years ahead. Perhaps Berthier's fidelity sprang from a sense of physical inferiority. Himself a small, undistinguished-looking man, with none of Murat's glitter or Lannes self-confidence, he never became reconciled to the fact that the most beautiful woman in Italy preferred him to any of the handsome young blades in the train of the conqueror. She was not only beautiful and was to retain her classic features long after her contemporaries had grown old and wrinkled, but she was also gay and amusing. She made great play of her inadequate French and was always saying something shocking and then apologizing with a pretty show of confusion, and blaming the gaffe on her unfamiliarity with the language. Nobody was taken in by these excuses but everybody liked to be present when she made one of her *risqué* remarks. It says a great deal for her charm that not one woman diarist of the period has written down anything liable to throw doubts upon the legend of her beauty.

Lovesick or not Berthier could read the signs of the times clearly enough. At the beginning of the campaign he was saying to Masséna: "We are about to make history!" A few weeks later he nodded his head in Napoleon's direction and remarked: "It will be a fine thing to be second to that man!" From the hour of Napoleon's first victory Berthier set out to be "second to that man." He never questioned his decisions, as did Lannes, or openly inveighed against him as did Augereau. Henceforth, whatever Napoleon did was right, even when events had proved him wrong. Patient, precise, and painstaking in every stroke of the pen, he walked in his master's shadow until it was dark. Then he went away and killed himself. There is only one recorded instance of Berthier disapproving of any action of his chief's and that concerned a matter far from the battlefield. When Josephine was at last persuaded to forego the fêtes in Paris and join her husband in Italy, the love-starved general caressed her in front of his chief-of-staff and his secretary. Berthier was greatly embarrassed by this and complained, in private, of "having to stand by with a smile and witness conjugal liberties!" It would be interesting to know how near the liberties approached licence.

Berthier's aide-de-camp during part of this campaign was the conceited innkeeper's son, Murat. Although Murat gained no prominence as a commander at this time he improved upon a reputation founded by his dash for the all-important guns during the "Whiff of Grapeshot." As a cavalry officer he was fearless, quick-thinking and impossibly gaudy. It was in Italy that Murat first met his future bride, Napoleon's youngest sister Caroline, sharpest and most treacherous of the Bonaparte brood. Murat was handsome and Caroline was willing but Napoleon, sure of his destiny after Lodi, hesitated to sanction the engagement. "After all, he is only an innkeeper's son," said Napoleon, whose family had once queued for municipal soup in Marseilles. However, he was persuaded by Josephine to agree to the match and he lived to regret it, for Caroline never ceased to encourage her vain, feckless husband to seek more and more power and in the end she nagged him into treachery. For the time being, however, and for many years to come, Murat could congratulate himself on his brilliant foresight: his entry into the Bonaparte family gave him precedence over all others, earning for him a crown and the cordial detestation of his colleagues.

One more obscure young man walked into the spotlight during the Italian springtime. Bessières, one-time barber of Languedoc, had forgotten his quixotic defence of King Louis when the Paris mob stormed the Tuileries in '92 and was now, outwardly at least, a staunch Republican. At the battle of Rivoli Captain Bessières was promoted Major and his subsequent rise was almost as rapid as Murat's for within seven years he was a duke. Perhaps he said nothing of his narrow escape from death as a Royalist but perhaps, more than any marshal, he deserved a title that was bestowed from a throne. He was the only man among them who had shed blood defending one.

Ex-gunner-cadet Marmont was another man who could congratulate himself on foresight during this campaign. Among the host of fighting men surrounding Napoleon he was the only one who could lay claim to youthful friendship with the great man. Before the first shot had been fired in Toulon harbor, and long before Bonaparte had earned the gratitude of Paris politicians by commanding a mob, Marmont had called him friend and taken him to his parents' home when they were garrisoned in Burgundy. In spite of Marmont's subsequent record (and no marshal emerges from this story with a grubbier one) there is no reason to assume that he had shown a lonely young officer this kindness with an eye to future preferment. He was a cautious, cold-blooded man but in these early days he had a genuine admiration for his brilliant and moody friend. In his assessment of the earlier victories he goes further than anyone in predicting the future and, what is even more interesting, in capturing the mood of the French camp when it was riding the flood-tide of victory. "We were like a big, happy family" he writes, looking back on those triumphant days when everyone about him was young and eager and full of promise. He was never to be so happy again but for this he had no one but himself to blame. Marmont was the kind of man who will never fully commit himself to one cause or one person. Such men are common enough but few are called upon to pay Marmont's price for half-hearted loyalties.

One other uncommitted man came down into Italy when the hottest of the fighting was over. This was ex-sergeant major Bernadotte, the cleverest fence-squatter of the century, the cleverest perhaps of all time.

Bernadotte was now enjoying high command in the Army of the Rhine, a much smarter outfit than the hard-fighting, hard-looting Army of Italy, and he had never met Napoleon until he arrived in September 1797. His officers and men were understandably jealous of the Italian Army's reputation and quarreling soon broke out on a vicious scale. Bernadotte even challenged Berthier to a duel and in combats between the two groups there were three hundred and fifty casualties before the idiotic strife was checked. Ex-journalist Brune, himself a hothead, was temporarily in command of Masséna's division when the trouble began and there was bad blood for a long time between the hook-nosed Gascon, who flatly refused to fall under Bonaparte's spell, and the man who had once written a military text-book to prove that he could become a famous general whenever he liked. It was here that bragger Bernadotte sowed the first seeds of discord among the "happy family." Nobody cared for him very much and he owed his subsequent rise less to his talents than to the fact that he married Napoleon's former sweetheart and sister-in-law, the pretty little brunette Desirée Clary. Fifteen years were to pass before Napoleon learned the lesson that one cannot necessarily trust a man simply because he happens to have married a relation.

Bernadotte did not remain with the Army of Italy very long. He further angered the Republican veterans by insisting on the reintroduction of the word *Monsieur* to replace "Citizen" and the order resulted in another challenge to duel, this time from outraged Brune. Augereau backed Brune but Napoleon later allowed the word to stand. Alone among them he could see that the time was approaching when courtesy would be more fashionable than fanaticism. Ultimately Bernadotte decided that he was bored by these bickerings and that his real talent lay in diplomacy. He got himself accredited to Vienna as French Ambassador but he was not an outstanding success. Austrians, humiliated by a series of crushing defeats in the field, thought they could win easier laurels by tearing down the Embassy tricolor, and Bernadotte, whose personal courage was beyond question, defended it sword in hand on the steps of his official residence.

So the first brilliant spring of the legend passed and for a short spell the men who had amazed a continent drank and whored, duelled and argued politics in billet and bivouac until fighting should begin again. Back in Paris the Directory that had succeeded the bloodthirsty Convention rocked before the blast of another counter-revolution and men began to look around for someone strong and successful enough to give France the sane, stable government it needed if the fruits of the Revolution were to be saved from the pockets of the seedy rascals who had stayed the guillotine.

Nobody had been more surprised than men like Barras and Tallien at finding themselves public heroes when the tyrant Robespierre was overthrown, and the smartest of them decided to make the most of it. Without Napoleon they would have been thrown down in a little over a year but his victories kept them in the saddle. It was proving, however, a very slippery saddle. Royalists, theorists, terrorists, and honest men were sick of mob rule and nepotism and all were trying, in their various ways, to unseat the government. If Napoleon had cared to cash in on his popularity after the Italian victories he could have made himself military dictator by marching on Paris. He was determined, however, to come to power by legal means and for the time being was content to humor the opportunists of the Directory. They exchanged polite letters to one another, each assuring the other of an unshakeable loyalty to the Republic, but Bonaparte had already made up his mind to rule France, whereas the Directors, dominated by Barras, were equally determined to remain in power as long as possible, some because there was money to be made but a few, like the patriot Carnot, because they were genuine Republicans.

On the eve of Lodi the Directors had sent Napoleon a letter ordering him to share the command of the Army in Italy with old Kellerman, victor of Valmy. Napoleon ground his teeth with rage but he kept his temper and wrote back saying that, whereas he felt sure Kellerman would lead the army as well as he was leading it, it would be suicidal to split the command in two. Before the Directors had thought out an answer to this Napoleon had entered Milan and there could be no question of superseding him as commander-in-chief.

In the meantime, however, Napoleon kept a close watch on the capital and very little escaped his eye while he was in the field. When things had quieted down somewhat he sent Augereau to Paris to insure that the Royalists did not organize a military coup aimed at reinstating the Bourbons.

This was the kind of job the soldier-of-fortune relished. Asked by the Directors why he had come to Paris he replied, very innocently: "Me? Why, I've come to kill Royalists!" The Directors took him at his word and he was given a free hand. Having investigated matters Augereau decided that he needed money to square the various factions and sent off posthaste to Bonaparte for an advance. Bonaparte dispatched funds but in so doing made a remark concerning Augereau's character that should surely go down in history as an outstanding understatement: "That fellow Augereau is rather warm!" he commented and one wonders if he was having second thoughts about his choice of emissary.

He need not have worried. Augereau knew his business. He posted his men, served out champagne, and set about rooting out the conspirators. In a matter of hours the danger was past and the surviving Directors were safely in the saddle again. They had two and a half more years of power before Napoleon judged the moment had come to have done with mobs and factions and political clubs and all the prattle and paraphernalia of revolutions. Nobody could time a positive action with the accuracy of Napoleon Bonaparte and he proved it that autumn, when he returned to Paris after an absence of more than eighteen months.

His bearing was modest. Nobody would have believed that he was proud of his achievements, and even schemers like Barras and Talleyrand were puzzled. Here was a soldier whose genius was already being discussed as far away as Moscow and Lisbon, a man just past his twenty-eighth birthday whom every honest citizen admired and every ranker in all the armies of the Republic adored. Everywhere he went crowds flocked to cheer and jostle him. He and his charming wife (whom he so obviously worshipped) were fêted and flattered wherever they appeared but he showed no sign at all of recognizing power that was his for the taking. Nervous politicians courted him and he ramained polite and respectful. Bystanders cheered him as he rode through the streets of Paris and he acknowledged their cheers with an absent-minded lift of the hand. His narrow, sallow face, burned by the Italian suns, was impassive and his dress soldierly and simple. His lack of ostentation supported the claim that he, alone of all the generals who had ridden down into Italy, had lived on his pay and allowances and left all the loot for the little men.

The act was an enormous success. The people loved him for his modesty and moderation. Here, they reasoned, was the man who could not only rescue France but rebuild her. It was exactly what he intended them to think. Like a twentieth-century stage star he chose a role that left the audience wanting more.

. . .

Wherever Napoleon rode he was attended by a small group of his close personal friends. Berthier was still in Italy, unable to drag himself away from the arms of Madame de Visconti, but most of the other veterans shared the victor's triumph. Prominent in the group was Cavalryman Murat, determined to get into the act and into the family, Lannes, who was spending with the carelessness of a man who knows that the next bullet may find a vital spot, Marmont, taking his cue from the man he had backed to win, and a few of the others who had won glory and riches in the cities of Piedmont and Lombardy. There was now talk of invading England and Napoleon traveled to the coast to study the project. Paris waited. France waited. Britain and the rest of Europe waited.

Then Napoleon made up his mind. An invasion of England without naval supremacy was impractical. A more indirect attack should be launched. Why not cripple the islanders by closing their trade routes to the East?

The Directors were delighted. At one stroke they would be rid of a man who could replace them by a word and embarked upon a campaign that would give them not only prestige but as much wealth as they had won in Italy. Happily they dragged out an existing plan for a descent upon Egypt and when Napoleon approved it they set about scratching round for backing.

Fortunately it was close at hand. The idea of a revolution had been occupying the minds of certain politicians in the cantons of Switzerland and text-book writer Brune was dispatched to the support of these partisans of liberty and equality. When he marched back again the Swiss treasury was empty. Brune was learning that there was a good deal more to being a general than knowing how to keep companies of infantry in correctly-dressed lines.

Almost the entire proceeds of the Swiss raid were earmarked for the Egyptian campaign but at the last moment the project collapsed. Bernadotte came pounding back from Vienna shouting of an insult to the French flag. Ships reported that the British and Russians were threatening a descent on the northern coastline. Rome revolted and a mob tore a French general in pieces. For a while it looked as if the Italian work would have to be done all over again. Napoleon, however, had set his heart on being a second Alexander. He sat down and wrote a threatening letter to Austria. Berthier was sent to quiet Rome, and close behind him (for Napoleon needed the map-wizard for his new campaign) went Masséna, rubbing his hands at the thought of all the gold lying about in the Holy City. The English, the Czar and the House of Hapsburg heard about the Eastern project and composed themselves to wait a month or so. They wanted to be sure that Longboots would be out of the way when they renewed the attack upon France.

In the early summer of 1798 Napoleon and his 45,000 sailed from Toulon. With him went Berthier, reluctantly but dutifully, Lannes to lead the infantry, Murat to lead the cavalry, and Marmont to direct the guns. One other serious-minded professional accompanied the expedition, the slovenly, humorless Davout. At this time Davout had never met Napoleon. He had very few friends and still kept himself very much to himself. Perhaps the abortive mutiny in the mess had taught him that impulsiveness did not pay.

Gaily and optimistically the army sailed away and Josephine, surrounded by tearful wives and sweethearts, called her farewell from the quay. The last words she addressed to her adoring husband were: "If you get to Thebes do bring me one of those pretty little obelisks!"

CHAPTER FOUR

FORTY THOUSAND CASTAWAYS

LONG before the French army set sail for Egypt Napoleon had come to terms with his destiny. History has represented him as a great believer in omens but there is not much fact to support this claim. His talk of his "star" was little more than a figure of speech and his announcement that it was his destiny to do this or that usually meant that he had selected a certain course and made up his mind to pursue it, no matter what obstacles intervened. He used this kind of phrase as a smokescreen. He was not only a brilliant general but for many years an extremely lucky one, and if faith in his luck, or "star," or "destiny" encouraged the men about him to attempt the impossible, then he was prepared to discourse for hours about omens and predestination.

By May 1798, when the Egyptian adventure was well advanced, he had gathered about him a group of talented officers who took his luck for granted. Their confidence in it, plus their faith in his ability, seeped downwards through the army's junior officers, sergeants, corporals, to the ranks. Today, we should call this confidence *esprit de corps* and the attitude of the men of the British Eighth Army towards Montgomery, or that of American troops towards Patton, are examples of what collective confidence can do for a fighting force. The German Africa Corps felt this way about Rommel and in Napoleon's own time the Peninsular veterans acquired the same faith in Wellington's luck.

By this time the men completely dedicated to Napoleon's future included at least six future marshals, namely Lannes, Murat, Berthier, Marmont, Bessières and Davout. All six were now with him, heading for Alexandria.

Of the future marshals left behind at least ten held a high opinion

45

of Napoleon's ability but it is doubtful if, at this stage, any of them guessed the heights to which the Corsican might rise in the near future. They thought of him not as the future master of Europe or even France but merely as an exceptionally talented leader in the field. These ten were to play various roles in checking the renewed attempts on the part of Russia, Austria, and Britain to take advantage of Hop-o'-my-Thumb's absence. This party included Masséna, Pérignon, Grouchy, Lefèbvre, Soult, Ney, Mortier, Oudinot, Suchet, and St. Cyr. We shall see how they fared when they lacked Napoleon's guiding hand.

Discounting for a moment the six future marshals not included in either group there remained four who thought of themselves as Napoleon's equal, or even his superior. They were ready to concede the Corsican's luck and ability and they would have agreed with anyone who said that France stood in need of a single strong man who could consolidate the social gains of the Revolution but they were not devotees like Murat and Berthier. These four were plain-speaking Augereau, ex-haberdasher Jourdan, blunt old Kellerman, and the shifty Bernadotte. Each fancied himself as the much-needed strong man and it would not have needed much persuasion on the part of Director Barras, of Talleyrand, or of the Abbé Sieyes, to convince any one of them that Bonaparte was now a dead letter and that it was their plain duty to come forward, throw out the Directory, and assume a military dictatorship under the able guidance of an experienced politician. The politician, of course, would be the man who organized the coup.

Augereau and Jourdan were both diehard Republicans. They still believed in riotous assembly, the Feast of Pikes and, if need be, a busy guillotine. Both had forced their way to the top in the days when a single step lay between command of an army and a brief walk up the steps of the scaffold. They accepted this risk. Augereau had walked a tightrope since the far-off day when he killed an officer on parade. He held life cheap, his own and everyone else's. But Jourdan was a different type. He believed very sincerely in the theory of revolution, and because of his beliefs he had thrown aside his peddler's pack, rushed into the army and risen by a series of remarkable chances to high command, with victories to his credit. He now saw himself as the leader who had thrown back the foreign invasions in the heat of the day. To the end of his life he could never quite understand how a mere traveling draper had attained such distinction but deep in his heart he was proud of his record and would have fought to the death to oppose the rule of an autocrat. Old Kellerman, ex-sergeant major, would have seconded him, for he too was a passionate believer in the rights of man, even if it meant imposing them on the masses with the cutting edge of a cavalry saber. After all, it had been he, François Kellerman, who had stood undismayed when the Prussian army swept majestically up the slope towards the mill at Valmy, and he who saw them march down the slope and disappear into the mist. That was nearly five years ago when young Bonaparte's name had never been heard. The victories in Italy had been welcome enough but they had not saved Paris from the returning *émigrés,* or Paris Republicans from the hangman who would have followed the Prussians and Austrians into the capital. Kellerman was a laboriously slow thinker but even he was beginning to wonder if it was not his duty to save France from anarchy as he had once saved it from foreign mercenaries.

Then there was Bernadotte, the handsome Gascon, the man who could never be persuaded to jump off the fence at all. Bernadotte heartily agreed with every politician when told that he was the future dictator of France and then let the deputations depart wondering if cannonades in the Lowlands had unhinged the general's brain. For Bernadotte was, and remained, the biggest enigma of all. Not a single schemer in Paris knew what to make of him. He bragged and postured until politicians were convinced that he was ripe for a *coup d' état.* Then, when they made certain suggestions, he merely smiled, agreed with them and disappeared. At last they gave him up, confident that in due course they could lay their hands on a soldier who was popular enough to carry the fighting forces with him but not clever enough to rule without a politician at his elbow. They were not seriously worried about Bonaparte any more for the little man was a long way off and most of his terrible friends were with him. In fact hardly anyone in Paris, including his wife, expected to set eyes on Napoleon again. What had he said when they asked him when he was likely to return? "Who knows? Perhaps never!"

They went back to the depressing task of combing the clubs and the barracks and the cafés for the right man.

.   .   .

Napoleon's luck held during the hazardous voyage to the Orient. The watchful Nelson missed him and he arrived on the last day of June, disembarking his force at Alexandria and marching inland towards Cairo.

It had been a tedious journey. At first Napoleon was seasick and very short-tempered but when he recovered they all sat around in his cabin and played endless games of cards. Napoleon cheated quite shamelessly but at the end of the game he always returned the money he won. He read a great deal, mostly philosophy and history, or worked at mathematical problems with some of the savants who had accompanied the expedition. He never read a romance and despised those who did. Poor, gentlemanly Bessières received a severe scolding when Napoleon glanced over his shoulder and saw the title of the book he was enjoying. "That," said the commander-in-chief witheringly, "is the kind of book a lady's maid would enjoy!" The ex-barber sighed and returned the book to his locker.

At this time Egypt, nominally Turkish, was ruled by the military caste of Mamelukes. They were splendid warriors and owed allegiance to no one but their captains, the Beys. To the wretched fellaheen it did not matter a handful of rice who ruled the Nile Valley. Whoever was in charge he led the life of a mangy, half-starved dog.

Thus it was that the veterans of Italy marched almost to Cairo before they met with serious opposition. Then, in the shadow of the Pyramids, Bonaparte's theories of modern warfare were matched with the spectacular but obsolete tactics of Oriental cavalry. The Mamelukes came thundering down on six compact squares of infantry and those who did not go down under the well-directed volley fire were scattered south and west by Murat's brilliant charges. Many were killed and more were drowned in the Nile trying to escape. The handsome innkeeper's son was under a cloud at this time. Napoleon had not forgotten some hesitance on his part under the walls of Mantua but at the battle of the Pyramids his work was faultless and he became the idol of the cavalry. After the battle it was the infantry's turn again. They found none of the promised loot in Cairo and went fishing in the Nile, using their bayonets as rods. Every now and again they caught a dead Mameluke, whose valuables, averaging ten thousand francs in gold, silver and precious stones, were carried on their persons in special belts. It was a very profitable day's fishing.

The French entered Cairo on July 21. On the night of August 1 Nelson sailed into Alexandria roadstead and blew the French fleet—ships of the line, frigates, corvettes and transports—to matchwood. It was more than a naval defeat, it was a disaster of the first magnitude. At a single stroke the victorious army was converted into a horde of castaways, with no means whatever of returning to France or getting reinforcements and supplies through the British blockade.

One of the first men to feel the full weight of the tragedy was the chief-of-staff, Berthier. Berthier had never wanted to go to Egypt in the first place. It was too far from the haunts of Madame de Visconti. He could bear the absolute dearth of military intelligence but the thought that his adored's love letters were now being studied and sniggered over in the cabins of English frigates made him very wretched. Two or three ships had escaped the general fate and were moored close inshore, the sole hope of a fraction of the army returning home. Berthier, made bold by intolerable heartache, began to plague the commander-in-chief for a passage and was so insistent that at last Napoleon handed him a passport and told him he might leave. He made it very clear, however, that Berthier's whinings had displeased him very much and that he was happy to dispense with his services. He also remarked that, while others might despair, he, as commander-in-chief, had every confidence in the successful outcome of the venture and intended to march across the Sinai Desert, up the coast of Palestine, into Asia Minor and home to France by overland route. Alternatively, he might even found an Eastern Empire and turn his back on Europe for good.

Berthier wrung his hands. It was plain that the decision of a lifetime faced him. If he used his passport Napoleon would soon find and train another chief-of-staff, whereas if his favorite pupil did succeed in dodging the blockage and getting home he would have forfeited all chances of fame under the greatest genius of the age. Berthier's love for the Corsican won and he threw down the passport. Napoleon at once embraced him and they sat down to plan the march to Jaffa.

Berthier was not the only grumbler. The glamorous East had disappointed nearly all the officers and they became quarrelsome and edgy. Bessières got into trouble again for acting as second at a duel and when Napoleon overheard a group of them grousing he suddenly lost his temper and strode into the middle of them shaking his fist and roaring: "If you are five feet ten inches I shall deal with you!"

Berthier, having made up his mind to deprive himself of Madame de Visconti's company, did his best to compensate for her physical absence. He erected an altar to her in his tent! Bourienne, Napoleon's grave and punctilious secretary, was amazed when he called on the chief-of-staff one evening and found him kneeling in front of the lady's portrait. The secretary coughed, discreetly, but Berthier made no sign and presently the embarrassed Bourienne stole quietly out into the desert, leaving the odd little officer to his devotions.

Part of the trouble during this period of inactivity was due to the acute shortage of women in the camp. Most of the French found the native girls too obese for their taste but the commander-in-chief, having learned that his wife in Paris had been unfaithful to him, solaced himself with the blonde wife of a chasseur, a girl called Fourés who had evaded the ban against camp-followers by disguising herself as a soldier. Berthier obligingly posted the husband to France with a large packet of "important dispatches" but the blockading British knew every detail of camp life, and when the wretched man was taken prisoner they set him on shore again as the best means of annoying the commander-in-chief. Marmont, in command at Alexandria, was unable to detain the poor devil without giving the game away and the cuckolded chasseur came hurrying back into Cairo to find his wife living openly with the commander-in-chief. Thoroughly disgusted he demanded a divorce and the provost marshal gave him one.

By this time, however, plans were advanced for the overland march and the army shook off its lethargy and set out for Syria.

Across the wastes it toiled, crossing the Suez Isthmus and pushing the feeble Turkish opposition before it. By the end of March 1799, the French were sapping the walls of Acre, which were defended by an English sailor (who had escaped from a Paris prison a few days before the French sailed from Toulon) and a French *émigré*, who had graduated from the same military school as Napoleon. These two men, with some captured French cannon and a mob of half savage Turks, now faced the most efficient army since Cromwell's Ironsides and the French never doubted the issue. Yet Sir Sidney Smith, Engineer Phillipeaux and their wretched garrison, with some help from the plague, successfully defied forty assaults in sixty-six days and pushed twenty-four sallies into the lines of the besieging army. Four thousand men and four first-class generals died in the breaches of St. Jean d'Acre. Many more were wounded and had to be carried back to Cairo.

Among the wounded was the impulsive Jean Lannes, leader of a dozen storming parties and at last left for dead on the slopes of the fortifications. In a final, hopeless assault Lannes got a bullet in the temple and the few survivors of his forlorn hope dived back into the trenches and left him lying in the open. Jean Lannes, however, commanded not only the respect but the friendship of his men. A captain ran out and dragged him back by his heels and Lannes never forgot his act of gallantry. He not only set the man up in business when they returned to France but frequently went to stay with him. One of the strongest characteristics of the French army at this period was the warm comradeship that existed between men of high and low rank.

With the camp crowded with casualties and the plague claiming more victims every day, there soon was no alternative but to retreat. Sullenly the French abandoned their trenches and Lannes and the other wounded officers were carried away in litters. Every horse, including the commander-in-chief's, was used for the disabled.

When the army trailed into Jaffa Napoleon walked through the wards of the hospital shouting: "The Turks will be here in a few hours! Whoever feels strong enough get up and come with us!" It says a good deal for the hardihood of the French soldiery that after a few days' rest in Cairo the survivors of the march were able to meet the new Turkish threat at Alexandria and hurl the Sultan's army of twelve thousand men back into the sea.

This battle, known as Aboukir, was one of the most spectacular of Napoleon's victories. Lannes, whose convalescence had been spent in a jolting litter over miles of burning sand, was fit enough to lead the infantry. In the pursuit that followed the victory he got another wound, this time through the thigh, and Murat, who also distinguished himself at the fight, was another casualty. The two future marshals, who already detested one another, were laid side by side in the hospital and Lannes must have taken full advantage of the fact that he could insult his rival with impunity, for Murat's jaw had been shattered by a pistol shot and his face was swathed in bandages.

After the battle of Aboukir another future marshal, so far utterly obscure, joined the inner circle of the commander-in-chief. The latecomer was Louis Nicholas Davout, twenty-nine years of age and serving his first campaign under Napoleon. The aloof, moody man had a grievance. Knowing himself to be a superior soldier to the majority of Napoleon's officers he resented his isolation and after a good deal of thought on the subject he demanded an interview. From the viewpoint of both men the meeting proved extremely fruitful. From that moment on Davout showed Napoleon unswerving loyalty and in the end Napoleon reposed more trust in him than in any of the men who had shared his early triumphs in Italy.

A thin trickle of European news was now penetrating the blockade. Lannes, for instance, had learned that his wife had given birth to a boy fourteen months after her husband's departure on the troopship. Napoleon learned that his wife was living with a cashiered officer and also that his Italian conquests had been lost and that the armies of Russia, Austria, and Britain were destroying the Republic.

For hours after receiving the newspaper reports that told of a disastrous defeat at Novi, of the surrender of the future marshals Pérignon and Grouchy, of the encirclement of Masséna in Switzerland, and a dozen other disasters, he and Berthier were closeted in their headquarters.

When they emerged it was to send for the Admiral in charge of the few vessels that had escaped destruction by Nelson. Napoleon justified his desertion by pressure of events. He had made up his mind to chance a return passage and leave the Army of Egypt to its fate.

Between them the commander-in-chief and chief-of-staff made out a short list of gauntlet runners—Lannes, still on crutches, Murat, still swathed in bandages, the well-mannered Bessières, and Marmont the gunner. Davout was not included. He remained behind to buttress the authority of Napoleon's successor, General Kléber, and as a kind of consolation prize the new commander-in-chief was given custody of pretty little Pauline Fourés, the divorced blonde of the chasseur.

Pauline failed to console the new man, for Kléber, who had never succumbed to the Napoleonic charm, was speechless with fury. In the trenches before Acre he had growled his contempt for the man. "There goes the little scoundrel," he had muttered, "he's no bigger than my boot!" Now, in command of thousands of disease-ridden, half-mutinous men, and with no hope whatever of getting home other than as an exchanged prisoner, Kléber cursed the commander-in-chief with a profundity that would have excited the admiration of Augereau. Perhaps a premonition lent color to his invective. In a few months he would be dead, stabbed to the heart by a fanatic as he walked on the terrace of his headquarters.

League by league, often moving at the speed of an oar-propelled boat, the tiny convoy crept westward along the coast of Africa, ready to beach and make a run for it if a British frigate made a grab at them. They were lucky. After weeks at sea they slipped across the waist of the Mediterranean and landed at Corsica, where Napoleon was astonished at the number of islanders who claimed kinship with him. Four days later they made another dash and finally got ashore at Fréjus.

The stage was set for a new adventure, this time in Paris.

.　　.　　.

Between the attack on the Bastille and the moment when Napoleon usurped power and made himself consul for life a large number of Frenchmen claimed to have saved the Republic. There was Danton, with his roars of defiance in '92, and there was Dumouriez, who had deserted the Royalists, there was Kellerman, who stood like a rock at Valmy, haberdasher Jourdan, victor of Fleurus, Hoche, Marceau, Moreau, and several other generals, including young Napoleon Bonaparte and his cronies. All these claims had a certain amount of validity but there is one that is unquestioned, even today. It is that of André Masséna, ex-sergeant major, fruit-seller and smuggler, who held the Swiss bastion against all comers during the advance of five allied armies in the last year of the old century.

If Masséna had not held onto Switzerland, or if he had made a single false move or error of timing, the fugitives from Egypt would have returned to a France occupied by British, Austrian, and Russian troops. There would have been no Marengo, no Austerlitz, and no Waterloo. Masséna was thus the midwife of the saga for by holding on to Switzerland he saved France for Napoleon and incidentally displayed a genius for defensive warfare that has not been surpassed by any soldier in any army in the world.

The Coalition, financed by £300,000 in English gold, reformed its ranks in the summer of Napoleon's departure. Anglo-Russians under the grand old Duke of York descended on the Dutch coasts. The Austrians, under the Archduke Charles, drove Jourdan back to the Lower Rhine. The savage Russian general, Suvorov, half-man and half-demon, planned to cross the St. Gothard and join forces with Austro-Russian troops in Zurich. With Masséna prostrate, there was nothing to stop a combined advance on Paris.

Brune hurried north-east to challenge the Duke of York and found a general who did indeed march his men to the top of the hill and march them down again. Brune was not a brilliant strategist but he was a genius when measured against the Duke of York. In a very short time he had not only defeated him twice but talked him into evacuating. The northern coasts were safe.

Down in the south, however, things were by no means as satisfactory. The situation moved from bad to worse. No one could make headway against the Russian Suvorov, who smashed every army sent against him and soon recaptured all the cities won by the Army of Italy. Sérurier and his command were taken prisoner and General Macdonald, the son of the clansman, who came up from Naples to stop the rout, was swept across the Apennines into Genoa. The French tried again at Novi but General Joubert was killed and the two ex-aristocrats, Grouchy and Pérignon, were taken prisoner when the rearguard was overrun.

Meanwhile, with yet another army, the Russian Korsakov was sitting in Zurich, awaiting the arrival via the St. Gothard of his countryman Suvorov. Watching him, like a professional poker player with a poor hand, was Masséna, his troops deployed in a semi-circle as he tried to look in every direction at once.

The miserly old rascal had two things in his favor, his own indomitable patience and the extremely high quality of his divisional commanders. Serving under Masséna in Switzerland at this time were no fewer than four future marshals. Acting as chief-of-staff was Oudinot, the tough, front-line fighter who once thought of being a brewer, and with Oudinot were Michel Ney, who might have been an Alsatian barrel-cooper. Louis Suchet, who should have obeyed his parents by becoming a silk merchant, and Nicholas Jean-de-Dieu Soult, who had wanted to be a baker. Also there were farmer's son Mortier, the big, jolly man whom everyone liked, as well as leaders like Lecourbe, Souham, d'Erlon and Vandamme, every one of whom was to write his name on the Arc de Triomphe. The roll call of the Army of Switzerland would have encouraged a less self-reliant commander-in-chief than Masséna as he sat still in his headquarters outside Zurich, holding his troops as a desperately anxious gambler holds his cards.

His task was beset with appalling difficulties. First he had to watch Korsakov and his allied Austrian army in and around Zurich, where the invaders had massed ready to enter France the moment Suvorov appeared. Then he had to watch Suvorov and let him get near his allies but not near enough to break through to them. Above all he had to persuade the panic-stricken politicians in Paris that the moment to strike was his, not theirs.

A string of couriers came galloping into his headquarters with despatches imploring him to strike but Masséna held on to his cards and waited. More and more enemy troops packed themselves into Zurich, until the city and the country outside were jammed with wagons and supplies. News came from mountain-fighter Lecourbe that Suvorov was forcing his way, yard by yard, up the St. Gothard, delayed but not checked by Lecourbe's skillful retreat. More dispatch-riders arrived with shrill messages that if Masséna did not fight now the Republic was lost. Masséna read them carefully but said nothing and did nothing. Quietly, without any sign of dismay, he waited for somebody to play the wrong card and at last somebody did, the Russian Korsakov, who extended his lines so much that he had his back to the lake.

Like a cobra Masséna struck. Pinning the Russian against the lake he sent Oudinot dashing to cut off the enemy's escape. The Russian knew he was trapped. Abandoning all the guns and stores he had, plus eight thousand prisoners, Korsakov burst through Oudinot's lines and fled. There would be no junction of Czarist generals now. On the day Masséna and Oudinot hit Korsakov, Soult fell on the Austrian army like a thunderbolt. The Austrians abandoned everything in a stampede to get out of Switzerland and back to their own country. All that was left of the three-pronged trap was the savage Suvorov, struggling up the pass. The victorious French turned on the Terror of Islam and gave him the hiding of his life. He was lucky to get back over the wild country of the Grisons with a battered remnant of his command and the Czar, his employer, was so dismayed that he at once abandoned the Coalition.

Horsemen dashed off to Paris announcing the deliverance but their arrival did not provoke as much excitement as it should have done. There was a reason for this. Another staff officer had arrived from the south with equally sensational news. Napoleon had landed at Fréjus and was on his way to the capital.

CHAPTER FIVE

"SECURITY FOR ALL!"

ONE did not have to be a politician to realize that something was stirring in Paris during the brief period between Napoleon's return to the Rue Chantereine (renamed Rue de la Victoire in honor of his Italian triumphs) and his seizure of power after the coup known in history as "Brumaire."

Anyone who lived in that quarter of Paris must have been impressed by the steady stream of distinguished visitors who passed in and out of the house that had once been occupied by the great actor Talma, the house to which Josephine had taken her husband after their wedding five years before. To have stood at the corner of Rue de la Victoire in November, 1799, and watched the carriages and the horsemen come and go, would have been to look upon most of the men who were to write the story of the First Empire. The story had begun when young Bonaparte directed artillery fire on the British in Toulon. It was to end twenty years later, when the last Imperial army rushed pell-mell down the road from Waterloo to Charleroi. They were all there, talking, gesticulating, courting and being courted, protesting, converting or being converted. It was more like a salesman's convention than a conspiracy and the principal salesman was Napoleon. The product he was selling? Himself, as Master of France!

In and out they went, passing the time of day with the charming, gracious Josephine or her sister-in-law, Julie, the soap-boiler's daughter whose dowry had rescued the Bonaparte clan from penury not long before, and while many of them stayed to drink a glass of wine and pledge themselves as Bonaparte's men, there were others who talked their way out again and drifted away to consider the wisdom of supporting a man who had just deserted his army and come home like a battle-shy recruit.

There were those, of course, who needed no persuasion that Napoleon was the man to control France. The converted included Jean Lannes, still hobbling about on crutches from the effects of his thigh wound at Aboukir, and his rival Murat, whose wound was healed and who was on top of his form, dashing about Paris at the head of jingling columns of hussars and dragoons. There was Gunner Marmont, oldest friend of Napoleon, who had long ago made up his mind to follow this man to the end—or almost the end—and there was the indispensable Berthier, planning the conspiracy as he would a battle, with stacks of neatly arranged papers and an infallible memory for the name and the present whereabouts of every potential supporter. There could be no doubt whatever about the loyalty of these men, or of some of the lesser known soldiers, like Macdonald and pedantic old Sérurier, who had never much liked the din and muddle of revolutions. These men, and most of their officers, could be relied upon to back any soldier against any politician, and at the crisis of a conspiracy that was to come within inches of failure they were to prove their worth.

There were, however, a number of uncommitted public figures who were yet to be convinced that it was a soldier's duty to overthrow his constitutional government and replace it with military dictatorship. Old Sergeant Major Lefèbvre, for instance, now Governor of Paris, who descended upon Bonaparte's house demanding to know what the hell was going on and why detachments of troops were marching and cantering all over the city. Were they or were they not bent on some kind of demonstration against the lawfully elected government?

Lefèbvre's misgivings did not worry Napoleon much. To a psychologist of Bonaparte's ability the old soldier was an easy victim. He took him by the arm, led him on one side, and talked in hushed tones of a threat to liberty by various unnamed factions in the slums. The old warrior nodded his head sympathetically and any questions he might have asked were lost in a wave of gratitude that swamped his honest heart when Napoleon made him a present of a magnificent sword, captured in Egypt. From then on, Napoleon kept Lefèbvre close beside him wherever he went and treated the old fellow with great respect. It was like the founder of a dubious firm of brokers printing the name of an impeccably honest old colonel on a spurious note-heading.

Some of the others were not so easily gulled and among those who gave the most trouble were Augereau and Jourdan who were beginning to wonder what had happened to their beloved revolution and whether

it had lost itself in a maze of proclamations about the dangers of invasion
and the threats of civil war. For the time being they refused to commit
themselves one way or the other but while they reserved the right to challenge the legality or necessity of the plot they did not denounce it and
were seen everywhere, talking to the troops, sounding public opinion and
weighing chances with the coolness of men who had already survived a
decade of rioting and disorder.

Bernadotte was an even harder nut to crack. All the blandishments
of Josephine, of Julie Bonaparte, the sister of Desirée, Bernadotte's wife,
and of Napoleon himself, backed by the persuasive Berthier and the impatient Lannes, failed to woo the big Gascon into the flock. On the morning the conspirators were due to strike he turned up at the house in the
Rue de la Victoire wearing civilian clothes, as though to disassociate himself from any idea of a military coup. Few who called at the house that
day got away without declaring for one side or the other but Bernadotte
managed it and even his brother-in-law, Joseph Bonaparte, was unable
to say whether the man was for or against Napoleon. In short Bernadotte
did what he had done on all previous occasions, he wore down everyone's
resistance, drowning them in a sea of wordy platitudes that meant absolutely nothing. Finally they left him sitting on the fence and got on
with the business in hand. Lannes limped across to take charge of the
Tuileries Guard and Murat marshalled the cavalry. Marmont won over the
gunners and made sure of their tools, and the conspiracy slowly gained
momentum. On the morning of November 18, the first legislative Chamber, the Council of Ancients, was accounted for. Then the plotters converged on the tougher opposition, the Council of Five Hundred, which
was adjourned to St. Cloud, outside Paris, to await the outcome of the
second day's maneuvers.

It was at this point that the conspirators ran into serious trouble,
for Napoleon had made a grave tactical error. He had taken it for granted
that an assembly of professional politicians could be conquered by rhetoric.

By early afternoon on November 19 troops had converged on the
Orangery at St. Cloud, and waiting to oppose or to fraternize with them
was a guard of Republican grenadiers, men whose duty it was to protect
the legislators. Nobody knew how these men would react to the threat
and while they were being sounded Bonaparte strode into the hall and
began a halting speech about the danger of a Jacobin revolt and a return
to the days of anarchy and the guillotine.

He had over-estimated his powers of oratory. A good enough speaker to harangue loot-hungry soldiers he was by no means good enough to dazzle professional talkers. Somebody asked for names and Napoleon began to stutter. In a moment there was uproar as deputies, enraged by this insult to their dignity, surrounded him, threatening and shouting and demanding over and over again to know what was happening to the constitution. Someone struck him a blow and another seized and disordered his uniform. All his life Napoleon hated and feared mobs and on this occasion he lost his nerve altogether. He gave ground, fumbling for words, and the chance was almost lost.

He was rescued by his brother Lucien, who, as President of the Deputies, began a frantic defence of the man who had tried Cromwell's tactics but rejected Cromwell's reliance upon force. A squad of men ran in and jostled their way to the half-fainting Bonaparte, dragging him and his brother Lucien clear of the press. Outside, the plain speaking Augereau summed up the situation. "You're in a fine mess now!" he jeered and was on the point of throwing up the whole business and going over to the opposition.

Lucien, however, had not lost his nerve. He piloted his brother across to the waiting grenadiers who were still paraded and undecided what to do. Pointing to his own and his brother's disordered clothes, and to a streak of blood on Napoleon's face, he made a ranting speech about an attempt on their lives by a minority of deputies, armed with daggers. Napoleon was popular with soldiers and the men began to mutter. The President of the Assembly, roared Lucien, was surely entitled to military protection from such an assault! Driving his point home, he seized a sword and held it within an inch of his brother's breast, declaring that he himself would kill him if Napoleon dared to challenge the liberty of France. The theatrical gesture was just what was needed. The grenadiers, now almost hemmed in by shouting pro-Bonaparte troops, were won over and the day was Napoleon's—or almost so.

There remained Murat's *coup de grâce*. All day long the handsome cavalryman had been urging Napoleon to throw aside the pretence of legality and rely on saber and bayonet as the only arguments that could not be misunderstood. But Napoleon continued to hesitate. He was determined, he said, to assume power by constitutional means. He did not want it said, once he was in power, that he had got there by attacking the elected representatives of the people. Yet this, in the ultimate, was what happened, for the furious deputies, voting Bonaparte an outlaw, would never be intimidated by any other means.

Murat ordered the drums to beat and their thudding carried across the court of the Orangery and into the Chamber. Timid deputies began to slip away but a majority still remained. The grenadiers began to file into the hall and an officer shouted "Citizens! You are dismissed!" More deputies slipped out but a large body stood its ground. Murat could wait no longer. "Chuck this rabble out!" he roared, and the soldiers advanced with bayonets. Sérurier drew his sword and joined in the fun. Bewildered Lefèbvre had the last of his doubts resolved by witnessing a soldier's sleeve ripped by a civilian. This was too much to bear. With a shout of rage he too joined in the fray and a moment later the last of the deputies were leaping from ground-floor windows and disappearing into the November dusk. Augereau, so far an uncommitted spectator to this extraordinary scene, now decided to come down on the winning side. Solemnly he walked up to Napoleon and congratulated him on organizing a long overdue spring-cleaning.

. . .

Night was falling over Paris. The rank and file of the conspirators went home secure in the belief that tomorrow would be a better and brighter day, ushering in a new and splendid era. Augereau, Murat, Lefèbvre and the others congratulated one another but Murat had other business. He called for four reliable troopers and sent them galloping over to Madame Campan's Academy for Young Ladies, where Caroline Bonaparte, youngest sister of the new consul, was learning arts and graces that are not usually taught in Republican schools. The troopers had orders to escort Mademoiselle Bonaparte to a place of safety. Having gambled heavily for forty-eight hours the innkeeper's son was not going home without making sure of his winnings.

Comparative quiet fell on the city. Jean Lannes threw aside his crutches, limped to his horse and trotted away from the Tuilleries. Jourdan, wondering perhaps if he should have stuck to haberdashery after all, went into hiding. Unlike Augereau, the other diehard Jacobin, Jourdan, could not quite bring himself to the point of congratulating a man who had smashed the Republic. Down in Italy, André Masséna, commander-in-chief of all French troops in the area since his victory in Zurich, locked his cash-boxes and turned his mind to pretty women.

Napoleon closeted himself with Sieyes and Ducos, the two surviving directors, and they set about drafting a new constitution and the first public
proclamation. The latter document announced that "there had been no victor or vanquished in the recent change of government but only security
for all!" This, it seems, did not apply to the two survivors of the Directory, or to the legislators who had leaped from the Orangery windows.
In the space of four weeks, Napoleon Bonaparte was chief consul, with
two nonentities for yes-men. There were to be legislative bodies of a sort
but NCO's in the barracks had more real say in what was written into
the statute books.

CHAPTER SIX

MASSÉNA HEARS THUNDER

THE popular conception of Napoleon Bonaparte is still that of a plump little man in a black hat who was good at war, was always waging war and therefore obviously delighted in war. Even after the passing of a hundred and fifty years few writers show much interest in his achievements off the battlefield and his creative work as a civil servant and administrator.

The facts are, of course, that as regards the waging of war he was less guilty than his opponents. Almost every war he engaged upon was forced upon him by others and while it is certainly true that he never hesitated to carry war into the enemy's country he was a sincere believer in the adage that the object of war is peace. If anyone doubts this let him read the text of the letter written by the victor of Marengo to his arch-enemy, Francis of Austria. It is the plea of a man who is fully aware of the bloody dispute that had been maintained for eight years and was to continue, with brief intervals of peace, for another fifteen years.

The purpose of this book is to follow the fortunes of his twenty-six marshals, not to submit an apologia for one of the most complex and able men in history, so it will suffice to say that the conqueror of "Brumaire" was obliged to drag himself away from the task of reorganising France from top to bottom and assemble an Army of Reserve within weeks of commencing his consulship. The reason for this was the relentless pressure of Austria in Italy and the fact that once again the French found themselves on the defensive in the south.

The Russians had retired from the ring for a while but Austria and Britain still clung to the hope that a successful invasion of France would put the clock back to July, 1789. Everyone in Paris had been too occupied with politics to consolidate Masséna's splendid victory at Zurich and the old smuggler was now boxed-up in Genoa, with an Austrian army on the land side and the British Admiral Keith's fleet within cannon-range of the waterfront. With him, as his right-hand man, was Nicholas Soult. The two men respected one another. Both were polite and both were very ambitious. Both, in a curiously shamefaced way, were patriots, but whereas Masséna had little to learn as a strategist his lieutenant was a comparative beginner. It was years before he would know enough to worry that other master of the defensive, the Duke of Wellington.

Masséna, Soult and a rabble of half-starved men were sealed up in a hostile city and it would be more than two months before Consul Bonaparte could lead his army down from the Alps and effect their rescue. In the meantime, as at Zurich, Masséna's duty was to sit still and by so doing prevent the Austrians from advancing along the coast into Provence.

It was an even tougher assignment than that given him in Switzerland, the year before. There was no way of getting a single sack of flour into the beleaguered city and for a time the garrison subsisted on horseflesh. Then the supply of horses gave out and they were given a loaf of bread each day. It is a courtesy to call the ration "bread." A young lieutenant has left us a graphic description of the ingredients of the fare issued to the soldiers. The loaves were a small quantity of damaged flour, sawdust, starch, hair-powder, oatmeal, linseed and rancid nuts. Such substance as they had depended upon cocoa! A general who sampled it likened it to peat mingled with oil.

On this fare Masséna's men held out in Genoa for exactly two months and during this period they not only beat off many attacks but carried out a large number of sorties. The civilians, who were reduced to eating cats and rats, sometimes took advantage of these sorties to gather weeds and nettles from outside the walls and from this they made soup. All ordinary provisions had disappeared at the outset of the siege, the local black market having cornered everything unclaimed by the military. It was now offering codfish, figs and sugar at prohibitive prices.

Typhus broke out and hundreds of civilians died each day, to be buried in a long trench sown with quicklime. Day and night fighting, and the naval shells lobbed into the town by British men-of-war, combined with sickness and privation to reduce the garrison to a few thousand combatants. But Masséna held on and Austrian and British envoys who came in under a flag of truce to suggest honorable surrender went away dumb-founded by the man's coolness and nerve.

In one of the sorties Soult, leading a charge, received a musket-ball in the knee and his men tried to carry him back on a stretcher improvised from musket barrels. The Austrians, however, were pressing hard and rapid movement caused the wounded man intolerable pain. So they left him alone with his brother and an aide-de-camp and all three were cap-tured and taken in triumph to the Austrian camp. The enemy's triumph was short-lived. Encouraged by having captured a famous general they pursued the French right up to the walls and were caught in a furious thunderstorm that drove both sides to shelter. Masséna took advantage of the storm to sally out again almost at once and under cover of the thunder, lightning, and torrents of rain the starving French pounced on the attackers and took a large number of prisoners.

Men died on the ramparts, the hospitals were crammed with typhus victims, and civilians dropped dead in the streets but Masséna went about his business with the preoccupied air of a merchant engaged in an impor-tant business deal. He even had the idea of stopping military funerals for fear they might depress survivors. Another order he issued was that only those capable of bearing a musket would be fed. Soldier-servants, grooms and valets became fighting men overnight.

At last an enterprising officer swam through the blockade with news that Napoleon, Lannes, Victor, Marmont, Desaix and the others had de-scended to the plains and posted themselves between the main Austrian forces and Vienna. Nobody had ever really believed that the French Army of Reserve would achieve the Alpine crossing— nobody that is, except the quiet man holding onto Genoa. When he heard the news he suggested to his emaciated lieutenants that it might now be a good idea to cut their way out, thus causing a major diversion to help their comrades further east. His officers demurred, pointing out that the garrison could not march, much less fight. Masséna reluctantly agreed that they had a point, so instead he sent a message to Lord Keith and the Austrians' saying that he was now ready to discuss surrender terms.

At the initial meeting between the three parties his impudence made them gasp. He would prefer, he said, to march out with drums beating and join Suchet's troops in southeastern France but as a concession to the allies he promised not to fight until he got there! The French, of course, were to retain their arms and he also required permission to send two officers through the Austrian lines in order to inform Napoleon what had happened! The Austrian general was so dumbfounded at this insolence that he was unable to utter a word but Lord Keith, who greatly admired his opponent's courage, bullied his ally into accepting the terms. Just as he was about to sign the agreement, however, Masséna heard what he felt sure was gunfire. "Why, there is the first consul coming now!" he exclaimed, laying down his pen.

But it was not the first consul, just a peal of Alpine thunder, and in the end Masséna signed and the garrison tottered out with all the honors of war, Masséna at the head of the column on one of the very few horses left in Genoa.

.   .   .

Napoleon, sharing a bed with the singer Grassini in Milan, was awakened in the small hours and told that Genoa had fallen. The news did not disturb him overmuch. The city had already held out much longer than he had any right to hope and his plans for beating the Austrians were now well advanced.

The Austrian army in Nice came pounding back to meet the terrible threat to its rear and the great battle that followed, Marengo, owes far less to Napoleonic inspiration than any of the great victories. Wellington might have called it "a damned close-run thing," and for a time it did look as if the French army was going to be caught in a trap of its own making. Napoleon had staked everything on success and if he was defeated then it would be the French not the Austrians who were cut off from bases.

Lannes had won a brilliant victory at Montebello (the town that was to give him his title when the new nobility was established) and on June 14, afterwards regarded as Napoleon's lucky day, the two main armies met and fought each other to a standstill. Then the Austrians threw their last reserves into a furious counter-attack and the French began to retire. In another half-hour it would have been over and a disaster on the scale of Waterloo would have engulfed them. The situation was saved by Marmont, the quick-witted gunner, and by a small group of cavalry under the command of Valmy Kellerman's son. With the few guns he had left Marmont poured in a point-blank fire of grapeshot and at the right moment Kellerman's heavy cavalry charged in the flank. Young General

Desaix was killed but the counter-attack was successful. By sunset the Austrians were everywhere in flight.

Soult, lying in hospital within sound of the gunfire, pictured the ebb and flow of the battle. By nightfall wounded Austrians were coming in with news of a French victory and the patient knew that he would not remain a prisoner for long. When Napoleon was looking about for deeds that could be used for ennobling a successful general he ruled out his four greatest victories as triumphs that belonged solely to him. No marshal was ever Duke of Austerlitz, Duke of Jena, Duke of Friedland or Duke of Marengo. As regards Austerlitz, Jena and Friedland he was justified in claiming the credit but concerning the Marengo he was not. The credit for this narrow victory was not his and neither, in the strictest sense of the word, was it Marmont's, or Kellerman's, or Lannes', or that of any man who actually fought in it. It was André Masséna's, who had made it possible by baking his revolting loaves in Genoa's public ovens and by prohibiting military funerals because they depressed his starving garrison. Masséna must have realized this but he never quarrelled with the titles that were bestowed upon him. After all, it was not titles that mattered to him but the revenues that went along with them.

CHAPTER SEVEN

THE UNWANTED MAP

"THERE are no such things as bad troops, only bad officers!" Napoleon had declared, and during the interval between the overthrow of the Austrians at Marengo and the formation of yet another Coalition aimed at bringing France to her knees, the First Consul set to work to insure that French armies should be led into battle by the cream of available officer talent.

The collapse of Austria in 1800 isolated Britain, and Napoleon, realizing that a prolonged breathing space was badly needed by a nation that had been fighting without pause for over seven years, bent his powerful will to secure a temporary peace with the islanders. For a time he was unsuccessful but at length in 1801 the peace party in England gained the ascendancy, and when hostilities ceased the future marshals were able to devote their energies to building up the instrument that was to dominate Europe for another twelve years. Three years were to pass, however, before eighteen of the twenty-six men under review became marshals and Napoleon, having already made himself life consul, crowned himself Emperor in Nôtre Dame.

During the greater part of this interval the men who had flung back successive invasions in the Lowlands, had twice overrun Northern Italy, had defied half Europe in Switzerland and Genoa, and had crossed the desert from Cairo to Acre, were quartered in a huge, convex arc along the northern coasts of the Continent. They were there with the avowed intention of invading Britain but one cannot help doubting the seriousness of Napoleon's intentions regarding an invasion, at least towards the end of the period. He had already learned the penalty of invasion without

adequate sea-power and as long as his standards flew from the cliffs of
Boulogne the British fleet, by far the most powerful naval striking force
in the world, remained within gunshot range, ready to sink his clumsy
barges the instant they put out into deep water. Nevertheless, he continued
to talk a good deal about invading England and in the minds of the corps
commanders there were no doubts that one day it would be attempted.
Probably Napoleon's primary purpose in keeping this host under arms
was to perfect the machine he needed to found a dynasty.

Viewed as a whole, this was a pleasant, hopeful and successful period
for the group of professional soldiers, ex-artisans, ex-lawyers, dyers, and
coopers who had followed the drum since the storming of the Bastille.

Brune, the only man among them who had already met and defeated
a British army, was sent down into the still troublesome west with the
object of making one final attempt to persuade the gallant, pigheaded
peasants of La Vendée that the Revolution was now a fact, and that the
Bourbon kings had no prospect whatsoever of returning to punish the
men who had guillotined Louis and his Austrian wife.

Napoleon gave Brune sixty thousand men to back his persuasions
and the General made moderate progress but after a time he was transferred to the Army of Italy and his place in the west was taken by Bernadotte. To everyone's annoyance the swashbuckling Gascon succeeded
where every other soldier had failed. For years the war in La Vendée
had been an open wound in the Republic. Column after column of "blues"
had been swallowed up in this difficult country, populated by fanatical
and improbably armed charcoal burners and carters, men who could not
or would not accept the fact that there was no longer a king at Versailles,
or a beautiful queen who played at being a shepherdess with her courtiers.
Some said that the evasive Bernadotte had been sent into the heart of
the smoldering provinces in the hope that a failure would provide good
excuse for breaking him and disposing of a very troublesome and unreliable fellow. Others suggested that he owed this second chance to his
wife's former friendship with Napoleon and her family relationship with
Napoleon's eldest brother. It is more likely that the second reason is the
truth. Napoleon had many faults but harboring malice was not one of
them. He was too big a man to bear a permanent grudge against an individual, sect, or even nation.

However that may be the Gascon hedge-squatter achieved a personal
triumph. He was at his very best when dealing with civilians and there

was no more trouble from the west. From then on, until his disgrace seven years later, Bernadotte enjoyed as much favor as anyone.

It was otherwise with Macdonald who, despite his assistance at the time of the coup, was still strongly suspected of Jacobinism and remained out of favor for a long time.

Perhaps Napoleon's distrust of this dogged half-Scotsman did have a personal element, for Macdonald had lately acquired a considerable reputation as a lover. His most celebrated mistress was Pauline, prettiest and wittiest of the Bonaparte clan. Pauline, an extraordinarily lovely woman, could never have enough male admirers and was credited with having indulged herself with five lovers in one week. She apparently devoted the maximum time to Macdonald for they are reported to have locked themselves up at St. Leu for three days, a supply of food having been sent in in advance. Napoleon loathed scandals that involved members of his family and he was extremely angry when he heard about this romantic weekend. He did not wholly forgive the future marshal until he handed him his baton on the field of Wagram, in 1809.

On the other hand Joachim Murat was riding even higher than usual. In the year of Marengo he married Caroline, Napoleon's youngest sister, the girl whom Murat had remembered to guard at the time of the *coup d'état* and had been angling to marry ever since they first met in Italy, four years before. Josephine favored his suit but she paid a high price for her sponsorship. Napoleon gave Caroline a dowry of thirty thousand francs but being short of funds he appropriated his wife's favorite pearl necklace in order to raise the money. Josephine was not slow to replace the loss. She sent for a famous jeweler and through him obtained a necklace worth considerably more, one that had once belonged to the unfortunate Marie Antoinette. It was necessary, of course, to persuade Napoleon that she had owned the replacement for a long time, so she told him it had been given to her in Italy. For corroboration she sought Berthier's help and the unfortunate chief-of-staff was persuaded to deceive Napoleon as to the worth of the new jewels. Berthier was very fond of Josephine and he stood by her, although the act of deception troubled his conscience and he was terrified of being unmasked as an accomplice. He never was. Napoleon had an eagle eye for terrain and the mistakes of his adversaries but as a husband he lost every engagement.

Not long after Marengo the Royalists made their final attempt to destroy the man whom they had hoped would use his power to reinstate the Bourbons. A few bold spirits manufactured an infernal machine consisting of a barrel of powder and placed it, with a slow fuse attached, on a cart along the route that Napoleon was taking to the Opera. The bomb exploded with devastating effect and a number of people were killed. Napoleon escaped but among the minor events triggered off by the explosion was the premature birth of Caroline's first child, Achille. Caroline had been traveling in a carriage immediately behind the consul's coach and was brought to bed within hours. In view of the fact that his wife's life had been endangered Murat showed remarkable restraint by asking the first consul to spare the lives of the conspirators. His plea was in vain but the attempt does him credit.

There was a good deal of coming and going among Paris conspirators in this period and much need for an efficient police force in the capital. Napoleon did not have much faith in professional policemen. "They invent more than they discover and only catch fools!" he grumbled. Fortunately a first-class military policeman was at hand. Davout had escaped from Egypt and arrived home after a series of hair-raising adventures and the humorless Burgundian made a very good policeman. He was not the type of man to waste time chasing fools or manufacturing evidence. He was attentive, thorough, and absolutely ruthless. He could not be bribed and it is impossible to play upon human sympathies that do not exist. There were no more infernal machines in Paris as long as the iron-willed Davout was sitting at police headquarters.

Lannes and Augereau had been in trouble as usual. Both took grave exception to Napoleon's reconciliation with the Church and, at the special service ordered to commemorate the Concordat with Rome, Lannes growled that all that was necessary now was the appearance of the million men who had died to get rid of this mummery! Augereau, still a Republican at heart, agreed with him and they salved their consciences by swearing all the way through the service.

About this time Lannes got into financial trouble by overspending on the uniforms of the Consular Guard. Napoleon was a very careful man with money and although he was obliged to shift his wife's mountain of debts every time he returned to Paris he had no intention of doing the same for extravagant generals. He told Lannes that unless he could make good the deficiency he would have him cashiered. Openhanded Augereau came to the rescue and loaned Lannes the money. Lannes was then given a lucrative embassy in Portugal but like his fellow Gascon,

Bernadotte, he was not suited to a diplomat's career. The Portuguese were terrified of him. Wherever he appeared he trailed an enormous saber that clanked and rattled like a specter's ball and chain. His principal victim was the Prince of Brazil, who trembled every time he came into contact with the terrible general.

Lannes thoroughly enjoyed himself down in Portugal. There was a dignified English ambassador in Lisbon and Lannes indulged his hatred of the British by driving his coach alongside the British official's in such a manner as to precipitate the British equipage into the ditch. In the intervals between saber clanking and reckless driving he found himself another wife to replace the lady who had been unfaithful to him while he was in Egypt. The new Madame Lannes was a very charming person and greatly beloved by everybody. Later on she reappears in the story as the chaperon of the Emperor's second wife.

Some of the future marshals were now approaching the age when most professional soldiers think of retirement. Kellerman was sixty-five and Sérurier was nearly sixty. Both had seen as much active service as they wanted to see and were looking towards a quiet life on their country estates. When the marshalate was announced, in May 1804, these two ex-Royalist officers, together with ex-grenadier Pérignon and ex-sergeant-major Lefèbvre, were placed on the retired list, although Pérignon was only fifty and Lefèbvre a year younger. Two other men who were named as marshals of the Empire were in their fifties, Berthier, the chief-of-staff and Moncey, the lawyer's son who had so often run away to the army and been rescued by long-suffering parents. Neither, however, was retired. Berthier served on for another decade and played a leading role in every major campaign. Moncey, honest, plodding old fellow, continued soldiering until he made a complete ass of himself in Spain and was fetched home and told to put his slippers on.

For the rest there were active days ahead. During the brief peace of Amiens, when Europe was quiet for the first time since the *émigrés* had marched on Paris, hundreds of wealthy English globe-trotters visited Paris and compared the good looks and soldierly bearing of the future marshals to the sallow insignificance of the man they called Master. The trippers, however, were soon scuttling back to London or resigning themselves to dreary years of internment, for the patched-up peace did not endure. Soon the trumpets were braying on the heights overlooking the Channel ports and two hundred thousand men were in training for a descent upon Kent and Sussex. By midsummer a fighting force was in being that was to become known as the Grand Army. It was composed of seven corps, made up of men with enormous experience in war and led by the most celebrated captains of the age.

War with Britain began again in May 1803, and nine future marshals took up their commands in the Army of the Coasts of the Ocean. The corps commanders were Bernadotte, fresh from his triumph in the west, Marmont, stationed in Holland, Davout, in the Dunkirk area, Soult and Lannes at Boulogne, Ney at Montmireul (where a hundred years later Haig was to preside over the slaughter of Englishmen in Flanders), and Augereau, stationed at Brest. They commanded, respectively, the first, second, third, fourth, fifth, sixth, and seventh corps. Bessières was in charge of the Consular Guard (soon to be known as the Imperial Guard) and Murat led the cavalry.

Then began a brief period of social and military splendor that advertised the assumption of hereditary power by the commander-in-chief. There were balls, concerts, and dances to offset the weeks of intensive training. Murat outbid Lannes as the army's most reckless spender on uniforms. In a single year he spent one hundred thousand francs on coats, cloaks, and spectacular additions to his gorgeous accoutrements. Léger, his military tailor, also supplied the well-dressed Berthier and is said to have made a net profit of nearly half a million francs in twelve months. Napoleon frowned at all this extravagance. He himself wore the simplest uniform and outraged the perfectionist Léger by asking him to put a patch on a worn pair of breeches. Léger's professional pride was equal to the rebuke. He would sooner, he told the first consul, go out of business altogether. Napoleon grumbled and ordered a new pair.

On May 19, 1804, the decree for which the entire army was waiting was published. Eighteen popular generals were created marshals of France, four of them honorary marshals and the remainder on the active list.

There had been lively speculation as to the names that would appear on the list and some of them puzzled the tipsters. Masséna was a certainty. His brilliant defence of Switzerland and Genoa had ensured that, but some of the high-ranking officers were disgusted to see Brune, Pérignon, and careful old Moncey enjoying equal rank with soldiers like Lannes and Augereau. The truth was hidden in Napoleon's intentions. He was determined to unite all factions in post-revolution France, and among the original eighteen we find Republicans, ex-Royalist officers who might still be wooed back to the Bourbons, uncomplicated moderates like Mortier, simple patriots like old Kellerman, and a group of younger men who had climbed the military ladder alongside Napoleon and owed their advancement to talents developed by him. Even Bernadotte was included; Napoleon wanted no possible rival in the political field. But perhaps the appointment that civilians found the most puzzling of all was that of Michel Ney, barrel-cooper's son of Saar-Louis, who had never served under Napoleon in the field.

We last met Ney as a divisional commander under Masséna in the Swiss bastion but prior to that his service had been carried out exclusively in the Lowlands and with the Army of the Rhine, which Napoleon had never won over. Moreau, its most famous commander, had recently been exiled to America after complicity in a conspiracy against the first consul's life, and some of the Rhine veterans who saw the way the political wind was blowing drifted over to Napoleon's camp at the turn of the century.

Ney had been the most prominent Rhine convert. He was already well known as a brave and intelligent soldier but so far his modesty had kept him out of the limelight, that and a far more serious attitude towards his profession than was held by, say, happy-go-lucky Jean Lannes, or advance-and-be-damned Augereau. Ney venerated physical courage and his attitude to war was that of a mystic. As a young hussar captain he had performed dozens of gallant exploits but as he rose in rank he began to apply his mind to the administrative aspects of campaigning, to the problems of transport, supply, the care of the wounded and above all what we should now call welfare and morale. The rank and file adored him. Strongly built, red-headed, an expert swordsman and a terrible opponent in hand-to-hand fighting, he was known to be excitable and hot-tempered but like many powerful, hot-tempered men he was also a sentimentalist and his attitude towards an opponent softened the moment he calmed down. He never understood politics, then or later. "Duty" was his watchword and after duty, "action." He never relied upon gallopers to find out what was happening in the skirmishing line but rushed forward to see for himself. He was absolutely impervious to shot and shell and wherever he appeared men pulled themselves together, climbed out of ditches and from behind walls and advanced shouting: "There goes *Le Rougeaud!* Things are hotting up boys!" Napoleon must have been quietly watching him for some considerable time. When a German-speaking officer was urgently needed for a diplomatic mission to Switzerland he sent Ney, who spoke German like a native. The red-headed young veteran was far more successful as a diplomat than was Lannes in Portugal, or Bernadotte in Vienna. He carried out his duties smoothly and efficiently and on his return Napoleon admitted him to the inner fold. He was to prove the most celebrated of all the men who acclaimed the new Emperor when the Imperial decree was issued on the day before the bulletin announcing the marshalate.

Another surprise was the elevation of ex-barber Bessières, the quiet, well-mannered man who had once fought the Paris mob on behalf of a Bourbon. There must have been something charming about Bessières' character, for although he had done nothing spectacular all these years Napoleon counted him among his closest friends and he repaid the Emperor with unswerving loyalty. Marmont, who was not made a marshal on this occasion, was bitterly jealous of Bessières and raged against his elevation. But in the end Napoleon's preference was justified. Bessières gave his life for the man who had befriended him whereas Marmont's name was to become a byword for treachery.

One of the first Imperial occasions to thrill Paris was a grand ball given to the new Emperor and Empress by the marshals, who pooled twenty thousand francs apiece and staged a brillant event at the Opera. It was the first real ball Paris had seen since the days of the old monarchy and there was tremendous competition for tickets. Admission was in charge of a committee of junior officers and one of them, serving in Augereau's staff, remarked shrewdly: "I never realized until then how many friends I possessed!" The ball was a great success and Napoleon was delighted because it proved beyond doubt that France was done with Republican austerity and wanted a return to graceful living, beautiful display, and a certain amount of pomp. There were still grumblers, among them Lannes, who persisted in wearing his hair in the old-fashioned military queue, but all the marshals, and more particularly their wives, welcomed the chance to parade their clothes and cultivate some of the manners and courtesies of the Bourbon Court. To behave impressively under these circumstances must have proved a strain on some of the ladies. Lefèbvre's wife had been a fat, jolly, loud-mouthed washerwoman and was extremely proud of the fact, but the younger set, women like Caroline Murat and Lannes' new wife, were quick learners and friction was eased by the charm of the new Empress, who had been trained in Court etiquette when she was the young wife of the Marquis de Beauharnais. She proved indispensable to her husband in teaching the would-be courtiers how to behave. Josephine made a warm friend of Ney by finding him an extremely pretty wife called Aglaé and the success of this marriage encouraged her to devote more time to matchmaking. Madame de Campan's academy for young gentlewomen was enjoying a boom at this period. Almost every pupil Madame turned out made a brilliant marriage and later on, when the daughters of the new nobility began to appear, she enrolled and trained a second generation as pretty and accomplished as the first.

So the summer and the autumn passed, with the army still strung out along miles of tented camp facing the Channel and English sailors following the training schedules through spyglasses and occasionally trying pot-shots at the harbor batteries. Every now and again there was a big stir ashore when Napoleon came down from Paris for a review, and pressed men aboard the English fleet were probably the first foreigners in Europe to hear the thunderous shout of *"Vive l'Empereur!"* roll across the downs when the pale, slightly-built man rode among his veterans, advising, criticizing, commending, and searching out talent.

When Napoleon was out of camp he was in Paris, working eighteen hours a day preparing for the coronation scheduled for December. No effort was spared to make the occasion one of the most spectacular in French history, and when the great day arrived the new marshals were there in full-dress uniform, some of them still inclined to be skeptical of pomp that savored of a dead century but each properly aware of the respect due to men who had fought their way up from the lowest ranks by their own courage and merit.

One future marshal did not attend the coronation and stayed away from choice. This was the cynic St. Cyr, onetime draftsman and actor, now recognized as an excellent strategist. St. Cyr's curious individualism was carried to dangerous lengths that autumn. He flatly refused to sign the petition passed around among senior officers asking Napoleon to make himself Emperor. He disliked Napoleon and did not give a gallery hoot who was aware of the fact. He had Bernadotte's temporizing technique but far more moral courage. He did not strut about making indiscreet speeches, or veer this way and that according to the company he kept; he went quietly about his own business, keeping his own counsel. Nobody, not even Napoleon Bonaparte, could tell St. Cyr how to vote or whom to support. In the whole wide world there was only one man who impressed St. Cyr—the man who had once been an engineering student, then an actor and was now a first-class general; to the end of his life Gouvion St. Cyr never changed his views about this.

Old Lefèbvre had no such reservations. He had put Republicanism behind him now and when the stately procession approached the altar in Nôtre Dame and Napoleon saved the Pope the trouble of crowning him by placing the diadem on his own head, it was Lefèbvre who carried the sword of state.

Even Berthier, the wizard with the maps, was growing a little more sure of himself these days and went so far as to advise Napoleon to marry his wife according to the rites of the church before he received an Imperial crown in Nôtre Dame. Josephine ardently desired this, for it made her position far more secure, and after some grumbling Napoleon gave in and arranged a private ceremony the night before the coronation. The Emperor must have remembered this pious advice from his chief-of-staff when, some time later, he sat down and wrote Berthier a testy letter urging him to put aside the bewitching Madame de Visconti and make a respectable marriage. "This affair has gone on far too long!" he declared, with his customary scorn for any romantic attachments but his own. "You are making yourself absolutely ridiculous!" It was high time, he added, that "a man who walked in an Emperor's shadow" should found a family and forget all about love! Berthier bowed under the storm and dutifully married the noble bride selected by his master, but he was not a staff officer for nothing and somehow managed to persuade his wife to accept Madame de Visconti into the house. The three of them lived in perfect accord for the remainder of his life.

.   .   .

So the Revolution died at last, not under the hob-nailed boots of a continental army or the flood of British guineas or indeed as a result of any action on the part of dismayed Hapsburgs, Romanoffs, Bourbons, and Hohenzollerns, but simply because the average Frenchman willed it so, voting for a return to order and brisk commerce under a régime that could offer steady prices, an end to land speculation, and good metaled roads free of highwaymen. The courtiers in London and Vienna and St. Petersburg studied the Coronation news with long faces, and even longer ones were seen at the Buckinghamshire exile of the remaining Bourbons, who saw an end to their hopes that Napoleon would reinstate the King on his throne. The reflections of professional soldiers in every European capital were equally somber. They had seen what was happening in the coastal camps of the French army during the last three years and even the most stupid among them realized that men who had beaten them when the French army was little more than a rabble were likely to prove invincible after thirty months of intensive training. Pitt, the great realist, was under no illusion at all as to the future. He worked day and night to organize another coalition and the flow of British gold poured into Vienna all that summer urging Austria to get up and fight again. Then the Czar was won back to the alliance and British agents were set to work in the Prussian Court. Every musket in Europe would be needed if the Powers were to halt the alarming growth of the country that was drunk with success.

Pitt had no luck in Berlin. Prussia was not ready to fight, never having recovered from the moral shock of Valmy. In addition, its territory was too near Bernadotte's veterans in Hamburg and Marmont's auxiliaries in Holland; and William, its sovereign, was a very timid man. In the end Austria advanced alone up the Danube valley with a promise that a huge Russian army would join in before the Hapsburgs came to grips with the little scoundrel who now called himself Emperor and seemed to have bewitched the entire French nation. Britain's contribution was to keep the seas and unloose the purse strings. The Czar's hordes began their long tramp westward and the sprawling Hapsburg empire forgot about Fleurus and Jemappes and Lodi and Rivoli and Arcola and Marengo, and drummed up recruits from every province. More drubbings were needed before the elderly Austrian generals learned that one did not necessarily have to be born a gentleman to deserve the rank of sublieutenant.

Four hundred miles to the north-west one hundred and fifty thousand sunburned men struck their tents and shouldered their knapsacks, relieved that there was to be no sea-voyaging after all and glad to be moving down into the soft campaigning country of Germany where there were always plenty of beer and women to be found. Not a single man in camp was disturbed by the prospect of a collision with Russians and Austrians. Some of them had helped to harry the savage Suvorov over the mountains and every man among them had seen the backs of Austrian troops during the last ten years. Like a pack of cards shuffled by an expert dealer the seven corps, the mass of cavalry and the Guard faced about and peeled off, dropping south, scutheast and east with mathematical precision. Civilians cheered them as they tramped and trotted across the wide French plain, dust rising in vast, billowing clouds about the long, smartly stepping columns. The thunderbolt was on its way and when it found its target, on the first anniversary of the Coronation, the dying Pitt was to speak a phrase that was remembered by successive generations. With far greater accuracy than is usually found in the prophecies of statesmen he was to say: "Roll up that map! It will not be wanted these ten years!"

CHAPTER EIGHT

"SOLDIERS, I AM CONTENT WITH YOU!"

BERTHIER was the hero of that long, dusty march. What he achieved had never been attempted before but it was performed with a perfection that sets Berthier apart as an organizer of genius and could hardly be improved upon by a twentieth-century general, with the modern aids of radio, telephone systems, and power-driven vehicles at his disposal. Berthier had none of these miracles to coordinate the movement of his nine huge units and many of the roads he used were forest tracks. He had no supplies of tinned foods, no traveling repair shops, no adequate signaling system and only horse-drawn transport for his ammunition reserves and baggage. Yet, in forty-five days, men who had been encamped at Brest, Boulogne, and Hamburg were in position as far away as Basle and Innsbruck and the great arc of the Grand Army was coiling round the Austrian General Mack, at Ulm, cutting him off from his base and from new armies trudging westward out of Vienna and the Russian Steppes. It was a faultless text-book concentration but it came from a better text-book than the one journalist Brune had written to impress his lady-friend. This was compiled by the founder of the new style of war and the Austrian generals would not have understood a word of it had it been explained to them phrase by phrase.

Throughout the whole of this five-month campaign Berthier hardly left Napoleon's side. Every major decision was taken in conference and their office was the Emperor's eight-horse coach. This vehicle was the last word in traveling equipages, a small, mobile hotel, with folding tables, a folding seat that could be converted into a bed for Napoleon, a large map compartment, a larder, and a small armory. When Berthier wanted

79

to sleep (which was not very often), he did so sitting upright, but apart from this the coach was fitted with every comfort and convenience. Wherever it went it was escorted by relays of chasseurs and orderlies, and whenever the commander-in-chief and chief-of-staff needed to alight and inspect the country the escort formed an outward facing ring about them. When dispositions had been made and the landmarks identified, Napoleon and Berthier climbed back into the coach, the coachman cracked his whip and the huge vehicle and escort moved on at a furious pace. To see the Emperor's coach pass through a village at full gallop was to witness something out of a fairy-tale or a nightmare, depending upon one's nationality.

By mid-autumn the Grand Army had stormed down to the Danube and the first that General Mack knew of its arrival was when its cavalry had debouched into an enormous arc through which his scouts could not penetrate, and its infantry was between him and all his sources of reinforcement and supply. Shut up in Ulm, the astonished Austrian asked Ney's chief-of-staff for eight days' grace, promising to surrender if the Russian army did not appear during the truce. General Rapp, the Alsatian aide-de-camp, gave him five days and at the expiration of that period Mack surrendered with thirty thousand men. Not one man in twenty of the Grand Army had discharged his musket.

In the meantime Augereau, who had come dashing down from Brittany, accounted for another Austrian division, whilst Masséna, advancing into Venetia with the veteran Army of Italy, scooped a further five thousand Austrians into the bag. In all, in the course of twenty days, Masséna, Soult, Ney, and Murat took a grand total of fifty thousand prisoners.

To Augereau's extreme indignation a regiment of his prisoners escaped. Among those who surrendered to him were two regiments of dragoons and hussars, who were sent to a rendezvous under the escort of a single officer. The hussars were spirited Hungarians, led by a fire-eating old colonel, and when the prisoners were at a safe distance from the French the old warrior announced that he, for his part, had thought better of surrendering and had decided it was more honorable to join the remains of the Austrian army. The dragoons would not accompany him but the hussars shouted their approval and galloped off into the woods. It was the kind of ruse Augereau might have employed in similar circumstances.

With Vienna open to attack the remaining Austrians joined the leisurely advancing army of the Czar. Together they still outnumbered the French, who were hundreds of miles from their base and uneasy about neutral Prussia in their rear. It was absolutely essential, if the allied army was to be brought to battle, to capture the great wooden bridge at Spitz and cross the Danube. The bridge had been minded by the retreating Austrians and was guarded, on the further side, by a formidable battery of guns. To rush it would have been suicidal, so Lannes and Murat, forgetting their hatred of one another for an hour or so, decided to win it by guile.

The success of this maneuver was a lesson in Gascon impudence. In full dress uniforms the two marshals approached the bridge supported by a storming party of Oudinot's grenadiers, who took cover in a plantation on the right bank. The marshals walked blithely onto the bridge, waving to the astonished engineers who were getting ready to destroy it. The weak pickets guarding the approaches fell back firing, but an odd musket shot or two did not concern Jean Lannes or Joachim Murat. When the main bridge was reached Lannes told the officer in charge that there had been an armistice and that under its terms the bridge was to remain in French hands. The puzzled officer scratched his head and said he would have to go into Spitz and get instructions from his general. "By all mean do that!" said Lannes and the man went. The two marshals then continued their advance in a casual and confident manner.

Meanwhile Oudinot's storming party had followed them onto the smaller spans and were now approaching the double. An Austrian officer, seeing them, grabbed a torch and tried to fire the combustibles under the main span but Lannes cried out that this was a violation of the armistice terms and such an act would get him into serious trouble. He then snatched the brand from the man's hand while Murat, concentrating on the NCO in charge of the guns, pushed him gently on the chest and continued to advance, the undecided gunner giving way step by step until the deputation had reached the battery.

At this stage in the comedy General Auersperg, the senior officer in charge of the bridge, put in a belated appearance. The poor old fellow was completely bemused by the two Gascons, and while he hesitated and stuttered one of his NCO's, with far more common sense than his superior, got ready to fire guns at the approaching grenadiers. Lannes put a stop to this by sitting down on the nearest gun, and in the end General Auersperg agreed to retire and the bridge was won.

There was an unhappy sequel to this episode. After the French triumph at Austerlitz General Auersperg was tried by court-martial and condemned to death, along with General Mack, who had surrendered so feebly in Ulm. Both, however, were reprieved but kept in prison for ten years. Utterly disgraced and shunned by their families they both died soon after their release.

At last, in the dreary country of Moravia, the two main armies came face to face, divided by a steep-sided brook. It was the eve of the first anniversary of the Coronation and the French were jubilant. After dark a fog came down and Napoleon's escort made pine torches to light the Emperor on his rounds. Soon everybody had recognized the Imperial staff and had improvised torches of their own, so that the Russo-Austrian army looked down from its position on the plateau opposite and saw the French camp blazing with light and heard the thunderous roar of *"Vive l'Empereur!"* The sun rose brilliantly that morning and was afterwards remembered as "the sun of Austerlitz," portent of triumph. And triumph it was, a shattering, overwhelming victory for the men who had marched and maneuvered all the way from the Channel ports.

Lannes held the left wing against all attacks and Davout, who had come up after some record-breaking marches on the night preceding the battle, played the role of the man who is being slowly pushed from his ground. The object of this feint was to encourage the enemy to deploy on marshy ground bordering the lakes. Murat's cavalry supported the hard-pressed Lannes and the center was firmly held by Soult, Bernadotte, and the cavalry of the Guard, under Bessiéres. Each phase of the battle went according to plan—Napoleon's plan. Lannes and Murat beat off attacks on the left and later advanced to Austerlitz, and Davout slowly retreated until his opponents were tangled up in the marshy ground alongside the lakes. Then Napoleon launched his furious frontal attack on the Pratzen plateau, where the enemy had concentrated his best troops.

The Russian Noble Guard under Duke Constantine made a spirited resistance and succeeded in capturing the eagle of the regiment commanded by Napoleon's brother, Joseph. Bessières, who was now making a reputation for himself as a clever handler of heavy cavalry, led the counter-attack in person and his horse grenadiers, thrusting their sabers into the bodies of their opponents, shouted: "We'll give the ladies of St. Petersburg something to cry about!" Soult moved in and occupied the plateau and then, with Oudinot's help, turned and attacked the advancing enemy left in the rear. Davout at once checked his sham retreat and counter-attacked from the other side.

The result was an utter rout. Abandoned by their right and center, now in flight beyond the plateau, the encircled left wing dispersed in confusion. Some companies ran into the marshes, while others tried to escape along the road between the lakes. The French cavalry charged them here and they were nearly all killed, as were the poor devils who tried to flee across the frozen surface of the lakes, for the French artillery fired on the ice and broke it up, destroying gun-teams, squadrons, and battalions at each salvo. That same night the Emperor of Austria sued for peace and another coalition was shattered.

.   .   .

There were some interesting sequels to Austerlitz. Soult, whose work in the center and on the right had been first-class, always considered that this battle was a personal victory and went on believing this to the end of his long life. Lannes, furious that his gallant stand on the left was not given sufficient praise, left the field of battle and went home to Gascony without the formality of Imperial permission. He rode so fast that he was probably the first man to bring France news of the victory. Mustapha, one of Napoleon's Mamelukes whom he had brought home from Egypt, disgusted his master on the battlefield by promising to bring him Prince Constantine's head as a battle trophy and General Morland, a French veteran involved in the attack on the center, started a marathon lawsuit by getting himself killed. Morland's body was sent home for interment in a contemplated Hall of Heroes and was preserved in a barrel of rum pending the building of the tomb at Les Invalides. The years went by and the Hall of Heroes was never built. Everyone forgot about the hero until one day, soon after Napoleon's first abdication, the barrel fell apart with age and the general's corpse, now decorated by long, sprouting whiskers, was sent over to the School of Medicine for dissection. The relatives heard about this and indignantly claimed the body for burial. The suit dragged on for years and the family won, so General Morland was laid to rest nearly ten years after his death in action. As a comment on the dividends of patriotism this is the most emphatic in history.

The victory at Austerlitz consolidated Napoleon's throne as nothing else could have done. When, amid the debris of overturned cannon, abandoned equipment, dead men, and bivouac fires, the new Emperor issued his proclamation beginning "Soldiers, I am content with you . . . !" he realized that with an army like this behind him it would take a world in arms to dislodge him. He had never had much faith in the popular favor of politicians and he had realized long ago that if he was to found a new order in Europe based upon the broad gains of the Revolution then the only instrument upon which he could rely was his army and, more important even than this, the men to whom the rank and file looked for leadership in the field.

Turning his back on warfare for a spell he begun to ponder means to bind these men to him for ever.

· · ·

Augereau was given a very congenial task in the New Year. He was sent to the city of Frankfurt with a special mission, that of making the prosperous Frankfurters eat their words.

Prussia and the other German States had remained neutral during the crisis but many Germans had secretly hoped for an allied victory. Not only were the aristocrats of Central Europe yearning to humiliate this cocky and apparently invincible army of ex-privates and tradesmen, the people generally were already feeling the weight of the French requisitions. In a year or so Europeans would be saying: "Even the rats starve where the Grand Army marches!" On the eve of Austerlitz a wishful-thinking Frankfurt journalist announced that Napoleon had been heavily defeated and all the other newspapers copied the story without waiting to check its accuracy. Frankfurt was a free city and its press made the most of the rumor. It was announced that not a single Frenchman had escaped the rout.

Napoleon read these reports with interest and then ordered Augereau to quarter his entire corps in Frankfurt, adding that Frankfurters were to present each private with one *louis d'or,* each corporal with two, each sergeant with three, and every lieutenant with ten, as a bonus for surviving the slaughter. The inhabitants were then to board and lodge the troops at exhorbitant rates. Any money left over was to be sent to the Imperial treasury.

The terrified citizens, seeing ruin staring them in the face, protested that they could not find such a vast sum. They were told: "The Emperor merely wishes to give Frankfurters a chance of counting a single corps that survived the crushing defeat. There are six more corps coming, plus the cavalry, plus the Guard!"

Augereau enjoyed this joke enormously and sent out his provosts to beat up the bonuses but soon he began to feel sorry for the townspeople and appealed on their behalf to the Emperor. Napoleon, having made his point, gave Augereau permission to modify the decree and the marshal contented himself with billeting his staff and a single battalion in the city. The Frankfurters expressed their gratitude by making the men of the Seventh Corps very welcome during their stay. It is interesting to surmise what the merciless Davout or the thrifty Masséna would have made of this opportunity.

The remaining corps went into billets elsewhere. Germany, in these early days, was a popular campaigning ground and in the years ahead the veterans were to look back upon this period with nostalgia. Many of them married German girls in the garrison towns and easy relationships between the men of the Grand Army and the southern Germans survived the direct clash with Prussia that same autumn. Seven years were to pass before retreating Frenchmen were to have German doors slammed in their faces but by then the chasseurs, hussars, cuirassiers, and guardsmen were already marching into legend.

CHAPTER NINE

TITLES AND TRIUMPHS

NAPOLEON, it is claimed, loved a lord and therefore must have been motivated by old-fashioned snobbery when he remodelled his court on the manners and customs of the old régime.

This, like so many judgments of Napoleon, is less than a half-truth. His real views concerning the trappings of kingship can be found in a brusque comment to his future father-in-law when Francis of Austria hunted among records for noble Bonaparte ancestors after assenting to the marriage between the French Emperor and his daughter. On that occasion Napoleon quietly reminded the snob of his own Hapsburg ancestor by saying: "Thank you but I prefer to be the Rudolf of my race!"

Napoleon reinstituted titles in 1806 for a different and far more important reason than the desire to have titled people about his person. He did it because he understood the strengths and weaknesses of mankind as few men of his generation understood them. He was aware that if his throne and dynasty were to endure they needed props that were proof against reaction. It was all part of his plan to extract the solid gain from the Revolution and discard elements of anarchy that were still capable of engulfing France in a second period of mob rule. Nothing extinguishes a revolutionary fire so effectively as a douche of privilege, administered here and there upon the heads of the most articulate agitators. This is true of the left-wing in every country today and it was true then, as Napoleon proved by his careful distribution of honors in the years following his triumph of Austerlitz.

Among the eighteen men he had already raised to the rank of marshal all but a handful were of humble origin. Of the first crop only Kellerman, Sérurier, Berthier and Davout had held commissions when the

Revolution broke out. Of the remaining fourteen at least five had been prominent revolutionaries and all the others, including Murat, Lannes, Masséna and Ney, were infected both by the political claptrap and the genuine idealism of the period. Only the gentle Bessières had been a Royalist and he had barely escaped with his life in the street rising of August '92. It was these men that Napoleon now sought to make his own. It was upon them that he meant to build a society in which a successful man of property might feel secure and not liable to wake up one morning with the rabble on his doorstep and a warrant for his arrest and the confiscation of his goods.

Brother Joseph was already a king. He had been escorted down to Naples by Masséna and placed on the Neapolitan throne alongside his plain, pimply, good-natured wife Julie. Louis, the younger brother who had married Josephine's daughter Hortense, was soon to mount the throne of Holland and within a few months of Austerlitz the marshals had the mortification of seeing the gaudy Murat, brother-in-law of the Emperor, become Grand Duke of Berg and Cleves, a tiny Rhineland duchy.

Murat was delighted, not so much with the prospect of revenues, which were small, but because the title ensured his precedence over all the other marshals except Berthier, who was given an even more splendid title, Prince of Neufchatel.

Nobody resented the Emperor's elevation of Berthier. Although he was not much liked among the senior officers of the Grand Army his talents were respected and he was recognized as Napoleon's right-hand man on the battlefield. Murat's elevation, however, caused a good deal of muttering until it was eclipsed, as a source of grievance, by the sudden elevation of fence-squatter Bernadotte who became Prince of Ponte Corvo! The murmur in the barracks now rose to a growl, for it was generally known that not only had Bernadotte done nothing whatever to seat Napoleon on a throne but had paraded an intense dislike of the man.

Even making allowances for Napoleon's need to eliminate this last possible rival from the ranks of the Republican fighting men, it is difficult to understand why Bernadotte was given this honor in preference to men whose loyalty was beyond doubt. The question was never really answered, not even on St. Helena, and one can only choose between two possible theories—the strength of the affection Napoleon retained for his former sweetheart, Desirée, now Bernadotte's wife, or his exaggerated idea of Bernadotte's popularity among the diehard Republicans.

It is true that Bernadotte had powerful friends (he even charmed Napoleon's secretary to a degree that is amazing considering his record) but the Gascon had proved such a waverer in the past that no intelligent plotter from the left, right or center would have chosen him as leader of a revolt against the victor of Austerlitz. However, there it was, Bernadotte was a prince and the remaining fifteen marshals grumbled and asked one another what kind of rewards were in store for men who had risked their lives over and over again in the Emperor's service.

Marmont was one of the principal grousers. He had missed being present at Austerlitz and this, coming on top of his disappointment at not being included among the marshals, made him very bitter. As Napoleon's oldest friend, one who had taken half-starved Captain Bonaparte home for a square meal when he was penniless nonentity, Marmont felt that he deserved something more spectacular than the command of a corps. He received elevation that summer. Napoleon sent him down into Istria, on the Adriatic, and gave him a free hand to employ his considerable creative talents in reorganizing the province. Marmont made the most of this opportunity and at once set about building roads and modernizing the administrative machinery with the energy and ability he had shown in standardizing the artillery of the Grand Army. He made a first-class job of the assignment and Napoleon noted and approved.

Other titles followed and it is as well to deal with them here, although many were not confirmed until Prussia had been overthrown and the new Russian attack ended in a partnership deed between Napoleon and the Czar, at Tilsit.

The more celebrated among the marshals received titles associated with notable feats of arms. Others had to be content with more conventional honors. The subtle distinction rankled throughout all the years of the Empire.

Kellerman became Duke of Valmy in honor of his stand against the Prussians on the day his ragged volunteers had turned the tide of foreign invasion. Bluff old Lefèbvre was made Duke of Danzig, Moncey received the title of Duke of Conegliano, and Mortier was made Duke of Treviso. Then came the titles that were to stamp French victories on the minds of succeeding generations. Masséna was made Duke of Rivoli, Lannes Duke of Montebello, where he trounced the Austrians before Marengo, Augereau Duke of Castiglione, in memory of his advice in 1796, and Ney became Duke of Elchingen, the battle that led on to the bloodless victory of Ulm. Davout's title was to come very soon and to arrive in a blaze of glory. Bessières was made Duke of Istria and Soult, who felt he had deserved more than any of them, was furious at not getting a battle honor and being made Duke of Dalmatia.

As time passed many of the famous generals who were not marshals received titles and the problem of choosing them sometimes taxed Napoleon's ingenuity. Victor, the redcheeked, garrulous ex-sergeant who had been such an enthusiatic upholder of liberty and equality in the old days, exploded with wrath when his title was announced. He was known throughout the army as *"Beau Soleil"* on account of his rosy complexion. Now he was made Duke of Belluno. The same kind of gaffe was averted in the case of Junot, one of Napoleon's oldest comrades and a man who only just missed becoming a marshal. Junot had greatly distinguished himself in action at Nazareth during the march on Acre and it was now rumored that the famous shrine would be added to his name. It was realized, however, that he would then become known as "Junot of Nazareth," so the title he eventually received was Duke of Abrantes.

As might be expected there was loud cackling among the wives when the new aristocracy was established, but among the old Republicans the Lefèbvres, man and wife, were the least repentant. The old warrior bought himself a fine house in Paris and a friend was sufficiently ill-advised to congratulate Lefèbvre on his extraordinary luck. "Luck?" exploded the old sergeant major, "Come out into the garden and I'll take twenty shots at you at thirty paces. If I miss, the house and everything in it is yours!" When the friend began to back away he added, "I had a thousand shots fired at me at much closer range than ten paces, before I moved into this!" Lefèbvre's charlady duchess regarded her title as an uproarious joke and went out of her way to embarrass dignified footmen who expected her to behave like a real duchess. Perhaps the best story of her comes from the witty pen of Madame Junot, who describes her arrival at the Tuileries to thank Josephine for the title. The usher announced her as *"Madame la Maréchale"* and she made no comment but as the flunkey was closing the door Josephine said: "And how is the Duchess of Danzig," whereupon the new Duchess winked at the footman and exclaimed, "Hey boy, what do you think of that?"

Between 1806 and 1814, when he abdicated for the first time, Napoleon made one marshal a king, two sovereign princes, three princes of the Empire, thirteen dukes and six counts. The remaining marshal,

Poniatowski the Pole, was a prince in his own right when he joined the Imperial Army.

. . .

It was time to be on the move again. Time to buy remounts and new field kits and engage servants and grooms who could speak German. For now, when one possible ally had been beaten to her knees and the other was hundreds of leagues to the east, Prussia at last decided to avenge the shame of Valmy and teach these braggart French how to fight battles. The Prussian Noble Guard had thrown down the gauntlet by sharpening their swords on the steps of the French embassy and the marshals learned of the certainty of war with grim satisfaction. Most of them had outfought Prussians in the days when the French went into the field shoeless. They were quite sure they were more than a match for them now, with or without Napoleon to plan the campaign.

Most of the star performers were available or within call. Lannes, sniffing a good fight from afar, came hurrying up from his native Gascony, where he had been spending vast sums of money among the friends of his youth in his native town of Lectoure, and Lefèbvre, in Lannes' temporary absence, took command of the Fifth Corps.

Davout and his veterans were ready and within a month were to perform one of the greatest feats of arms in the history of France. Berthier was there, busy with his maps and parade states, and Murat, wearing yet another new uniform, as befitted a Duke with his own gorgeous livery. Victor signed on as Lannes' chief-of-staff and Ney harangued his Sixth Corps veterans on the glory that awaited them. Bernadotte and Soult set their men in motion and Murat threw out his vast cavalry screen as the Grand Army pushed into Thuringia in glorious autumn weather, reminiscent of the spell that had preceded last year's swoop upon Ulm.

There was only one marshal who set out with a heavy heart. Pierre Augereau had just come from the funeral of his wife, the pretty Greek lady with whom he had eloped in his vagabond days and whom he had taken home to France after his escape from the Inquisition. It is typical of this huge, loud-mouthed roisterer that he was a gentle and considerate husband. When he had invited his young officers to make free of his rented château in Brittany two years before he had laid down a single condition. "Make as much noise as you like but keep clear of the wing occupied by my wife," he told them. "She is a lady who likes to be quiet!"

Now she was dead and he was inconsolable. All his staff grieved for him, for he was as popular as Ney with officers and men. He was still the same Augereau when it came to a fight but the approaching campaign was to show that his personal loss had done something to soften him a little.

The state against which the Grand Army was now marching was probably the most despotic in Europe, not excluding Russia. Its lower classes were little more than serfs and its army was held together by a form of discipline that verged on the ludicrous. No one would serve in the Prussian army from choice so it was recruited from the riff-raff of central Europe, men who signed on while they were drunk and sobered up to face a non-stop nightmare. For every seven men in the Prussian army there was a merciless Prussian corporal and every corporal carried a cane. Men were flogged insensible for the slightest fault and during their service they were issued with no warm clothing and no blankets. They slept on straw and their food was as meager as their pay. When they were too old to fight they were given a licence to beg and Marbot tells us that most of them did not wait for the licence to begin begging. He was surrounded by half-starved wretches the moment he arrived in Berlin. As there were not enough drunken sots in Europe to keep the battalions up to strength press gangs were kept at work sweeping peasants and artisans into the ranks. After a month or so in the Prussian army there were few who thought of mutiny or desertion. The penalty for either was a cruel death.

On the other hand, the officers, with few exceptions, were either arrogant coxcombs or doddering old fools. One of the exceptions was Marshal Blücher, already an old man by military standards but full of fire and patriotism. In the years ahead he was to give a better account of himself than any ten thousand Prussians.

Napoleon's plan was not merely to defeat Prussia but to annihilate her and he thought that this might be achieved in a month. In the event it was done in twenty-four days. The Grand Army began its advance on October 8. By the first week of November there was not a single Prussian force in existence and every gun and supply wagon was in French hands. It was an even greater triumph than that of the previous autumn.

Bernadotte, Soult, Ney, and Lannes were in at the death but Augereau and Davout, with Bessières of the Guard and Berthier, chief-of-staff, were only a day's march behind them. It was a triumph, not so much of hard fighting, but of marching, maneuvring and almost faultless staff-work. Once again the cool brain at the source, and Berthier, that brain's administrative outlet, showed that wars were not won by slogging away with the saber and musket-stock. They had to be worked out like complicated mathematical problems and in Napoleons's traveling coach the calculations were made, down to the last horseshoe nail.

The first clash came at Saalfield, where the impetuous Prince Louis, thrown back by Lannes, was killed during a hand-to-hand encounter with a sergeant of hussars. In the old, professional armies an NCO would have started such a fight under a serious psychological disadvantage but in the army Napoleon had forged in the crucible of the Revolution a good sergeant was worth two princes of the blood.

The French then rushed on to the Saxon town of Jena, beyond which the Prussian army, or what was thought to be the major part ot it, assembled across the one good road out of the town. Between the suburbs and the Prussian position was a steep-sided plateau called the Landgraftenburg. Its flat crown would ordinarily hold about ten thousand men, standing shoulder to shoulder. A Saxon parson who was opposed to Prussians involving his countrymen in an unwanted war, came forward with an offer to lead Napoleon's storm troops onto the plateau by a narrow path ascending the town side of the slope. Napoleon and Lannes explored the path and within an hour thousands of men were at work widening and leveling it by the light of torches that were invisible against the glare of burning Jena. Each relay of men worked without pause for one hour, then moved forward to take their places on the crowded plateau within cannonshot of the Prussians. By dawn on October 14 forty thousand men were massed there, while Soult was working round to the right of the enemy, and beyond Soult, the corps of Davout and Bernadotte were positioning themselves to deliver additional right hooks. The plan was to smash through the Prussian center and drive them into the triple trap from which hardly a man could escape.

The first part of the plan succeeded to perfection. When the morning fog was dispersed by cannonfire the astonished Prussians saw a ghost army of forty thousand men arrayed on the plateau. So sure had they been that the cliff was inaccessible to armed men that no one had thought of mounting a guard to watch it.

The issue was never in doubt. Augereau swept down on the Saxons holding the Prussian right, Soult stormed into the village on their left, and Lannes hit at the center, with Murat's cavalry in support. Ney had come up well in advance of his corps. Fearful of seeing all the glory go to the impetuous Lannes he lead his advance guard into the thick of the fighting, leaving desperate staff officers searching for him to take command of his leaderless men as they hurried onto the field.

For a time Ney was hard-pressed but Soult soon came to his aid and the Prussian left and center were broken. Ney, incidentally, resented Soult's advance and grumbled that he could have done the job himself if they had given him another ten minutes. The reluctant Saxons on the left fought better than their allies and their infantry formed square to meet Augereau's assault. Seeing that they had no hope of staving off disaster Augereau halted his men and sent officers to tell the Saxons what had occurred elsewhere and advised them to surrender and avoid useless butchery. At that moment, however, Murat dashed up with his dragoons and cut his way clean through the Saxon squares, breaking them up in a matter of minutes. Thousands of Saxons surrendered and Napoleon, determined to make an ally of their sovereign, treated them well and released them the following day. The battle was over and the great pursuit began.

While this was happening outside Jena, Davout, in command of the most isolated arm of the double right hook, was fighting for his life in the little village of Auerstadt, just across the Saale. For what had happened there was the result of a miscalculation on Napoleon's part and might have cost the French the fruits of their great victory at Jena. Davout had run headlong into what his chief had imagined to be a single Prussian corps but was, in fact, the main section of the Prussians led by the king himself.

With twenty-seven thousand men Davout now faced fifty-three thousand and there was nothing to do but stand and fight it out. The outnumbered French formed square and all day long, while Napoleon and the other marshals were smashing through the Prussians at Jena, the baldheaded, humorless disciplinarian was galloping from square to square exhorting his men to hold on until help could arrive.

Over and over again cavalry and infantry tried to overwhelm this man but every attack was thrown back by Davout's solid ranks. Every moment Davout expected Bernadotte's corps to appear and save the day but attack succeeded attack and Bernadotte did not appear. One of Davout's staff declared that he actually located Bernadotte sitting his horse in a field and explained what was happening. He says that the Gascon's calm response to his frantic message was: "I shall be there!" In the end the Prussians abandoned the fight, turned their backs on this indomitable man and his immovable squares and hurried off to the north. The breathless Davout was left alone to attend to his wounded and send a courier off to headquarters to ask, in crisp, icy terms, why a single corps had been left unsupported to fight more than half the Prussian army.

Where was Bernadotte? What had happened to the corps that should have marched to the sound of the guns and trapped the greater part of the Prussian army according to plan? Strategists and historians have argued this point for a century and a half. Bernadotte's original orders were to make for Naumberg, and Napoleon's dispatch suggested that he and Davout might, if they fell in with one another, march together. While Napoleon was shattering the Prussians at Jena, and Davout was defying furious attacks at Auerstadt, Bernadotte was about eleven miles distant from the latter place and, according to him, heard no sound of either battle. His orders, he agreed afterwards, were certainly to make for Naumberg but this was exactly what he had done. He always obeyed orders to the letter. There was no love lost between these two marshals but it is inconceivable that Bernadotte would have let his personal dislike of Davout (whom he had reason to believe had spied upon him while he was acting as chief of military police) prevent him from coming to his support when he was facing such tremendous odds. It is far more probable that Bernadotte heard both cannonades but on thinking matters over decided to play for safety and obey the letter of his instructions. Whatever the cause of his failure, the army and Davout never forgave him, and Napoleon was furious at his miserable lack of enterprise. "He ought to be court-martialed and shot!" he roared, when it was clear that his carefully-thought-out encircling movement had failed and that Davout had met and defeated more Prussians that day than had all the remaining corps of the Grand Army.

Bernadotte was undismayed by the ill-will his inaction had earned him. Asked point blank whether his non-appearance on the battlefield had anything to do with the fact that he had been jealous of Davout he replied, "I might have been piqued at getting something like orders from Davout but I did my duty!" The phrase "something like orders" suggests that at least Davout's couriers had found and explained the situation during the day's fighting. Bernadotte was rather like the traditional

Englishman in Bernard Shaw's *Man of Destiny*. You could find him in all sorts of unlikely places but never outside his private citadel of principle.

The French pursuit thundered through every city and fortress in Prussia. There had never been a follow-up as sustained and relentless as this and the fleeing Prussians were prised from stronghold after stronghold until their remnants reached the sea, at Lübeck.

Prominent in the French van was Murat, waving his gold cane and summoning castles to surrender to his light horsemen, while awaiting the arrival of the infantry of Lannes and Soult with their siege trains. As soon as they put in an appearance Murat galloped on to the next strongpoint, flourishing his wand and pouncing on the most comfortable billets in the district.

Lannes, who was developing an almost pathological hatred for this prancing mountebank, quarreled with him incessantly, but charges and accusations could not cloud the spirits of the innkeeper's son. He was enjoying life as never before and even his sullen enemies were fascinated by his panache and shameless theatricality. He behaved more a like a daring boy of seventeen than a grand duke and brother-in-law to an emperor, but Napoleon, who never approved of personal adornment, was beginning to realize that whatever Murat's faults he was the best cavalry leader in the world. "At the head of twenty men, he is worth a regiment in the field!" he told Berthier. Berthier made no comment. His brain was probably occupied with the problem of discovering the mathematical worth of Murat in firepower.

The spearhead of the pursuit was Bernadotte's corps. It had not fired a shot on October 14 and was as fresh as when the campaign commenced. It was Bernadotte who rode into Lübeck at the end of the long chase and here he had the greatest stroke of luck of his career. Among the prisoners he took was a party of Swedish soldiers who had just disembarked to assist the Prussians. The Prussians were now beyond anyone's help and as the newcomers left their transports they were gathered into the net. Bernadotte behaved towards them with faultless courtesy and he made a very deep impression upon their officers, who returned to Sweden with wonderful stories of this charming French marshal, who had fed them, flattered them, and made them feel that they had taken part in a summer excursion rather than an abortive campaign. These Swedes must have been convincing talkers for some years later, when Sweden was looking for a crown prince to succeed her childless king, all the prominent men of the country voted for Bernadotte, soldier and charmer. Today, the house of Bernadotte continues to rule Sweden.

Bernadotte achieved yet another distinction during this campaign. He caused the loudest laugh ever heard among the old moustaches of his corps. While entertaining the Swedes he had mislaid a wagon crammed with his Lübeck loot and he was extremely upset about the loss. "I don't mind the personal forfeit," he remarked plaintively, "but I was counting on all the money in that wagon to give every private in the corps a little bonus!" One wonders if this statement reached Masséna in Italy and if so what his comments were.

Because of Davout's gallant stand at Auerstadt his corps was given the honor of leading the victory march into Berlin. Davout's bands played Republican songs and the Prussian bourgeoisie gathered in glum silence to watch them pass. Seven years were to elapse before they again took the field against these men, but this time they made sure the rest of Europe marched beside them.

During the Grand Army's stay in the Berlin area the kind-hearted Berthier again showed a propensity for getting people out of unpleasant situations. Prussian Prince Hartzfeld wrote a chatty letter to the defeated king describing the French entry into the capital and the letter was intercepted by the French provosts. Napoleon was furious and declared that he would have the prince shot as a spy. There seems to be no doubt that he would have done so had not Berthier begged for the prince's life.

It was from Berlin that Napoleon issued the famous decrees aimed at throttling Britain's overseas trade and forbidding any continental power to trade with her. The first to benefit from this ban was Masséna, who at once started selling trading licences for cash and soon built up a fortune on the proceeds. But Napoleon was watching him and waited until the hoard was large enough to be worth confiscating. Marshal Brune, who took over in Hamburg, managed things rather more skilfully. Playing for somewhat lower stakes he milked a modest private income out of the sale of confiscated vessels but soon he too was detected and left the city in disgrace.

Back in Paris pretty Aglaé Ney, the marshal's wife, had fallen under a different kind of suspicion, that of setting her cap at the Emperor and reducing Josephine to hysterics. Madame Ney, who adored her famous husband, was extremely indignant at the charge, and it was soon obvious to Josephine that she was on a false scent. The real adventuress turned out to be the lovely, blonde Madame Duchâtel, wife of an elderly politician. Madame Ney's name was not cleared, however, until Josephine caught husband and mistress in circumstances which brooked no denial. It is not recorded what the hot-tempered Ney thought about this slur on his wife's character. He had fought several duels with far less provocation.

Apart from the sick and wounded none of the veterans returned to France that winter. There was more work to be done in the field, for the Polish patriots had now made up their minds to throw in their lot with the French and welcome Napoleon and his men as liberators. Russian armies were on the move again and there was the certainty of a winter campaign. The Grand Army looked to its boots and marched into Warsaw, where one more future marshal, whose name was mentioned at the very beginning of this book, waited impatiently for the victors of Austerlitz and Jena to restore the ancient kingdom of Poland to full independence. This man was Prince Poniatowski, the hope of every patriotic Pole, and as the year 1806 went out in a flurry of snow he came to offer his sword to Napoleon and pledge him the loyalty of his countrymen. Poland was not to be free for another century but in the next few years Poniatowski and thousands of his fellow Poles sacrificed their lives honoring this pledge.

CHAPTER TEN

THE ROAD TO THE RAFT

THE first role in which Poniatowski served Napoleon was that of procurer-in-chief. He was called upon to use his influence to persuade the hesitant Marie Walewska to desert her aged husband and become the Emperor's mistress. He performed this small service gladly. In his opinion a woman's marriage vows did not amount to much when weighed in the balance against the friendship of the man who had promised to liberate Poland.

It was a blithe New Year for patriotic Poles. The undefeated army marched into Warsaw with Murat at their head and everyone who witnessed the entry was tremendously impressed by the Grand Duke of Berg and Cleves, trotting at the head of his hardbitten cavalry. For the occasion Murat had donned a Polish uniform consisting of a green velvet tunic, trimmed with fur and gold brandenburgs, embroidered boots, and a Polish cap studded with gems and crowned by a nodding white plume. One would never have imagined that he and his cavalry had been having a terrible time in the Polish bogs since the Prussian campaign had been wound up, or that his horses and men had been desperate for forage and rations in that poverty stricken country. For Poland was not proving a popular campaigning ground and discipline went to pieces when men scattered far and wide to comb the hovels for bread and vodka. In addition there had been several collisions with tough Russian columns and on one occasion Murat had had to take refuge in one of Soult's squares. On another occasion four famished aides-de-camp had stolen Murat's supper (consisting of a roast goose, white bread, and a bottle of wine) while the marshal was sound asleep in a stable.

There was little time for rest and recreation in Warsaw, for the Czar's armies, well accustomed to this pestilential climate, were massing in the northeast and soon the veterans were on the move again, Murat and his cavalry, Ney, Lannes and Soult with their footsloggers, Bessières with the Guard, Augereau and Bernadotte bringing up the rear, one and all ploughing through endless mud in search of another Austerlitz or another Jena but having to be content with indecisive actions that cost men but yielded neither glory nor loot. Bickering was frequent and tempers were badly frayed. Bernadotte quarreled with Berthier, Ney quarreled with the patient Bessières, and Soult quarreled with everybody, but somehow the army kept on the move and at last the Russians were brought to bay near the little town of Eylau. The advance guard of the Grand Army piled arms in the graveyard and it proved a prophetic choice of bivouac. Fifteen thousand Frenchmen were to leave their bones in this gloomy backwater.

A variation of the Jena plan of attack was tried, with an attempt by Augereau to drive in the center and incline to the left, while Soult moved out to the right and hammered the Russian left, hoping to roll it up and drive it into Ney's corps. Ney was too far off to be of much help and so was Davout but it was anticipated that rapid marching on their part would result in blocking the retreat.

The grand design was a costly failure. Heavy snow began to fall and Augereau, advancing with a white scarf wrapped round his head, lost his direction in the blizzard and led his men slant-wise through a tornado of Russian artillery fire. The corps of fifteen thousand men withered away in a few minutes. Augereau went down with a grapeshot wound and twelve thousand of his veterans were soon piled on the trampled snow. Only the gallant 14th of the line held out on a hillock, charged by drunken Russian infantry and raked by a crossfire of Russian guns. The remnants of the corps staggered back and the wounded marshal despatched a string of messengers into the mêlée to tell the 14th to retire. Young Marbot finally reached the survivors and was told that if the regiment descended onto the plain it would be overwhelmed in a moment and that the survivors might just as well die where they stood. Marbot carried away their eagle in an attempt to save it from the enemy but he was severely wounded on the way back and was only saved by a miracle. Augereau's corps, that had marched all the way from Brest to Switzerland, and then fought its way from billets in Southern Germany to Lübeck in the north, and after that had crossed the muddy plains to Eylau, ceased to exist. So few were left that after Eylau it was broken up and its remnants distributed among the other corps.

Complete disaster was averted by Murat. Men lying out in the no-man's-land between the two armies raised themselves to watch ninety squadrons of reserve cavalry gallop across the frozen ponds and hard-packed snow to check the Russian counterattack. Then the winter's daylight faded and darkness fell on thirty thousand men lying out in sub-zero temperature. Only the luckiest of them, like Marbot, were carried back to the field ambulances and dressing stations.

After darkness Soult left his post on the right and sought out the Emperor and chief-of-staff. The man who had once wanted to be a village baker had been badly shocked by the slaughter but he was still defiant. When Napoleon remarked gloomily that the Russians had done them serious harm Soult snapped: "And we them! Our bullets are not made of cotton!" He then put his ear to the ground and listened. From the far side of the stricken field came a long, persistent rumble. "Anyway, the enemy is retreating!" he said briefly and went out to make his rounds of the picquet.

Soult was one of the few senior officers who emerges from Eylau with credit. The others had been staggered by their losses and by the apparent hopelessness of crushing these stubborn Northerners in this frozen wilderness, but Soult, after a grueling day, spent all night on the field. Even Ney had been sickened by the slaughter, and at the crisis of the battle there had been a minor panic among the Imperial Staff when the Russian infantry surged right up to the knoll occupied by Napoleon, Berthier, and Bessières. The two marshals, terrified at the prospect of seeing the commander-in-chief taken prisoner, had dragged at his bridle but Napoleon refused to withdraw. Instead, as though mildly surprised, he kept looking down on the mêlée and murmuring to himself over and over again: "What boldness! What boldness!"

There is a confused but likely story of a furious quarrel involving Lannes, Augereau, and Murat immediately after the disaster. It is stated that Lannes and Augereau joined forces to attack Murat, whose squadrons had averted a crushing defeat and who, therefore, gathered to himself all the credit in the bulletin Napoleon issued. According to Madame Junot, Lannes grossly insulted Murat in the Emperor's presence, calling him, among other things, "a pretending knave and a dancing dog in pantomime dress and plumes!" "Is it to stitch his mantle to yours that you steal glory from Augereau and me?" he is reported to have shouted at the Emperor and when Napoleon made no reply: "Very well then, we can spare it!"

There is something wrong with this story for Lannes, who was sick, was not present at Eylau. It is probable, however, that a quarrel on these lines involved Augereau, who was in great pain from his wound and most certainly resented the wording of a bulletin which estimated French losses at a modest twelve hundred killed and five thousand wounded! What is certain is that, just before or just after Eylau, Murat's obsession with uniforms called down the wrath of the Emperor on his head. When he tried to dress his staff in his ducal colors of amaranth, white, and gold the young officers refused to wear such fancy attire and one of them, de Flahault, resigned from Murat's staff and joined Berthier's. It was the small, neat chief-of-staff who was the real leader of fashion, and young officers on the staffs of the other marshals were usually at their wits' end to keep pace with his sudden changes in cut and style.

．　　．　　．

There was no more fighting for several weeks after the terrible check at Eylau. The army went into winter quarters and Napoleon, in intervals between furious stints of desk work, amused himself with the demure Madame Walewska, now won over by a combination of Napoleonic persistence and the pleas of the patriotic Poniatowski. "Surrender to him and he will free Poland," Poniatowski had urged. She surrendered, fell deeply in love with the man, and forgot all about Poland.

Augereau went home to recover from his wound, traveling by sledge across the wilderness crossed by the army in its winter advance. Masséna, cursing his luck, came up from sunny Italy, and Lannes shook off his illness and got ready for the spring campaign. Slowly the army recovered its confidence and when the snows melted and new drafts of recruits came in to fill the gaps in the ranks, it marched off to seek a final decision with the Russians.

The climax of the long struggle came at Friedland, where once again both armies fought with desperate courage.

Friendland was a head-on, bloody affair. The Russians endeavored to hold the town while their army crossed the river and the French pounced on them in the act. The four heroes of this engagement, fought on Napoleon's lucky day, June 14, were Ney and Lannes, of the infantry, and Victor and Grouchy of the cavalry.

Lannes, with the advance guard, carried out the initial attack and successfully pinned down the main forces of the enemy while Ney stormed into the town and cut off their retreat. To achieve this Ney completed a twenty-four hour march in twelve hours. Describing Ney's attack in a letter home Berthier wrote: "You can form no idea of the brilliant courage of Ney—it resembles only the time of chivalry. It is to him chiefly that we owe the success of this memorable day!"

At Freidland Ney was in his element. A dispatch-rider sent to find him and deliver fresh orders met him in the town square where he was sitting his horse among the blazing buildings and under a heavy artillery fire. He sat quite still, reading the dispatch as though he was studying a newspaper on a summer afternoon in the country. Roundshot crashed down on all sides but the young man who was watching the marshal reports that he was completely relaxed.

Friedland gave *"Beau Soleil"* Victor the chance he had been awaiting for years. Bernadotte had been wounded in an earlier engagement and Victor, to his great delight, was given command of Bernadotte's corps. He handled it very effectively and after the battle Napoleon presented him with his baton, so that the talkative NCO, who had once ridden into Paris alongside the silent Davout, now held equal rank with famous men like Lannes, Soult, and Ney. He proved unworthy of it.

Ex-marquis Grouchy, the man who failed at Bantry Bay, came into prominence when the cavalry charges were needed to complete the rout. A soldier who witnessed them has described the advance of Grouchy's massed squadrons at the height of the battle as an enthralling spectacle. Cuirassiers, dragoons, lancers, and hussars flowed into the fight like a torrent, the sun catching casques, steel breastplates, and sabers, and the entire plain echoing with the thunder of hooves and the steady roar of *"Vive l'Empereur!"* By evening the Russians were in full retreat. Two days later Soult captured Koenigsburg and all its stores and munitions, and the Czar sued for peace. The Russian war was over. Imperial France had reached the zenith of its power and once again Britain was the sole challenger to the man who had inherited the Revolution.

.   .   .

Just before Freidland, old Lefèbvre distinguished himself by capturing the city of Danzig. Lefèbvre never did anything in a hurry. When, as a new marshal, he had been complimented on his splendid coat, he remarked: "It should look well, I've been thirty-five years stitching it!" It did not take him as long as this to reduce Danzig but Ney or Lannes could have captured the city in half the time.

The peace negotiations between Napoleon and Czar Alexander were convened on a raft, moored in the center of the Niemen, at Tilsit. It was a splendid occasion, with everyone in his best uniform and almost everyone on his best behavior, but Lannes disgraced himself by exploding with rage when he saw Bessières chosen as the Emperor's personal attendant. So far most of Lannes' invective had been reserved for Murat, who was also in attendance upon Napoleon on the occasion, but now Lannes' cup of hatred of the Gascon Grand Duke was so full that it spilled over onto the urbane Bessières. From that moment he abominated both men equally and the quarrel with Bessières was to flare up again on a battlefield of the future.

Hatreds, as well as friendships, were beginning to harden among the marshals. Lannes and Augereau, always firm friends, could not bear the sight of Murat or Bessières. Ney abominated Masséna and Davout loathed Bernadotte. Victor and Soult disliked them all. Davout's best friend in the army was the brewer's son, Oudinot, but even this friendship did not survive the Empire. Soult made no firm friends, although he admired Ney's dash and courage. St. Cyr and Marmont, neither of them marshals as yet, shared with Masséna a steady contempt for almost all the others. The only man among the original creation who seems to have been genuinely liked by every marshal was Mortier, the tall, genial farmer's son. Mortier was also liked by his British opponents. He could not only speak their language but came nearest among the marshals to looking and behaving like an English fox-hunting squire! "Any officer would be proud to serve under him!" wrote a British contemporary who met him in Paris during the Armistice.

With full agreement reached between the Emperor and the Czar the army, or most of it, turned for home and the succeeding twelve months were to witness the social heyday of the Empire, with a galaxy of balls, theatricals, soirées, concerts, and receptions, and Paris shopkeepers rubbing their hands as money poured into their tills. The salons and illuminated fêtes were now settings for rivalries between the ladies of the new nobility.

There was jealousy and scandal to spare and a great deal of it stemmed from the childish antics of Napoleon's brothers and sisters, each of whom had a coterie among the courtiers and all of whom were forever getting into situations that raised the blood heat of the Emperor to boiling point.

Sister Caroline, Murat's wife, was the most troublesome, and there was the devil to pay when Napoleon discovered that she had seduced one of his closest friends, General Junot. Her follies were seconded by those of her husband of whom Napoleon was to say: "Titles turn that fellow's head! He is a wonderful man on the field of battle but off it he hasn't the brains of a goat!"

Murat's love of finery did not stop at uniforms. He carried his extraordinary tastes into the ballroom, where his curls, feathers, and furs properly belonged according to a lady who watched him. "His clothes would grace the wardrobe of a strolling player," was her acid comment. A scene that took place at one of his wife's masquerades was in keeping with this role.

Napoleon did not dance and was a poor participant in all drawing-room accomplishments but he liked to see others enjoying themselves, feeling that the splendor of the social events reflected credit upon the Empire. He therefore ordered that his sisters and his pretty step-daughter, Hortense, should take turns to give weekly balls. Pauline, the most attractive but laziest of the clan, declined. In spite of her reputation as a nymphomaniac she was always pretending to be ailing, but Caroline and Hortense played hostesses at a whole series of brilliant events that year. Caroline entertained on Fridays and Hortense on Mondays. Two hundred guests attended and the ladies were always outnumbered by three to one. At one of these masques the dancing was suddenly interrupted by an imperious female voice shouting: "I desire that she shall instantly quit my house!" Embarrassed guests pretended not to notice that the voice belonged to Caroline, the hostess. The order, addressed to her husband at the top of her voice, concerned a certain lady who happened to be Murat's current mistress. The girl had been introduced into the Murats' ball by Hortense, who pretended to be indignant, but one cannot help feeling that this was Hortense's way of repaying the ill will shown by Caroline towards Hortense's mother, Josephine.

Hortense herself was not always discreet. She attended one of the masques dressed as a vestal virgin, which might have passed unnoticed but for the fact that she was in her eighth month of pregnancy. Scandals, however, could not check the feverish gaiety of the Paris hostesses that season. On the very night of the slaughter of Eylau there was a glittering ball in the capital and many of those present eventually learned they had been widowed while they were dancing.

Bernadott's wife, Desirée, was a frequent guest at these events and so was the new Maréchale Lannes. This charming women was quite unaffected by the scramble for titles and told Madame Junot that her husband felt the same way. "There are others," she sighed, "who hold opposite opinion—look around you!" Lefèbvre's washerwoman duchess attended the balls but seldom danced. She much preferred sitting out and telling scandalized guests amusing stories of her charring days before the Revolution. Napoleon's mother, the grim-faced Letizia, was a silent spectator. She considered balls, masques, and concerts evidence of flighty, improvident minds and sighed over the ruinous extravagance of her children.

Sometimes the court went down to the Palace at Fontainebleau and there were hunting expeditions and big-scale shoots. On one of these occasions the Imperial party went out rabbiting and the foresters, anxious that His Imperial Majesty should have a good day's sport, loosed thousands of tame rabbits. Unfortunately, when Napoleon's party appeared in bright green coats, the rabbits swarmed towards them under the impression that keepers had arrived with armfuls of lettuce. They had to be driven off with whips before they could be shot. There was always something slightly farcical about the new nobility's pursuit of these gentlemanly sports. On another occasion, Napoleon loosed off his fowling-piece at the wrong moment and a chance pellet deprived the unfortunate Masséna of an eye. Napoleon at once blamed Berthier, and Masséna does not seem to have borne either of them a grudge. From then on, he always wore a patch over the injury but he could still see far more than most men.

At length, in the summer of 1808, many of the officers began to drift away from Paris, heading southwest in the train of the Emperor. The Spanish War was on the point of beginning and of all the gay young men who took that road at this season there can have been few who guessed that they and their kind would be drawn into the vortex and swallowed up for six long years and that hundrds of thousands of them would die in the squalid villages and on the bare uplands of the Peninsula. For the war down here was soon to be known as "the ulcer" and in the end it was to bleed the Empire to death. Several of the marshals were to spill blood in Spain; more were to squander their reputations here.

CHAPTER ELEVEN

THRONE TO LET

THE curtain raiser on the Spanish tragedy was General Junot's descent upon Portugal, in the autumn of 1807.

Affairs in Spain were extremely complicated without French intervention. The Bourbon King Charles and his hideously ugly Queen were dominated by the Queen's favorite, an ex-guardsman called Godoy, who strutted about under the title of "Prince of the Peace." Prince Ferdinand, the King's son and heir, hated his mother's lover and was, moreover, extremely popular with the Spanish people. The sudden entry of the French into Spain touched off an explosion that, given time, would have occurred without assistance from Napoleon.

Junot was promised his baton if he succeeded in arriving in Lisbon in time to capture the Portuguese Royal Family and the English shipping in the harbor. Desperately anxious to atone for his dangerous flirtation with Caroline Murat the general did his best. He maintained such a rate of march across the Peninsula that he arrived outside Lisbon with a few hundred men, the remainder having fallen exhausted by the road, but his haste was vain. The Portuguese notables, with memories of Marshal Lannes' clanking saber to speed their packing, had fled aboard the English ships and the vessels had put out to sea.

Junot set himself up as governor and with better luck he might have won his baton after all. Considering the difficulties that faced him he achieved wonders. It was not to be, however, and Junot was never to win more than a dukedom out of the wars, for a certain Irish soldier known as "The Sepoy General" was already approaching Portugal. His name, not yet mentioned in the camps of Europe, was Sir Arthur Wellesley and his first action on arrival was to destroy all hope of Junot's advancement.

In the meantime dramatic events were taking place in Spain. By the spring of 1808 three French armies had massed on the Pyrenean borders. The first of them, grandiloquently styled "The Corps of the Coasts of the Ocean," was under the command of Marshal Moncey. Moncey was now fifty-four years of age and it is difficult to understand why Napoleon dragged him out of retirement and sent him off on this new adventure. It was getting on for forty years since young Moncey had driven his family half crazy by tossing his law books out of the window and running off three times in succession to join the army. Notwithstanding pluck and persistence he was not the man to contend for glory against the younger veterans of the Grand Army. Napoleon gave him Grouchy, the heavy cavalry leader, as his second-in-command and the pair entered Spain cautiously and by no means sure of a welcome.

Their fears were groundless. The bewildered Spaniards assumed that the Frenchmen had come marching down into Spain to help them in a revolt against King Charles, his ugly Queen, and the hated favorite, Godoy and Moncey did nothing to disillusion them. The French were welcomed everywhere, although the Spaniards, who had heard all about the Grand Army's astounding feats in Bohemia, Egypt, and Poland, were puzzled by the youth and poor physique of the conscripts Moncey led down onto the plains. The Spaniards, however, were due for a second surprise. On the heels of Moncey and Grouchy came Murat, whose brilliant staff dazzled the Spanish peasants as the Grand Duke pranced and curvetted his way through Burgos and Valladolid to El Molar, a town just outside Madrid where he established his headquarters.

Then, as though Moncey and Grouchy and Murat were insufficient for the job, a third army began to edge across the border, this time under Bessières, with the dashing Lasalle of the light cavalry in support. Spaniards living along the route to the capital began to ask one another what was afoot, but they were not long in doubt. The French occupied the open towns but the citadels were garrisoned by Spanish troops. Soon, however, some very robust-looking invalids began to be sent into the various citadels to convalesce and when there were enough of them they suddenly regained their health and took over the fortresses, together with all the military stores the Spaniards had placed there.

Affairs were now coming to a crisis in Madrid. The mob rose in favor of Prince Ferdinand and a lynching party went looking for Godoy, who rolled himself in a length of matting and hid in a loft. Emerging after a two-day fast he was seized and nearly killed before Murat's troops rescued him and lodged him in jail to await the French Emperor's decision. Then, to save Godoy's life, the Queen persuaded the doddering Charles to degrade the favorite and ultimately to abdicate in favor of his son, Prince Ferdinand.

Murat, dashing in and out of the storm center, did not like this at all. He had come down into Spain convinced that there would be a throne to let and he was quite sure that he would be chosen as tenant. It seemed to him, as an interested observer, that his chance of becoming a popular king of Spain were far more promising if he replaced the feeble Charles than if he followed the popular Prince Ferdinand. The Emperor, who usually decided this kind of thing. was a long way off, and in the meantime Murat, Generalissimo of Spain, was without definite instructions. He decided to continue treating the prince as a prince and the king as a king.

The smoldering quarrel now burst into flames that threatened to engulf the nation. King Charles, his queen, the battered Godoy and the hot-tempered King (or Prince) Ferdinand, were all persuaded to hurry to Burgos to consult the all-wise Emperor Napoleon. The rival parties vied with one another in efforts to reach him first but when they arrived at Burgos Napoleon was not there and Ferdinand, his Castillian pride smarting, refused to go any further. Fortunately Bessières was there to convince him that it would be very foolish of him to leave the field open to his parents and Godoy, so Ferdinand not only pushed on as far as the border but actually crossed it, placing himself completely in Napoleon's power. In any event caution would not have saved him for Bessières had secret orders to arrest him if he refused to continue the journey.

The master chess player now had all the Spanish pawns under his hand and he swept the board clear, offering the furious Ferdinand a choice between abdication and a handsome pension or a few moments in front of a French firing squad. Ferdinand chose the pension, and his parents, who blamed him for their plight, resigned their hereditary rights. Godoy, thankful to have escaped with his life, retired from the complicated game without a protest. A château in France was better than a roll of matting in a Spanish loft. So the throne in Madrid was to let after all.

But was it? There was still three members of the Spanish Royal

Family in the capital, Charles's youngest son, the thirteen-year-old Prince Francis, and his uncle and great-aunt. Murat, feeling that there were too many claimants in the offing, made haste to pack them off to join their pensioned-off relatives in Bayonne but the Spanish mob had other ideas. Aware at last of what was taking place and not being disposed to watch the last members of the royal family set out for the border, the angry citizens rushed into the streets, and on May 2 Murat had a full-scale revolution on his hands.

Nothing could have distressed him more. He was not in the least afraid of a city mob, not even a bloodthirsty Madrilean mob that took pleasure in hunting down every stray Frenchman in the capital and slicing him into small pieces. What did worry the Grand Duke of Berg and Cleves was the odium he must incur by putting down such a revolt and hanging hundreds of his future subjects. For the moment, however, his soldierly instincts won and he set about restoring order with a promptness and efficiency he had shown thirteen years before when he had dashed across Paris to fetch guns to use against a similar rabble. Most of his units were posted outside the city and Murat sent an orderly officer galloping through the sunbaked streets to fetch the Mamelukes and the dragoons, while he himself held the revolutionaries in check in the Puerta del Sol.

The cavalry had a difficult job to reach him. Every window of every street concealed an amateur sharpshooter and the streets were thronged with screaming partisans, who cut and stabbed at every French uniform within reach. Among those who were dragged down in the furious ride into the city was Mustapha, the Mameluke who had been so distressed at Austerlitz because he had failed to present the Emperor with the head of a Russian Grand Duke. His comrades swore to avenge him and they were soon given the opportunity. Dashing into the square they had lopped off a hundred heads in a hundred seconds and the insurgents scattered, leaving fifteen hundred dead on the paving stones. By sunset the Revolution was over but in crushing it Murat's worst fears had been realized. He was now the best hated man in Madrid.

Did the innkeeper's son really lose the Spanish crown that day or had Napoleon already made up his mind to give it to brother Joseph, the King of Naples? Even today nobody can be sure. All that is certain is that Murat, vain, strutting peacock that he was, would have made a far better King of Spain than plump, lethargic Joseph. The army thought so anyway and resented Napoleon's elevation of his brother. In the years of savage fighting that lay ahead Murat, superb judge of terrain and expert handler of cavalry, would have been worth a thousand Joseph Bonapartes in Spain.

Some kind of consolation came to Murat with the offer of Joseph's empty throne in Naples, and after a severe bout of colic, caused through celebrating in advance with too much Spanish wine, the disappointed Gascon rode sadly out of the capital and up Spain's one good road to Burgos and the border. He was one of the few fighting marshals who never returned to Spain and in this he was more fortunate than he knew. The Peninsula was to prove a graveyard of military reputations.

The Spanish adventure had got off to a very poor start but far worse was to follow and that almost at once. By the end of May, Spain had emerged from its stupor and almost every province was in revolt. Open towns and third-rate fortresses became formidable citadels overnight and the French discovered they had entered upon a kind of war that had hitherto escaped their experience. So far they had fought professional armies. Now they were fighting a people whose arrogance, religious fervor and racial background combined to make them the most merciless opponents the imperial troops had ever encountered.

The Spanish army was of little account. Even Bessières and his conscripts made mincemeat of it in the field, but the trouble with the war in Spain was that it was so rarely fought in the open. It was an affair of ambushes, of sudden descents upon stragglers and lightly-guarded convoys, of useless pursuits over ranges of mountains and gorges and river crossings, all defended by skilled mountaineers. It was the kind of war the Republican blues had fought against the peasants of La Vandée and, as one marshsal put it years later, "In Spain a small army is defeated and a large one starves!"

Bessières' victory was more than offset by the shameless surrender of nearly twenty thousand men under General Dupont, at Baylen, in Andalusia, and at the same time came news of Junot's defeat by Wellesley, in Portugal. Under the terms of the subsequent armistice Junot and his men were transported back to France in British ships, but the Invincibles had not only been beaten in open battle at Vimiero but bundled neck and crop out of Portugal. The loss of face was considerable.

A third setback followed with the escape of a Spanish army from Denmark, where it had been sent by Napoleon in the previous year, when Spain was supposed to be an ally. The man who let it escape was Bernadotte, Sovereign Prince of Ponte Corvo, who had replaced the disgraced Brune in the Hanseatic Cities. The Spaniard who organized this remarkable escape of eight thousand men was De La Romana, and British vessels set him down right where he could be calculated to do the most damage— in his own resurgent country. Finally, as though to advertise to the world that Spain was now a stage for French disgraces, brother Joseph, who had never wanted to go there in the first place, suddenly bolted like a rabbit for the comparative safety of the Ebro. Moncey, who was called upon to escort him, was for once obliged to ride at a canter.

Napoleon read these successive dispatches in a cold fury. It must have seemed to him incredible that, in a few short weeks, one French army had surrendered with arms in its hands, another French army had been beaten and shipped home by the English, a Spanish army had sailed out from under Bernadotte's hooked nose without anyone lifting a finger to stop it, and his own brother, whom he had just made King of All the Spains, had scuttled from Madrid like a terrified conscript under his baptism of fire. Yet the facts were indisputable, and at last the Emperor decided that if this was the cost of leaving important matters to a pack of bungling subordinates, he had best do what he should have done at the outset, travel down into Spain in person.

He ordered up three veteran corps of the Grand Army, a huge cavalry reserve and part of the Imperial Guard, and in advance of the veterans, as they came swinging across France from German billets, rode the most formidable array of officer talent in history, Ney and Lannes, the infantry sloggers, tough old Lefèbvre, fifty-three but still spoiling for a fight, Victor with his brand new baton, Soult, Mortier, and the supreme individualist St. Cyr, still only a general but scenting promotion. With them, marched all the best and brightest of the reserve talent, men who, although not yet thirty, had already fought on fifty fields and shared in a dozen brilliant victories, in all about one hundred thousand men and almost every one a veteran. Quietly and without fuss the Grand Army smashed clean through the center of the enthusiastic Spaniards and was in Madrid within a fortnight of the first exchange of shots.

That should have been the end of the war. Joseph was reseated on his throne and almost a quarter of a million Frenchmen, half of them highly-trained shock troops, were occupying Spain. All the previous wars had ended at this point but this one did not. The Spaniards fled but they did not lay down their arms, go back to work, and await brother Joseph's proclamations. Instead they took to the mountains or dived into fortified towns, from which they had to be ejected by murderous assaults and weeks and weeks of siege warfare. Saragossa was a case in point. Moncey, sent against it, could make no headway at all and its motley garrison, entrenched behind stone walls ten feet thick, crowed defiance at the Imperialists outside. Brigands began assembling by the thousands in the stark mountains of Navarre and Galicia. No one could imagine how they survived in such inhospitable places but they did and were frequently pouncing on supply trains and small bodies of troops and dispatch-riders. If they were in a hurry they cut their prisoners' throats and scuttled back to the mountains but if they had an hour or so to spare they crucified their captives, or boiled them in oil, or suspended them upside down from trees over fires. Within a few weeks of the outbreak of full-scale warfare all trace of civilized conduct disappeared. The Spaniards murdered a batch of stragglers and the French, maddened by this kind of frightfulness, set torch to every village through which they passed and massacred all the inhabitants. More than a century and a half was to elapse before Europe was to witness this kind of warfare under Hitler's bullies.

Yet, in spite of every evidence to the contrary, the French High Command was slow to realize the truth of the situation. At the outset of the campaign, Lannes had written home: "They are everywhere in flight, we shall be back by the spring!" and this attitude of mind was to persist for another year, until the hopelessness of the struggle began to break through the thick crust of self-confidence baked by the years of success. The marshals and their senior officers did not seem to realize the fundamental difference between fighting a government and fighting a nation and their master was equally short-sighted. He made the idiotic mistake of supposing that a war on this scale could be conducted from Paris and without unified command. In the next few years Napoleon made a great number of mistakes but never one on this scale. The war in the Peninsula was to cost him not merely his throne, but, in a sense, his unique military reputation. For all but two of the marshals who served there it was to bring nothing but wounds, despair, and disgrace.

· · ·

Having replaced the breathless Joseph on his throne, and scattered the miserable professional armies of the Spanish Bourbons, the Grand

Army prepared to give its full attention to the English, who had shown such foolhardiness in coming ashore after all these years. They had done so once before and had been soundly beaten by ex-journalist Brune, one of the most undistinguished of the marshals. They had, it was true, given General Junot and his sixteen thousand men a beating at Vimiero, in Portugal, but they would now discover that an army under the direction of men like Lannes, Soult, Ney, and St. Cyr was a far tougher proposition than one commanded by a Brune or a Junot. With Madrid secure, Saragossa invested, and a central reserve building up in the heart of the country, Napoleon set the army in motion for Portugal.

He did not advance very far. News came that the British could be hounded out of the country by a thrust in the northeast, where Sir John Moore, the man who had taught the British infantry how to shoot accurately and had laid the foundations for the most mobile striking force in the world, had struck at Soult and in so doing had walked into a trap from which there could be no escape. Turning away from Portugal Napoleon summoned up every unit within call and flung his army over the Sierra Guadarrama into Old Castile.

It was not the kind of weather for a campaign that necessitated the crossing of a mountain range. Ney, with the advance guard, crossed without much trouble but then the blizzards came down and blocked the passes and men and horses of the Guard were flung over precipices by the raging wind. To reach the crest the cavalry had to dismount and lock their arms and the infantry followed, Napoleon walking in this fashion between Lannes and his palace marshal, Duroc. Step by step, the veterans staggered to the summit, the officers in their jackboots having to ride the last few miles on guncarriages. At the summit a halt was made at a monastery and wine was issued. Then these men of iron pushed on down the northern slope. But the storm had done its work and Moore was aware of his peril. With his whole force he bolted for Corunna and the French went tumbling after him into a tempest of sleet and rain and a wind that came shrieking out of the mountains like an army of Cossacks.

It was a horrible ordeal for pursued and pursuers. The discipline of the British broke under the strain and Moore had the greatest difficulty in holding his men together in order to fight delaying actions and break down the numerous bridges over which they passed. Napoleon, fearful of seeing his archenemies escape him, hounded his troops along the dismal roads like a man demented, but even under these appalling conditions the war did not degenerate into the kind of savagery that was now commonplace whenever the French clashed with the Spaniards. At one town the French advance guard heard the cries of women and children coming from a large barn and on opening the doors they found over a thousand half-starved and half-naked camp-followers who had been unable to keep up with the British rate of march. The poor wretches were fed and warmed and a message was sent ahead under a flag of truce to say that they would be returned unharmed the moment the weather mended.

Then, with dramatic suddenness, the driving force went out of the pursuers and the urgency out of the chase. Napoleon learned from a courier that intrigues were afoot in Paris and that Austria, cheered by the news from Spain, was mobilizing for yet another war. The English were in full flight and could be finished off by one or other of the marshals. His own presence was imperative in Europe if he was to hold down the conquests of the last eight years. He turned away with Lannes and dropped back to Valladolid. In a few hours he was on the high road to Paris.

Soult hounded the British into Corunna and then sent off a flag of truce, asking Moore to surrender. "No damned fear!" Sir John retorted and turned to fight while his army made ready to embark. The battle should have been an overwhelming victory for the French but it was bungled. Moore was struck by a cannon ball and died the same night but the English had badly mauled their enemies and embarked unmolested, Soult moving down to Oporto.

The islanders had escaped by the skin of their teeth but the moral victory remained with the French. After all, they had achieved their object and driven their opponents into the sea and the Imperial prestige had been restored. No one could foresee that this kind of hit-and-run warfare could continue indefinitely and that in the end it would be the big battalions who would suffer most.

Jean Lannes, having parted from his chief at Valladolid, went over to have a look at Moncey and Mortier, who were supposed to be investing Saragossa. He was not at all happy about what he found there. The siege was being conducted in a very half-hearted manner. Not only had the garrison loopholed every building but the French were having to defend themselves from the waspish attacks of roving bands in the surrounding countryside.

Lannes went straight to work, calling in outlying troops and settling down to conquer the city by blowing up every house with a separate mine.

It was the only way to capture Saragossa. Every floor of every building was manned by half-crazy patriots, fugitives, priests, and frenzied women, using stones, brickbats, and ancient firearms that fired nails, stones, lumps of iron, and flattened-out bullets cut with serrated edges in order to hook in the muscles of the men they hit.

It was a nightmare siege, bloodier and more bitter than at Genoa. The great convents of the Inquisition and St. Eustacia held out for weeks, yet here again, in the midst of these horrors, the French showed compassion. In one of the captured cellars they discovered three hundred noncombatants and treated them with every kindness, a fact that paid an unexpected dividend, for the town surrendered the next day and typhus was found to be raging among the garrison. The defenders told Lannes that fifty-four thousand men, women, and children had died during the siege.

The prisoners, some forty thousand of them, were sent to France but most of them escaped en route and joined the partisan bands. Palafox, the heroic commander, was treated as a state prisoner and spent the next six years in a French fortress.

. . .

While Lannes and Moncey and Mortier had been chipping away at Saragossa a future marshal had been having an almost equally difficult time outside another fortified town, Gerona, in Catalonia.

Catalonia was a sideshow in the war but the Catalan is an obstinate fellow, as was demonstrated to this generation when he defended himself with such stubbornness against Franco's troops during the Civil War of the thirties. He was no less obstinate a hundred and fifty years ago, and the ex-engineering apprentice, ex-actor, ex-artist St. Cyr could make no impression at all upon Gerona. His most elaborate drawings of siege works were of no avail. Gerona was impregnable. Napoleon, hearing of his lack of progress, lost patience and sent for old Augereau, who had only just recovered from the serious wound he had received at Eylau. The former waiter and seller of watches came to Spain reluctantly, pleading gout, but he arrived at last and took over the siege, St. Cyr returning home as a failure.

The city held out even longer than Saragossa, and Augereau was disillusioned about Spain far more quickly than were most of the marshals. The weather was vile and the loot paltry.

Masséna had managed things far better by remaining in southern Germany, although his turn was to come. Gerona surrendered in mid-December and Augereau showed its garrison no mercy. The Spanish temper and the Spanish weather seemed to have soured him somewhat. After Jena, he had captured the Prussian regiment in which he had served and had given every man he remembered a gift of money but he was losing his reputation for bluff, hearty sportsmanship and was now behaving like a sullen, brigand chief. He was down in Catalonia a long while and soon decided that war was a young man's game and that it was high time he retired from it and settled down to enjoy middle age in comfort. He had married again, an aristocrat this time, and he had accumulated almost as much wealth as Masséna. He was done with glory and yearned for leisure to enjoy what he had striven so hard to acquire. From now on Augereau was only half a soldier. Never again was anyone to say: "There goes the man who won Castiglione!" but rather: "There goes old Augereau, fed up to the teeth and looking for an excuse to be out of it!"

Soult was having a far better time in Oporto, where he settled himself after driving the English back to their ships. He was no longer interested in baking and not noticeably interested in soldiering but he still had ambition. He was absolutely determined that before he died those about him should address him as "Your Majesty" and it seemed to him, isolated in Portugal and far from his restless chief and all the other clacking competitors, that he might be chosen as the new Portuguese sovereign. The hope pricked him so sharply that he lost his customary good sense. He went out of his way to be kind and friendly to everybody and even so far as to organize little squads of cheerleaders, who marched about Oporto shouting somewhat forlornly: "Long live King Nicholas the First!" His staff began to fear for his sanity and seriously considered arresting him. It was, of course, Napoleon's fault that he was a victim of this obsession. Napoleon had made his brother-in-law Murat a king and at the same time had refused to make him, Soult, His Grace the Duke of Austerlitz. If Murat could rule Naples then Nicholas Soult was sure that he could rule Portugal and the marshal began to cast about for a means of so ingratiating himself with the Portuguese that Napoleon would realize the war could be wound up in these parts at once if a strong, wise, sensible man was put at the head of affairs and given the dignity of royalty.

The dream was shattered by the same man who had snatched Junot's baton away just as that general had it in his grasp. Wellesley appeared one morning with an English army and Soult left Oporto in such a hurry that he had to abandon not only his guns and baggage but, what was far worse, his accumulation of loot. He rushed back over the mountains and joined up with Ney, in Galicia, but the two men had never trusted one another and now they could not agree for an hour. After various disagreements they split up again, Ney to search for glory in the barren mountains, Soult to search for valuable pictures and church plate to replace the booty abandoned in Oporto. By this time Napoleon had heard all about Soult's vision and the little tricks he had employed to convert the dream into reality. Berthier was told to write him a severely worded warning and order him to stop making an ass of himself. Berthier wrote: "I am enclosing some proclamations which you will recognize as the style of him born to rule well!" It was one of the neatest snubs ever administered by the shock-headed chief-of-staff.

In March, 1809, Spain ceased to be the focal point of the struggle against Napoleon. This had shifted, once again, to Bavaria and the Danube Valley. For the time being, the scattered marshals in Spain had to be left to cope with their difficulties as best they could. Far more urgent problems were presenting themselves in the Viennese storm center, and Napoleon summoned Lannes, the best of his lieutenants in the Peninsula, to come and take part in what was to prove the Gascon's final campaign. Lannes and his staff left Spain with relief. By early spring, 1809, the greater part of the Grand Army was moving down on Austria, with Davout descending from the north that he had held so successfully all this time and Masséna pushing up from the south. In Napoleon's temporary absence from the field Chief-of-Staff Berthier took charge of the army and the immediate result of this was first a terrible muddle and then a furious quarrel with Davout, who considered Berthier an excellent staff officer but unfit to command a squad in the field.

CHAPTER TWELVE

THE BIG RIVER

THF River Danube played the most dominant role in that campaign, a wide, tumbling torrent at this time of year, its brown flood-water carrying tons of debris round the wide curves and cutting into the banks of the islets where the pickets of both armies played hide-and-seek with one another and the main forces assembled on either bank. For the Danube, an Austrian river, was now Austria's ally and the first to realize this was Napoleon as he probed and maneuvred and rained down questions on the patient head of his chief-of-staff. Looking out over the broad torrent, and watching the tree trunks and shredded foliage rolling down to the sea, Napoleon said: "They have a new ally today, Berthier: General Danube!"

Berthier said little. He was still smarting under the severe scolding he had received from his master when Napoleon came bustling down from Paris and joined issue with the acid Davout in a violent argument that had broken out between the two marshals. For Berthier, temporarily in command, had ordered the army to concentrate upon Ratisbon but Davout had angrily declared that it was vital to concentrate upon Donauworth. When the Emperor arrived he took a single glance at the maps and dispositions and declared that Davout was right and that Berthier was an idiot. Davout did not crow over the chief-of-staff, he was not that kind of man, but he never again trusted Berthier's judgment. Berthier who was not given to harboring grudges, nevertheless found it very difficult to forgive Davout for being so right.

It required great skill on the part of the Emperor and enormous exertions on the part of the troops, to correct Berthier's error but at last it was achieved, largely through Davout's superbly efficient marching and fighting. The enemy was whipped at Eckmuhl, where Davout earned himself a battle title to add to that of Auerstadt. From now on he too could be reckoned among the princes, for he was made Prince of Eckmuhl.

Victory notwithstanding, the main Austrian army, commanded by the talented Archduke Charles, had to be brought to battle, Vienna had to be taken and, if the campaign was to be rounded off, the flooded Danube tamed. It was not the slightest good trying the bluff of Lannes and Murat again and capturing the Spitz bridge by a mixture of boldness and guile. The Austrians were slow learners at war but not as slow as that and this time their army was not under the direction of dotards, like Mack or General Auersperg who would believe everything that was said to them. The Archduke Charles was as cool, resourceful, and resolute as Lannes himself, and so far his handling of the troops had been very imaginative. Neither then nor later did he commit a single mistake of any consequence.

Several of the fighting marshals who had contributed to the old-style triumphs at Ulm and Austerlitz were now far away in Spain, struggling against guerrilla bands, sullen, vindictive peasants, or the persistent Sir Arthur Wellesley. Ney was missing, and so were Soult and Augereau, as well as many of the more talented of the divisional commanders, men like Colbert who had been killed and Lefèbvre-Desnouettes, who now was a prisoner-of-war in far-off Cheltenham.

But others were there, eyeing one another watchfully and ready to fight the enemy or one another as the occasion presented itself. Lannes and Oudinot were up in front with the advance guard. Bessières was commanding the cavalry of the Guard. Davout was once again demonstrating his first-class strategical ability, and with Davout was Marmont, fresh from administrative triumphs in Ragusa. Also there was the clansman Macdonald, who had been in disgrace for years for plotting against Napoleon or for seducing (or being seduced by) the Emperor's sister, Pauline. Berthier was in his usual place, closeted in the traveling coach and snatching an hour or so of sleep when he could. Bernadotte came up with his corps of Saxons, and so did Masséna, whose tenacity was to save France yet again. Puffing along slightly in the rear of these star performers was old Lefèbvre, who had made such a poor show in Spain but could never have understood why or how. The army went forward with confidence under these men, for the muddles and frustrations of Spain had done very little to lower its morale. Because a second-rate general like Dupont had surrendered to a Spanish rabble it did not mean that the Grand Army had forgotten how to beat Austrians.

At Ratisbon Jean Lannes re-enlisted as a grenadier. The town was well manned and its walls were very high. In front of the walls was a wide ditch and to carry such a place by storm promised to be as costly as an assault upon Acre or Saragossa. Lannes directed the artillery to concentrate on a house projecting over the ditch and when a corner of the building collapsed into the fosse he called for ladders and storming parties. The first volunteers were swept away by the fire from the ramparts and hardly a man survived to dash back to the shelter of the outworks. Lannes called for a second and third group of volunteers but at last no one stepped forward. The men looked at the bodies of their comrades and were silent. "Very well," said Lannes, shortly, "I was once a grenadier myself!" and he shouldered a scaling ladder and marched into the open. His staff rushed after him, seizing the ladder and trying to pull it away from him. Lannes held on grimly and the group jostled each other across the open ground, swept by Austrian fire.

The sight of a marshal of France competing with his staff for the possession of a scaling ladder was too much for the infantry. They poured into the open and rushed under the walls, planting a dozen ladders side by side and vying with one another to be first on the ramparts. Two of Lannes' staff were the first on the walls and in ten minutes the storming party had poured down the far side and taken the main gate defenders in the rear. Thirty minutes later Ratisbon was in French hands and on May 10 the French were in the suburbs of Vienna. It was twenty-three days since Napoleon had left Paris.

There was no abject surrender on the part of the Austrians. They abandoned their capital and prepared to defend the crossing of the Danube to the last man. This time there was no mistake about the destruction of the famous Spitz bridge. The victorious French were on one bank and opposite, in unknown numbers, were the Austrians under the Archduke Charles. There was nothing Napoleon could do but undertake that most hazardous of all military operations, the crossing of a broad river in the face of a resolute enemy.

The problem taxed his ingenuity but he set about it with customary dispatch. Two crossing-points were selected, one slightly above Vienna, the other a greater distance below, where the large island of Lobau divides the stream into two branches. Lannes was ordered to go to work on the bridge above Vienna, while Masséna's men built a second bridge opposite Lobau.

Lannes' enterprise was a failure. The Austrians got wind of it at once and the French were thrown back with heavy losses. Hurrying up to discover what had happened Lannes fell headlong into the Danube and Napoleon, who was close beside him, had to wade in waist deep and drag him out. "The accident" comments an observer mildly, "did nothing to improve their tempers!" Lannes' bridge was then abandoned and the army concentrated on the Lobau crossing. The island was occupied in strength, and before the Austrians could concentrate on the left bank, Bessières and part of the Guard were across, occupying two villages the names of which were never to be forgotten in the story of the Empire. The villages were Aspern and Essling. Of the two Essling was the better suited for defense, for it possessed a tileworks and an immense three-storey granary built of stone. As soon as the crossing had been strengthened by engineers, Lannes' corps passed over and occupied Aspern. Shortly afterwards Masséna's corps took up its position in Essling. The scene was now set for one of the bloodiest and most obstinate contests of the Napoleonic wars.

On the morning of May 21 before Lannes, Masséna, or Bessières, who occupied the space between the villages with cavalry, could be reinforced, the Archduke attacked. Forced on the defensive, their flow of reinforcements and ammunition dependent upon a single bridge, the French were soon extremely hard pressed. Again and again the villages were taken and retaken. Troops worked like madmen to bring up fresh ammunition, and while Lannes clung desperately to the ruins of Aspern, Masséna fought it out in and about the great granary at Essling. The losses on both sides were terrible and at one time the head of the bridge was almost taken. Seeing an opportunity for a cavalry charge Lannes sent an urgent message to Bessières in the center, "ordering" him to "charge home!" The aide-de-camp, a tactful young man, had the sense to soften the message somewhat, but on hearing of this Lannes exploded with rage and at once sent another aide-de-camp, this time Marbot, with the strictest instructions to emphasize the words *"order"* and *"home."* Bessières, who in any case resented being under the orders of Lannes, was grossly insulted. "Is that the way to address a marshal?" he snapped, with uncharacteristic asperity. *"Orders! Charge home?"* The unlucky Marbot mumbled that by using these words he was obeying explicit instructions of his chief and on his return to

Lannes reported how the message had been delivered. Lannes was delighted, especially when the resultant charge was successful. "You see what effect it produced," he remarked; "but for that, Bessières would have fiddled about all day!"

When night fell the French still held onto their ground but the entire army, from marshals down to the newest conscript, was shaken by its losses and its dangerous situation. There was now leisure, however, for Lannes and Bessières to extend their private quarrel and that night witnessed one of the most bitter disputes that had ever occurred between senior officers of the Grand Army. Lannes chanced to meet Bessières face to face when the latter was in the act of rating Marbot for his rudeness earlier in the day. Lannes at once rushed to Marbot's rescue. "If the Emperor had placed me under your command I would have resigned!" he shouted, "but so long as you are under me I will give you orders and you will obey them!" He then went on to explain exactly why he had worded the message in this form. "It was because you were parading about all day without approaching the enemy boldly!" he said. "But that's an insult!" snapped Bessières, "and you shall give me satisfaction!" and his hand flew to his sword-hilt. "This very moment if you like" said Lannes and began to draw his own sword.

There is not the slightest doubt that a duel to the death would have taken place on the spot had it not been for the stern intervention of Masséna, who was senior to both men. "Put up your swords this instant!" he thundered. "You are in my camp and I shall certainly not give my troops the scandalous spectacle of two marshals drawing on each other in the presence of the enemy!"

Sulkily the two adult children obeyed and Masséna, taking Lannes on one side, succeeded in quieting him somewhat, while Bessières returned to his own quarters. Later the Emperor sent for them both but he came down heavily in favor of Lannes and issued a stern reprimand to the ex-barber. There is no record of what passed between them that night but Bessières must have received very definite instructions regarding the attitude he was to maintain towards his immediate superior. The following morning he approached Lannes and asked for his orders, without waiting for them to be issued to him. It would be pleasant to record that the easygoing Gascon took advantage of this approach and did something to repair the breach between them but the exact opposite is the truth. Lannes eyed Bessières coldly and then grunted: "As you await my orders sir, I *order* you to place them at such a point. . . . !" and went on to outline his tactical dispositions. By now, however, Bessières had got himself well in hand. He listened and made no reply.

Before the sun was high the desperate fighting began again and at first it looked as if the French were going to break out of their bridgehead and drive the Austrians away from the river. They almost certainly would have done so had it not been for the alarming news that floating tree trunks had severed the one link the troops maintained with their comrades on the far bank. The flow of reinforcements and fresh ammunition suddenly ceased and the French fell back, pressed hard by a savage counterattack.

The bridge was patched up and, with the arrival of help, the French surged forward again but now General Danube's caprice brought them to the very edge of disaster. The Austrians upstream towed a floating mill into deep water and it swept downstream and crashed right through the overstrained pontoon bridge, tearing it to pieces. Every man with his back to the river was now cut off in the face of the enemy and likely to remain so for hours.

The Archduke took full advantage of the French dilemma. He threw the whole of his strength against the contracting bridgehead and Aspern was again retaken. Simultaneously, Essling was stormed and the French were ejected from the granary.

Lannes took the offensive. It was the only thing he could do and he launched Bessières on a series of furious cavalry charges. There was no need to tell the marshal to charge home now. Every man in the French advanced divisions was fighting for his life, and Davout, who had been on the point of crossing when the bridge was shattered, improvised a shuttle service of boats to send over every bullet and powder barrel he could lay his hands upon.

The French line held and the engineers worked furiously at the bridge. General St. Hilaire was struck down in the presence of Lannes and so was Lannes' old drillmaster and friend, General Pouzet. Then there was a lull and Lannes, greatly upset by the death of his old comrade, walked away towards the village of Enzersdorf in advance of the Essling tileworks and sat down on a bank, lost in gloomy reflection. A few minutes later a squad approached him, carrying his dead friend in a cloak. Lannes got up and moved a few yards away, where he sat down again.

At that moment, as he rested with one leg crossed over the other, the ball that had hunted him down through Italy, across the deserts of Egypt, over the bogs of Moravia and Poland, and across the plains of Spain, found its mark. It was a mere three-pounder, fired from a gun near Enzersdorf, and it struck him at the point where his legs crossed, smashing one knee and tearing through the back tendons of the other. "It's nothing much!" he said, trying to rise, but it was and he could not rise. Covered with blood they carried him towards an ambulance but the movement caused him agony. Marbot, his aide-de-camp, fetched the cloak of the dead Pouzet to make a sling but Lannes, although in terrible pain, recognized it and refused to use it as a stretcher. "That cloak is covered with my friend's blood," he protested. "Just drag me along how you can!" Finally they constructed a rough stretcher from boughs and got the shattered man to the bridgehead, where Surgeon General Larrey applied a field-dressing. Later, as the fighting around them died down, they moved him across to the island of Lobau over the rebuilt bridge, and the survivors of the men who had held Aspern and Essling for thirty hours followed him under cover of night. They were beaten men and they knew it. For the veterans of the Grand Army it had been the costliest thirty hours since Eylau.

.   .   .

The Austrians occupied the bloody rubble of Essling and Aspern and the French fortified the island of Lobau with a hundred heavy guns. For the next five weeks the two armies watched one another across the narrow arm of the Danube, squatting like a pair of wounded dinosaurs awaiting the moment to renew the struggle for mastery.

Neither had experienced this situation in the past. For the one it had always been swift and crushing victory, for the other confusion and inevitable defeat. Now they were so evenly matched that a trivial mis-judgment on one side, or a spurt of energy on the other, might result in disaster or triumph, not only for the combatants but for Europe. It was an anxious time for the High Command but the blazing sunshine that beat down on the tents and bivouacs encouraged lassitude rather than activity.

The humid temperature killed Jean Lannes, lying crippled in a house in Ebersdorf. There had been a heated argument between the surgeons as to whether both, one or neither leg should be amputated. The opinion of Surgeon General Larrey, the senior man of the group, prevailed and the leg with the shattered knee-pan was taken off. Lannes bore the operation stoically but as the fever rose he pleaded for water. He was surrounded by water but it was undrinkable. The floods, and the constant passage of armies, had turned it dark brown. Marbot, the faithful aide-de-camp, made a strainer out of one of the marshal's cambric shirts and they got him a drink of sorts. Napoleon came twice a day and knelt beside his friend, telling him that he would live to fight again and for a time the indomitable Gascon believed him and sent for Mesler, the celebrated Viennese mechanician, who was reported to be the best manufacturer of artificial limbs in the world. But long before Mesler could measure him Lannes was delirious, calling on ghost battalions to fill the gaps in the line, and ordering up divisions of cuirassiers to turn the tide of battle, trying all day and all night to rise from his bed and take command of the crisis that still tormented his brain. Then, quite suddenly, the fever left him and he recognized the men about his couch. He spoke of his wife, the amiable Duchess of Montebello, and of his five children. The same day, at dawn, he slipped quietly away and Napoleon wept. The stocky, hard-swearing Achilles, who might have been the master-dyer of Lectoure, had now gone after Kléber and Desaix and Muiron and poor General Morland, still waiting in a barrel of rum to be built into the Hall of Heroes at the Invalides. The one man in the Grand Army who was never afraid to tell Napoleon the truth was dead and the army was to find him irreplaceable.

They embalmed his mutilated body and sent it on its long journey to Paris. For the time being it was laid in the cemetery of Père Lachaise and the infantry momentarily forgot its beloved corps commander and turned its attention to bridge building. For the Austrians were still just across the river and there could be no rest for anyone until they were beaten.

Masséna was the next casualty. His horse put its foot into a rabbit hole and threw him so heavily that he was unable to ride for weeks. He kept mobile, however, by means of a light carriage and was driven everywhere by his faithful coachman and postilion, both civilians. Between them the wily ex-smuggler and the commander-in-chief began to hatch a plot that was calculated to catch the watchful enemy at a fatal disadvantage. The Austrian dispositions were carefully reconnoitred, Napoleon and the marshal posing as a couple of sweaty sergeants preparing for a swim, and when they were satisfied that a frontal assault on the fortified village would be fatal the engineers were ordered to begin reconstructing the bridge that led straight into the enemy positions. In the meantime materials for another bridge, the one Napoleon meant to use, were made ready several miles downstream, in the neighborhood of Wagram.

This time the French enjoyed a little luck. On the night chosen for the crossing a violent storm broke and torrents of rain descended, masking the dash across the river. On the morning of July 5, when the storm rolled away and the sun rose on the cornfields, the Austrians gazed at the historic Marchfield, where the battle that placed the House of Hapsburg on the throne had been fought six hundred years before, and faced one hundred and sixty-five thousand men in the open.

The frightful losses of Aspern-Essling had been made good, all but the loss of the incomparable Lannes. Men had come in from the north, the west, and the south. Marmont, Duke of Ragusa, came hurrying up with a corps of men who had not fired a shot in three years. Davout was there, grimly holding the French right, and with him Macdonald and Grenadier Oudinot. Masséna, riding into battle in a carriage, held the left close to the river, and in support were Bernadotte and his Saxons and Bessières and his Guard. It was to be a battle in the old style, a heavyweight contest between columns, and to make sure that it went according to plan Berthier was there with his compasses poised ready to exploit the first false move spotted by the man in whose shadow he had stood for thirteen years.

For a long time there was no error to exploit. Davout, on the right, forged steadily ahead, but at the crisis of the battle matters stood badly for Masséna against whom the Austrians pushed the main attack, riding over Bernadotte's Saxons and driving the fugitives into Masséna's men, who began to give ground and fall back on the river.

Staff officers about Napoleon panicked. It looked like Aspern all over again but the Emperor seemed unmoved and kept looking to the far right. Back went the disordered Saxons and back went Masséna's columns, carried away in the rush. On went the exultant Austrians until they were within close range of the enormous masked battery on Lobau and here their lines halted, mowed down by the most intense artillery barrage ever seen on a Napoleonic battlefield. The great moment had arrived. The smoke of Davout's guns could now be seen beyond Wagram church tower and it was clear that he was pushing the Austrian left off the battlefield. The Emperor gave the command for which everyone around him had been waiting: "Counter attack with all the reserves!" he said, quietly.

Nearly forty thousand fresh men were flung against the Austrian center, led by Macdonald, the man whom Napoleon had never trusted. With Macdonald went Oudinot and Bessières, commanding the Cavalry of the Guard. With majestic force the central reserve rolled across the blazing cornfields and the battle was won, a victory but not a rout, for the Austrians drew off in good order and the French were far too exhausted to pursue. Once again the battle had been too costly. Thousands of veterans had died, among them several generals including the gallant Lasalle, a man whose élan epitomizes the Napoleonic legend. Among the wounded was Bessières, who was struck down almost in the Emperor's presence.

"Who is that!" Napoleon asked as he saw a flurry among the marshal's staff and when they told him it was Bessières he said, "No time for tears!" and flung himself into the work of pushing the stubborn enemy from the field.

But Bessières was not mortally hurt. A ball had struck his pistol holster and run along his thigh, hurling him from his saddle. He escaped with shock and severe bruising and when they saw him struggling to his feet the chasseurs of the Guard cheered, for they loved this unobtrusive, even tempered man.

Masséna fought the entire battle from his carriage, still attended by his faithful coachman and postilion, who had their hands full that day, for the Austrian gunners, guessing that the carriage contained someone of importance, directed a terrific fire upon it when the French left wing gave ground. Balls and shells fell all round the plunging horses but the one-eyed Masséna made no mistakes in his direction of the Corps. The one error that he did make that day was of a different nature and it involved his honor as a man not a soldier. For serving on his father's staff at Wagram was Prosper Masséna, his son, a youth of about twenty, present at his first engagement, and the marshal's main concern was to keep the boy out of harm's way. His natural desire to do so came near to compromising the lad for the rest of his life.

At the height of the battle, when the Austrian cavalry was cutting away at the routed Saxons, it was necessary to send an aide-de-camp to direct the fugitives to rally on General Boudet. It was Prosper's turn for duty but the assignment looked so dangerous that Masséna shirked sending him and chose instead Marbot, who had recently joined his staff. Marbot galloped off but the indignant boy dashed after him, thoroughly shamed by his father's protective action. Both got through safely but Masséna was furious and asked his son what had prompted him "to stick his nose into a mess like that?" The boy's answer was cutting. "My honor!" he said. "This is my first campaign and I already have the Legion of Honor. What have I done to earn it? Besides, it happened to be my turn!"

Masséna won fresh laurels for his brillant handling of men at Wagram but he also reinforced his reputation as the meanest skinflint in the French army. When it was suggested to him that he should reward the civilian coachman and postilion for their gallant behavior in the field he suggested giving them a present of two hundred francs. His staff, among whom his avarice was a standing joke, pretended to believe that he intended giving the two men *annuities* of two hundred francs. Masséna flew into a frightful rage at the very mention of such extravagance. "I would sooner see you all shot and get a bullet through my arm!" he raved. "If I listened to you I should be ruined—ruined you understand?" In the end, however, he was obliged to grant the annuity, for the story got back to Napoleon, who entered into the conspiracy and gravely complimented Masséna upon his generosity.

Wagram was not Bernadotte's lucky battle. The panic among his Saxons might have led to very serious consequences, and the marshal was obliged to shoulder the responsibility although no one doubted his personal bravery. Any commander can command troops who run away but Bernadotte was not content to leave it at that. He made the idiotic mistake of issuing a private bulletin to his men after the battle and in the bulletin he praised them for their gallantry! Napoleon, learning of this, lost his temper. It was a grave breach of professional conduct to publish a bulletin supplementing the Emperor's. Summoning Bernadotte he expelled him from the Grand Army.

The Gascon's skin was a thick one but this was a terrible blow to his pride. He wandered miserably off the field and took up temporary quarters in a small château. Presently Masséna arrived and Bernadotte made ready to abandon the lodging. Masséna, however, had not yet heard about the Gascon's disgrace and suggested they should share the billet. As soon as a staff officer acquainted him with what had happened, however, he hastily changed his mind and departed without saying a word to his fellow marshal. This action hurt Bernadotte far more than his expulsion and he left for Paris, arriving a few hours ahead of gossip.

For three future marshals Wagram was a day to remember all their lives. On that day they were given their batons on the field and joined the company of the score of men now holding the highest rank.

When the Austrians had fallen back and the luckiest of the wounded were being rescued from the blazing cornstalks, Napoleon sent for his oldest friend, Marmont, for the hard-fighting grenadier, Oudinot, and for the neglected Macdonald, who on that day had covered himself with glory. Marmont and Oudinot were given their batons without comment but to Macdonald Napoleon made honorable amend. "Come, let us be friends from now on!" he exclaimed, seizing the veteran's hand. It was a wise decision. Five years later, when the Empire was crashing round him, Macdonald was the very last among the marshals in personal attendance to turn his back on the Emperor.

The following morning the pursuit began but it was not the thunderous chase that had clinched the victory at Jena. The enemy retained his organization and when peace came it was by negotiation. One of the terms of the agreement was the Austrian Emperor's consent to the marriage of his eldest daughter to Napoleon.

The army was cynical about the proposed match. Only sixteen years had elaspsed since some of the men in the Grand Army had watched the girl's great-aunt, Marie Antoinette, ride in a tumbril to the guillotine, but apart from a natural antipathy for a Hapsburg bride, the rank and file were fond of the gracious Josephine. For a long time now, ever since the Italian triumphs, the old moustaches regarded her as a good luck charm. "We've never had a day's good fortune since we lost the old lady!" they were to say later, but Napoleon listened to the men who urged him to insure the succession and father a legitimate son. Even the Emperor Francis was in favor of the arrangement, acting, no doubt, on the precept "If you can't beat them, join them!" His daughter, Marie Louise, was a dutiful Hapsburg. Ever since her nursery days she had regarded Napoleon as the Fiend Incarnate but she had no objections to marrying him if Papa said so. In the House of Hapsburg Papa's whim was law.

Negotiations for the marriage were set afoot and divorce proceedings began in Paris. Josephine moved out of the Tuileries and a vast wagon train, containing a fabulous trousseau, began its journey to Vienna. To Berthier, senior among the marshals, was given the honor of representing the Emperor at the proxy wedding and he performed the task with tact and kindness. When he saw Marie Louise disconsolate at the prospect of abandoning her home and family he took her aside and comforted her, telling her that Napoleon was a very good fellow indeed and would do everything in his power to make her happy. Then, as she dried her tears, he issued secret orders for the transfer to Paris of all her personal treasures. The result of this thoughtful act on his part was apparent when Marie Louise withdrew from the balcony on which Napoleon had displayed her to the Parisians. The young Empress was greeted by a series of short, joyful barks and her pet dog ran to greet her. With the dog were her caged birds, her little sister's amateurish drawings, and all the objects of sentimental value that had stood in her suite at the Hofberg Palace, in Vienna. The methodical Berthier had packed every one and sent them to Paris in advance of the bride. Napoleon was very struck by Berthier's thoughtfulness, and when Marie Louise went into raptures he insisted that she should embrace and kiss his old friend.

.   .   .

Fortune was beginning to smile on Bernadotte again. No sooner had he arrived in Paris after the terrible disgrace at Wagram than he was called upon, as the only first-class soldier present in the capital, to march out and face the English who had once again made a landing on the northern coasts. They had already taken Flushing and were now embarked upon what was to prove the disastrous Walcheren expedition.

Bernadotte did not even have to fight a major engagement. The English, commanded by idiots, succumbed to fever at an appalling rate, and the strength of their battalions drained away under the eyes of the rag-and-bobtail that Bernadotte had been able to scrape together from the garrison towns.

Of all the expeditions planned or executed by the British in the war against Napoleon the Walcheren expedition was the most ineptly handled. It was a disaster from start to finish. Two of the biggest fools in uniform, Lord Chatham and his adviser, Sir Home Popham, were in command of forty thousand troops, a larger British army than that which was to win Waterloo. The naval forces were under the command of Sir Richard Strachan. Almost incredible muddle and delay inspired the well-known stanza that sums up the failure of the miserable enterprise:

The Earl of Chatham, with his sword half-drawn,
Stood waiting for Sir Richard Strachan.
Sir Richard, longing to be at 'em,
Stood waiting for the Earl of Chatham.

The timing of the attack was bad. When the Grand Army had been locked in its death-grapple with the Austrians on the Danube, British troops were idling in barracks on the coast. As one rifleman put it, "When Napoleon was winning Wagram we were killing cockchafers in Deal!" On the day the news of the Austrian armistice reached Britain the fleet sailed for the fever-stricken marshlands of the Scheldt. Napoleon, hearing of this, warned the local garrisons not to attempt a fight but to sit still and wait for fever to defeat the invaders. His prophecy was fulfilled with terrible accuracy. Of the forty thousand British who landed thirty-five thousand had hospital treatment before they re-embarked. Seven thousand died and many of the others became permanent invalids. Bernadotte watched dead Englishmen being shoveled into vast trenches and decided that there was no need to waste an ounce of powder. When the last of the poor devils had tottered down to the beach and been taken home to die the Prince of Ponte Corvo, so lately in deep disgrace, went home to be fêted in Paris. He was the only man, other than Brune, who had succeeded against the English.

Napoleon growled when he heard about the reception Paris had given its savior, wishing, no doubt, that the victor had been anyone other than Bernadotte, but another cause for Imperial displeasure was on its way. In due course a Swedish deputation arrived, seeking a crown prince, and had, in fact, already made up its mind to choose the gallant, hook-nosed marshal who had been so courteous and generous to the Swedes taken prisoner in Lübeck three years before. Their king, they pointed out, was not only childless but unpopular. What Sweden needed was a tall, dashing soldier who could reorganize their army and lead them on the field of battle. France was full of dashing soldiers now that men were coming home from the Danube fighting, but apart from Bernadotte, none of these made much impression upon the strangers. Napoleon put forward several suggestions but the Swedes shook their heads. It was Bernadotte or no one and surely it would be advantageous to France to have a Frenchman as future king of Sweden?

Napoleon raged inwardly but was in a curious situation and there

was very little he could do about it. So, the following year, Bernadotte
and his pretty wife Desirée packed their trunks and set off for the north.
The Gascon had got his throne after all and fate had compensated Desirée
for losing Napoleon to Josephine all those years ago.

.   .   .

By the close of 1809 preparations for the Imperial wedding were
in full swing. Napoleon, in a fury of impatience, tried to learn to dance
but there is no record of the fact that ex-dancing master Augereau was
called upon to give him lessons. Perhaps Augereau did not volunteer.
He was avoiding the limelight these days and hoping to enjoy a little
well-earned peace and quiet.

When the news came that Marie Louise was across the frontier Napoleon's impatience broke the bounds of dignity and he rushed down to
Soissons where the meeting between bride and groom was scheduled to
take place. Flustered officials told him she was still a day's journey off,
so he changed into a simple artillery uniform and galloped off towards
the frontier. With him, as escort, went a single man, and the Emperor's
traveling companion on this occasion was our old friend Joachim Murat,
King of Naples, the designer of dazzling uniforms and brother-in-law of
the bridegroom.

The weather was foul and rain fell in torrents. Napoleon, never a
good rider, must have found it difficult to keep pace with the best horseman in Europe. Along the slushy roads they cantered, two men who had
begun life respectively as attorney's son and innkeeper's son but who were
now Emperor and King. Startled mayors, and children rehearsing speeches
of welcome, saw them pass, a pair of breathless, mud-bespattered horsemen, and mistook them for a couple of hard-pressed couriers. At the village of Courcelles, while sheltering from a particularly heavy downpour
in the church porch, they saw the bridal coach lumber into view and at
once spurred into the escort of cavalry. The Master of the Horse recognized the Emperor and let out a great shout of welcome. Murat, grinning,
dismounted and watched his brother-in-law scramble into the carriage to
plant a resounding kiss on the bride's cheek. Sitting beside her, in the
role of wardress-de-luxe, was Murat's wife and there is no record that
the dripping King of Naples showed any eagerness to kiss his spouse.
This surprised no one for it was common knowledge that there had been

violent quarrels between man and wife, and the court at Naples was tittering over the shabby little artifices they employed to score over one another. Murat had got his throne but was discovering the truth in Shakespeare's observation touching its disadvantages. He had recently set out on an expedition to conquer Sicily but the bulk of his army refused to advance, its officers having received counter-orders from a somewhat higher level. Furiously Murat tried to combat this unseen influence by making Frenchmen residing in the kingdom of Naples adopt Neapolitan nationality but once again high authority intervened. A letter arrived from Paris signed with a large sprawling "N," pointing out that "the Emperor was surprised to learn that Murat no longer regarded himself as a Frenchman and he should try hard not to forget the fact that he had risen from stable to throne on the backs of Frenchmen!"

Murat, speechless with rage, tore off his Legion of Honor ribbon and spent the entire night reading police reports. His wife, secretly delighted by the snub, offered no wifely sympathy but gave a good deal of thought to the problem of how she would keep her crown if Europe arose one day and swept the entire Bonaparte family out of the palaces they occupied.

Rivers of blood were to flow before that happened but Caroline bided her time and went out of her way to welcome the new Empress. After all, the girl's presence in Paris was something of a personal triumph for Caroline and her sisters. They had been trying to unseat the hated Josephine for thirteen years.

CHAPTER THIRTEEN

THE ROAD ACROSS THE MOUNTAINS

SPRING, 1810. Napoleon was divorced and remarried and Europe (Spain and the high seas excepted) was at peace. For Napoleon it was to be a year of progresses, summer fêtes and winter firesides, the first year of peace he had enjoyed for seven years, his last until he reached St. Helena. For the majority of the marshals also it was a time to relax, sit back, and enjoy their wealth and titles, a time to hunt or grow fat at administrative desks. Those who were outside the Peninsula made the most of the lull. Like their chief, it was a long time since they had been beyond bugle call of the picket lines.

Kellerman, Pérignon, and Sérurier, long since retired, read the war news in the *Moniteur*, and Lefèbvre, who had campaigned down on the Danube, was inclined to hang up his sword and follow their example. The average age of these four Republican veterans was now sixty-three. They were not much use in a modern war but any one of them would have proved a formidable opponent in single combat with saber or pistol.

Moncey, too, had faded out, and old Jourdan, of Fleurus fame, home from Spain where he had made a dreadful mess of things. Moncey turned back to the desk he had forsaken in his youth and Jourdan, with his professional eye for haberdashery, was content to forget Spain and estimate cost and sources of the expensive garments worn by the ladies at the balls given by the marshals' wives in honor of the Imperial wedding.

The rest were still enjoying good health but even Davout, holding the north at Hamburg, spent most of his time at his desk, making sure that a steady stream of smugglers trying to turn an honest guinea by trading with England, were caught, tried, and shot. Davout was an excellent soldier but he was an even better policeman. Those he caught could be sure of two things, a fair trial and the maximum penalty if proved guilty.

Murat was busy down in Naples, designing new liveries, quarreling with his wife and studying police reports with rather less than Davout's flair for this kind of informaiton. Murat was not cut out to be a policeman. Neither, for that matter, was he cut out to be a king.

Lannes was dead and Bernadotte was captivating Sweden, whither he had now departed as heir to the throne. Berthier accompanied the Imperial couple on some of their royal progresses and lucky Brune was still in disgrace for selling confiscated cargoes taken from men that Davout was now shooting and hanging. Marmont was enjoying his recent promotion and so was the sober Oudinot, though with less ostentation. Only the eight unlucky ones—Masséna, Soult, Ney, Mortier, Bessières, Augereau, Victor, and Macdonald, were involved in the hideous, blood-curdling, wearisome, futile, never-ending business in Spain. The years 1810 and 1811 are exclusively a story of French disasters, large and small, within the compass of the detestable peninsula.

.   .   .

Masséna, perhaps, was the most unhappy of this luckless group. He had deserved well of the Emperor in the recently concluded Danubian campaign. He was feeling old and tired. At fifty-two he was a fabulously rich man and second only to Napoleon in military reputation. But what on earth was the good of wealth and veneration if one was obliged to struggle across the scorched uplands of Spain, warding off hit-and-run attacks by guerrillas, camping in burned out villages, and listening to the complaints of sullen subordinates all day and despairing mistresses all night?

When Napoleon told him that he must go and finish the war in Spain and hound the arrogant British across Portugal and into the sea he made all manner of excuses. He was not the right man for the job. He was too old. He did not feel well. A fitter and younger marshal would succeed where he must inevitably fail. Napoleon pooh-poohed these protests and resorted to flattery. "Your reputation alone will finish the business!" he declared, so Masséna, by no means taken in by the compliment, had no alternative but to set off for Salamanca with a baggage train that included an extremely pretty girl whom he seldom let out of his sight.

The old libertine had told the truth when he said that he was slowing down. He pottered into Salamanca days behind his staff and weeks behind his troops and then, instead of advancing before the partisans and Wellington could prepare a reception, he dawdled about the city making sure that the army was in a first-class state of preparedness for the campaign. Men who had served with him at Genoa and Zurich counted the days and wondered what had become of the mongoose who had pounced on cumbersome beasts like Korsakov and Suvorov, and sent them scuttling home to their native lairs.

Masséna was additionally unfortunate in Napoleon's choice of the men who were to serve under him. Ney's explosive temper had not been improved in Spain and Masséna's methodical approach to the campaign soon began to irritate him. Divisional Generals Junot and Foy did not help matters either, for Foy was a close friend of Ney's and Junot, who had lost his chance of a baton in this corner of Europe, had been wounded in the head and was behaving erratically. From the very outset of the expedition these three men formed a kind of junta to do everything possible to thwart their commander. Their disgraceful behavior was to make a notable contribution to the disasters that lay ahead.

Masséna was now generalissimo of the armies in Spain but if Napoleon had really intended him to enjoy supreme command he should have done something to insure that his orders were obeyed. As it was each marshal was supreme in his own area and even had they been disposed to co-operate with one another the trackless distances and the swarming guerrillas that isolated the various commands made co-operation extremely difficult. If Napoleon had been commanding Masséna's army in person the scattered marshals might have overcome these difficulties by sheer will power. As it was they were not disposed to attempt miracles on behalf of a one-eyed miser who had brought his mistress along with him and was known to be getting old and slack.

Soult was down in sunny Andalusia, where he was supposed to be besieging Cadiz. He had replaced Jourdan as military adviser to the unhappy King Joseph but he did not take this appointment seriously. Wellington had shattered his dream of becoming King Nicholas of Portugal but he could still be Viceroy Nicholas of Andalusia.

He was a long way from Madrid and even further from Paris and nearly all the messages sent to him were opened by the men who had butchered the dispatch riders. Nobody bothered him very much and he ruled like a viceroy, fighting when he had to but giving more attention to a systematic collection of works of art. One of the few cheerful aspects of campaigning in Spain was the number of works of art that were awaiting appropriation by a man of taste and culture.

Rosy-faced Victor was supposed to be helping Soult but Victor had ideas of his own about how a marshal of France should conduct himself in Spain. He and Soult got along reasonably well together. Each kept a pretty mistress and the two mistresses were sisters. Victor was not specially interested in pictures, or gold chalices, or crucifixes studded with stones mined in Spain's overseas empire but he was very interested indeed in acquiring the kind of military glory that had been enjoyed by Jean Lannes and still seemed to be the perquisite of men like Masséna and Ney. In pursuit of glory he had tried conclusions with Wellington at Talavera the previous year, but had been soundly beaten. It was typical of the talkative ex-sergeant that he claimed Talavera as a victory but unfortunately Napoleon thought otherwise. That was why he recalled Jourdan, who was present at the battle, and sent Masséna into Spain at the head of a new army.

Bessières, his Wagram hurts healed, was holding down the northern provinces and Suchet, the silk-merchant's son, was earning his baton in Valencia and Aragon. Augereau, fed up with it all, was still in Catalonia and brother Joseph was back on his throne in Madrid, so that it might be said, with certain reservations, that the French really did occupy Spain or such areas of it as were within a couple of days' march of their various headquarters. The rest of the country had degenerated into a kind of desert, where peasants dragged out a miserable existence evading the demands of the French and the partisans for their dwindling reserves of drauft animals, poultry, grain, wine, leather, and paltry personal treasures. Every now and again there was a clash between armed detachments and then the combatants moved on somewhere else. If the local inhabitants had been able to hide themselves and their livestock in time, they returned to their ruined village and tried to pick up the threads of their existence. If they were less lucky, their livestock was driven off or slaughtered, their womenfolk raped, and they themselves were either shot or pressed into service as beasts of burden. Whole areas of Spain were now looking like the landscape of Dante's Inferno, an impression conveyed to later generations by the painter Goya's "Disasters of the War."

About the middle of June Masséna continued his leisurely progress as far as the Portuguese frontier, where Ney sat down in front of Ciudad Rodrigo, the last border citadel. The place was very strong and might have held out a long time but the English did nothing to relieve it and an explosion of powder blew down thirty-six feet of the counterscarp, so the Spanish general surrendered. Anticipating a long siege, Masséna's young staff officers had built themselves a cosy little billet in the siege lines but just as they were settling in the marshal appeared rubbing his hands and exclaiming: "Well, my lads, you've got a nice place here!" The aides took the hint and vacated it while Masséna moved in. He might be growing old and lazy but he was still well able to take care of himself in the field.

After getting possession of Ciudad Rodrigo Masséna moved on to Almeida, another strong fortress. Here again he was lucky, for in August the place blew up killing six hundred of the garrison and the way into Portugal was open. So far, the army had not come to grips with Wellington who retired slowly, wasting the country as he went. It was one of the most notable examples of the "scorched earth" policy used with great effect by the Russians in World War II, and it succeeded beyond Wellington's expectations. The French crossed huge tracts of country without meeting a single inhabitant, or being able to lay hands on a single cow or chicken. In one city even the lunatics were freed from the asylum and driven over a mined bridge by the British rearguard.

The march was painfully slow, partly on account of the commander-in-chief's concern for his mistress. She had remained in Salamanca during the two sieges but she now followed the advance on horseback. At one point, when she was greatly fatigued, the considerate Masséna kept the army immobile for a week. Relations between the chief and his immediate subordinates deteriorated. Ney, already disgusted with the campaign, was furious when Masséna asked him to conduct the lady in question to luncheon. He escorted her to the table with the tips of his fingers and made it perfectly clear to everyone present that he was utterly contemptuous of this way of making war. He then sat through the meal and refused to address a single word to her and the wretched woman was obliged to faint in order to cover her embarrassment.

Things had come to this pass when the British made a stand on the ridge at Busaco. There was a road round the position and they could have been prised out of it by a flank march but Masséna took no steps to attempt this and Ney's smoldering temper induced him to advise a savage frontal assault up rocky slopes manned by the best marksmen in the world.

The result was disastrous. At the end of the day the French counted five thousand men and two hundred and fifty officers killed, wounded, or prisoners. The British continued their retreat towards Lisbon and the French followed, Masséna having indignantly refused to abandon the enterprise and take the army back into Spain. Ney, who had urged the suicidal attack, now protested that an assault upon such a strong position had been an act of crass stupidity. Masséna said nothing. He was not an easy man to provoke.

Horse, foot, and guns of the two armies went tumbling down to Lisbon. Masséna established hospitals at Coimbra and those among the wounded who survived the journey from Busaco were left here under guard while the rest of the army went doggedly after the English. In the first week of October, just as the rains began, they came up with them outside the city allegedly open on the landward side. It was here that the victor of Zurich and Genoa, the man whose name was respected all over Europe as a master of field strategy and dogged defense, received the shock of his military career.

Every single approach to Lisbon was blocked by a vast chain of expertly prepared fortifications, so strongly built and so cleverly designed in and around the hills, that it was obvious an attempt to storm them would be fatal to the attacker. For years, it seemed, British engineers and Portuguese civilians had been as busy as moles, converting barriers into small forts and linking them, at every possible vantage point, with bastions, trenches, underground galleries, and artificial landslides. The lines of Torres Vedras were impregnable.

Masséna sat his horse and stared at this vast labyrinthine citadel. Attached to his staff were several Portuguese officers and Masséna sent for them. "Did you know of this?" he asked quietly. No, they said, they had not known of it, nobody had known of it, but it had not been there a year ago. The English, added the Portuguese, must have been very busy indeed making such wonderful fortifications.

"Doubtless they were," said Masséna, grimly, "but Wellington did not make the mountains!"

He took a closer look and was amazed. Every possible approach had been blocked, here with barricades constructed from full-grown oaks, there with loose stone walls forty feet high. The lines were bristling with over five hundred guns, sited for cross-fire.

For six weeks the meticulously thorough marshal poked about looking for a chink, while his troops starved and his horses died for want of fodder. Then, with despair in his heart, he swung aside and edged round to Santarem on the Tagus. He knew enough about fortresses and fortifications to estimate how many men it would require to storm Torres Vedras and he knew also that he had not got that number of men under his command and would never have them, not even if reinforcements poured down from Spain or up from Andalusia. Ney knew it too and so did every man in the French army who had toiled all the way from Salamanca to chase the English into the sea. Now it was clear that the English would never be chased into the sea and that the most that could be achieved was the face-saving manœuvre of a protracted blockade.

The exhausted army lapped over the desolate country on the outer edge of the tight circle of which Lisbon was the hub. In front of it were miles and miles of strongpoints. To the west was the broad ocean, dotted with British supply ships. To the south ran the broad Tagus, patrolled by British gunboats, and behind it, denuded of population, produce, livestock, and fodder, was an empty, forbidding landscape. It was the terminus of Masséna's career.

. . .

Soult was always promising to come and help but he never appeared. Ney's insubordination grew more and more insupportable and his detestation of Masséna became almost pathological. He even tried to persuade a general in charge of some reinforcements from Spain to withhold his battalions from the commander-in-chief in order that Masséna might not be tempted to attack. The horses died from want of provender, the men grew haggard and wasted for want of rations. Across the breastworks scarecrow French sentries exchanged news and wry jokes with robust British redcoats, growing fat on regular supplies of beef, bread, pork, and beer, landed daily from their transports in the harbor. Masséna's information as regards what was happening in Paris came from British newspapers tossed over the barriers by friendly infantrymen.

Day by day, week by week, the strength and morale of the French army drained away, sapped by want of food, want of news from home, want of new clothing but, above all, by want of hope. Even had the fortifications confronting them been hastily dug trenches they would have been too sickly to assault them. By February, 1811, the man who had held out in Genoa against such desperate odds realized that he was beaten. Quietly and without fuss he gave the order to retreat and on March 3 the army began its long march back into Spain.

Now, the sullen, intractable Ney pulled himself together and became a soldier once more. All through the advance into Portugal and throughout every day of the long, hopeless siege of Torres Vedras, he had been carping and criticizing. Sometimes his behavior had verged upon mutiny and it must have tested the temper of patient Masséna to the utmost. Faced with the task of covering the retreat Ney's better qualities emerged. Every morning Wellington found himself confronting a resolute rearguard and every evening found the French occupying a position where they had to be outflanked all over again.

Johnny Kincaid, an exuberant British rifleman who rode with the Light Brigade in the van of the pursuit, learned to respect the French soldier during this long, toilsome and often bloody retreat. Never once were the Imperial soldiers hustled or chivvied. Always, with Ney well to the fore, they were sharp-eyed, aggressive, and ready to exploit every act of rashness on the part of the pursuers. It was a dress rehearsal for Ney's *tour de force* in Russia. If the Light Division advanced too rapidly the French turned and pounced. If it lagged the French gained a day's march to the river crossings. At one point a British regiment marched straight into a trap and was almost overwhelmed. "It looked," said an eye-witness, "like a red pimple in the dark masses of the enemy."

There was evidence, now and again, of a savagery not usually associated with the men of Napoleon. One day Kincaid came across the remains of a Portuguese civilian. He had been squashed flat under an enormous block of stone and laid out in the center of a village street as a warning to other partisans. Such reprisals were the legacy of the relentless cruelty of the Spanish guerrillas.

At another point Masséna was almost overrun and captured. Ney sent him a message that he was abandoning a position but the message did not arrive in time and Masséna, who pursued the art of good living even in the midst of a retreat, had found a pleasant spot for an open-air luncheon and was on the point of sitting down to the meal when English hussars rode over the hill and cantered to within eighty yards of the table.

The astonished commander-in-chief, who had supposed that several divisions separated him and his staff from the enemy, ordered his escort of dragoons and a dozen or so staff officers to mount and charge the hussars. The British turned and fled but the staff officers soon realized that they were riding right into the British advance guard. Hastily they wheeled and galloped back. Luncheon was left for the sharp-set men of the Light Division and Masséna and his staff rushed after the French rearguard shrouded in an opportune mist.

It was during this mad scramble to safety that the tough little lady friend of the marshal had to endure the maximum pain and discomfort. Until then she had kept up very well, riding dressed as a dragoon captain and sharing the hardships of the retreat with great fortitude. She must have been very attached to Masséna or to Masséna's money for she uttered no complaint when her horse stumbled and fell several times in succession. At last, however, she was so bruised that she was unable to mount and had to be carried by two soldiers. Masséna, desperately anxious about her, was honest enough to admit his folly in encouraging a girl to make the campaign. "What a stupid idiot I was to bring a woman to war!" he remarked to one of his staff.

When the border was finally reached the old smuggler's pride flared up and he suddenly decided that he would not quit Portugal after all but hold on and prepare for another invasion later in the year. This decision was the final straw for Ney who argued that it was absolutely impossible to maintain the troops in such a sterile country and that he, for his part, intended marching his corps back into Spain where there was bread. Even the long-suffering Masséna could not turn his sightless eye to defiance such as this and he did what he should have done months before, removed Ney from his command.

For a while Ney refused to accept dismissal but in the end he had to go and his veterans assembled on parade to say goodbye. He had commanded the Sixth Corps since the days when the Grand Army had been formed along the Channel coasts and he had marched it to Austerlitz, to Jena, across Poland to Eylau and Friedland and down into Spain at the outset of the war. The rank and file wept to see him go for now that Lannes had died he was the most popular man in the Grand Army.

Freed of his main opponent Masséna set about reorganizing his command. In spite of the failure of the campaign and the miseries it had brought in its train, his losses were moderate. He still had sixty-five thousand effectives in hand, together with the possession of fortresses like Ciudad Rodrigo and Almeida. Moreover it was Wellington who was now a long and weary march from his base, and Masséna was prepared to take his revenge on the man who had smashed his reputation.

The British had sat down before Almeida and the garrison was reported to be at its last gasp. Masséna was determined to relieve it and do battle with Wellington in the open but he was occupying territory that was technically under Marshal Bessières, so he asked the polite ex-barber for supplies and reinforcements. Bessières was not fond of Masséna but he was much better mannered than the red-headed Ney. He received every request for help with assurances of full co-operation. The only thing he did not do was to send troops or guns or supply wagons or powder.

Masséna waited and waited and the starving garrison in Almeida hung on day after day. At last the commander-in-chief could delay no longer and in late April he set out to do what he could with his own limited resources. At that precise moment shouts of joy rose from Masséna's outposts. A column of horsemen appeared on the road leading from Bessières' headquarters and at length fifteen hundred cavalry, six guns and thirty gun-teams approached the camp. At their head, looking extremely virtuous, was Bessières himself.

Even the iron-willed Masséna was shocked out of his impassivity. He gazed at the tiny column in utter astonishment, suspecting for a moment that he was looking at the advance guard of the long-awaited reinforcements. No marching columns appeared behind the cavalry however and with this miserable addition to his forces, Masséna moved against the British.

He made no attempt to conceal his bitter disappointment but Bessières was imperturbable. In all his dealings with the senior marshal he was not only polite but extremely helpful. He kept following Masséna about and making various little suggestions as to how the impending battle should be conducted, and at last Masséna could bear it no longer and broke his habitual silence. "I could do with far more troops and far less Bessières!" he told his staff.

In early May the two armies clashed and the result was a narrow victory for Wellington. With a little more luck Masséna would have won and Wellington, in later years, admitted as much. Bessières was no more help in the field than he had been during the preparations and Fuentes d'Onoro proved to be Masséna's last battle. Yet he went down with an odd but somehow typical gesture of defiance. After the battle he paraded all his best troops past the exhausted victors and an English officer said: "It made us proud to think we had just beaten such splendid fellows!" The marshal-prince who had done more than any other to win for the French army the legend of invincibility returned to headquarters to find himself not only disgraced but superseded. Gunner-cadet Marmont, one of the three most junior marshals, had been sent down into Spain to replace him. In the opinion of Napoleon a Peninsular general was only as good as his last success.

·　　·　　·

After his fine performance at Wagram Marmont had gone to Dalmatia as an administrator and here he had continued his imaginative constructive work that had begun in Ragusa after the Austerlitz campaign. He was delighted to take the field again and on his arrival in Salamanca it was plain that he had soon learned how to conduct himself as a marshal. He brought along a magnificent dinner service and an army of cooks and valets and threw himself into the work of reorganizing Masséna's dispirited army with the efficiency of a brand new broom. By June he was on his way to help Soult take Badajoz, the southernmost of the Portuguese border fortresses.

The man who had once wanted to be a baker and then a king and was now a real viceroy in Andalusia, was one of the few senior officers in the Imperial Army who enjoyed service in Spain throughout the disastrous year 1810. Still with him in this land of sunshine and orange groves were his colleagues Victor and Mortier. All three had been living comparatively tranquil lives since Soult had established his headquarters in Seville and had laid siege to Cadiz.

Time and again messages had been received from the luckless Masséna, starving to death before Torres Vedras, but Soult was even less co-operative than Bessières and had not even sent Masséna fifteen hundred horsemen and thirty gun-teams. Soult was mainly occupied in looting and by this time he had collected a very valuable assortment of old masters. There had been a battle every now and again and the dreary siege of Cadiz went on and on and on, though with far less ruthlessness on either side than at Saragossa or Gerona. Once Soult had almost defeated the British at Albuera, where the proportion of losses suffered by the islanders, two out of every three men engaged, was higher than in any battle of modern times, but he failed to exploit his gains and victory had been snatched from him by the stubborn gallantry of seven thousand redcoats. Albuera, like the fight at Fuentes d'Onoro, was almost lost by the British general and was saved by the gallantry and steadiness of the rank and file. Victor had tried conclusions with the British at Barosa but was heavily defeated. The British general, Graham, slipped out of Cadiz and caught Victor napping, and as a result of his victory the Scotsman was given a Spanish title "Duke de la Cerro de la Cabeza del Puerco." He was somewhat startled when he learned that this meant "Duke of the Hill of the Pig's Head"—a local name for the site of the battle. Mortier, the one marshal in Spain whose natural amiability prevented him from working off his private grudges on colleagues, had tried very hard to persuade Soult to help Masséna outside Lisbon but his advice had not prevailed and in the end he was recalled to France. Victor soon followed him and so did Bessières in the north. Bessières left the Peninsula in semi-disgrace for Napoleon had heard all about his modest contribution at Fuentes d'Onoro. Macdonald too was withdrawn from Catalonia and most of his men were handed over to a newcomer.

Macdonald's successor was Louis Gabriel Suchet, who might have been a silk-merchant but who had proved in a dozen campaigns that he was a clever strategist and a first-class administrator. That year, when most of the marshals were in trouble, Suchet's ability was recognized and he was awarded his baton at the age of forty-one.

Suchet was an intelligent, even-tempered man, unostentatious and eminently reasonable in his judgments and decisions. When he took charge of affairs in Arragon and Valencia he had everything against him, sullen troops, shortage of supplies, and a population that were ready to massacre French soldiers who turned their backs on them but Suchet changed all this. He was so tactful and reasonable, and his efforts to limit the horrors and vexations of war were so successful, that soon his was the only area in Spain where a Frenchman could walk unharmed among Spaniards. Napoleon watched his work from afar and ultimately placed his full trust in a man who could run a conquered province like a business house and show a profit without upsetting the employer, customers, or employees. He is reported to have said that if he had had two Suchets he could have held Spain indefinitely. This is an exaggeration but it says a good deal for the administrative ability of the new marshal.

Spain, however, was now becoming a sideshow once again. Great events were stirring nearer the center of operations and as the year 1811 ran out only a handful of marshals were left in the Peninsula. Bessières, Macdonald, Mortier, Masséna, and Ney were gone, withdrawn as failures. Victor was going without having taken Cadiz. Disgusted Augereau and blunderer Jourdan had both been recalled after making a bad job worse. Suchet was established in the southeast and Soult in the southwest. Marmont commanded the central army and brother Joseph was still sitting on the very edge of his throne in Madrid. From now on these men, and the skeleton divisions they commanded, would have to suffice. The Emperor had other and larger fish to fry.

CHAPTER FOURTEEN

THE ROAD ACROSS THE PLAINS

THE fruits of the agreement between Czar and Emperor on the Tilsit raft had promised to be sweet. It had taken the Little Father of All the Russias five years to discover that they were too sour to be swallowed.

After Friedland Alexander and Napoleon had decided to partition Europe. They talked of spheres of influence and what later generations would call "co-existence" but in the end their discussions and mutual flatteries resulted in nothing more than an extended truce, the bargaining factors being a pledge on Napoleon's part never to make Poland independent and a promise on the part of the Czar to exclude British merchandise from his realm.

The pact worked well enough for a time. While Napoleon was pounding Spain and stamping out the embers of Austria's patriotism on the Danube, the Czar had stood aside. They said that he was captivated by the personality of the French Emperor and perhaps he was. He was a strange man, tall, effeminately handsome, half romantic and half despot. He was also suspected of being a parricide.

There had been talk of Napoleon marrying the Czar's fifteen-year-old sister instead of the Austrian Archduchess but the project did not mature. Napoleon saved his face by marrying Marie Louise and the Czar saved his by announcing that his sister was too young to marry. The alliance survived this tiff but there was more trouble over Napoleon's decree to ban British shipping from Russian-controlled ports. The Russian aristocrats had never quite forgotten the fearful drubbing they had received on the heights at Austerlitz and at Friedland, and in the spring of 1812 the long truce broke under the strain and the two countries drifted into war. What astonished Europe was not the war but the magnitude of Napoleon's effort. A diversity of the races went to make up his huge army which was the largest assembled in Europe since the Persian Darius had invaded ancient Greece.

The core of the army was French, men who had marched and fought under the eye of Napoleon for fourteen years. They were the growlers, the old moustaches, the leather-skinned survivors of Arcola, Lodi, the Pyramids, Marengo, Austerlitz, and the German and Polish campaigns. The army was their home and fighting for loot and glory was their way of life. Many of them had won the cross and almost all of them boasted of several scars. They came trudging up from the hateful Peninsula and across France to the rendezvous at Dresden. They poured in from Italy and the German garrison towns, from the remount and recruiting centers in eastern France and from the seaports of the west. They were contemptuous of the polyglot allies who awaited them, Dutchmen, Italians, and Wurtemburgers, Saxons who had fled at Wagram, and Badeners who had fled at Jena. Only the Poles were welcome under their blue-blooded leader, Poniatowski, and this not because the Polish fighting record was excellent but because it was clear that the Poles saw in this new war the freedom for which they had been praying for generations. This, argued the veterans, would make them fight to kill. The French could count on Poniatowski and his lancers in a war against the Czar, but the others, the contingents from the little German states and from satellite territories, would surely not be called upon to do much more than act as wagoners, flank guards, and convoy escorts. The veterans looked beyond these hirelings and scanned the bulletins for up-to-date information regarding the names of the corps commanders who would lead them into battle.

They were soon reassured. The efficient Davout was there, relieved for a time of his task of supervising the north of Europe and punctual at the rendezvous with a splendidly equipped corps. Ney was coming and it was therefore obvious that Napoleon had thought little of Ney's flagrant insubordination to Masséna in Spain. Every infantryman in the army was delighted to see *Le Rougeaud*. His presence meant that they could count on seeing a marshal's coat a few paces in advance of the skirmishing line. Oudinot was there, the hard fighting ex-grenadier with a reputation among the infernal columns second only to that of Lannes. Talkative Victor was at headquarters already wishing that he had remained in sunny Andalusia with Soult. Macdonald was present and Bessières, commanding the Imperial Guard. Berthier was in his usual place and Mortier, another

Spanish veteran, was in command of the Young Guard. Royalty was well represented. In addition to Napoleon's youngest brother, King Jerome of Westphalia, Joachim Murat came prancing up from Naples with a glittering staff and a determination to win the hearts of all the Russian ladies and the respect of all their menfolk. The prospect of crossing hundreds of miles of first-class cavalry country put Murat in an excellent humor. In an advance across the plains he could see nothing but a wonderful opportunity to dazzle the Czar's Cossacks by the splendor of his uniform.

One other marshal reported, fifty-seven years of age and still following the drum. He was the miller's son, Lefèbvre, and the men cheered him as he rode into Dresden.

The vast multitude advanced eastward and crossed the Niemen at the end of June, beginning a campaign that was to hold pride of place in the calendar of military disasters for exactly one hundred and thirty-one years. Not until the débâcle of Stalingrad was a blight of this magnitude to strike an army of invaders.

Oudinot and Macdonald held the left wing, remaining in Lithuania and protecting the main body as it pushed through clouds of choking dust towards Smolensk. With Oudinot was a man whom we have met several times but who was still not a marshal, the ex-draftsman St. Cyr. This campaign was to present him with his opportunity to write his name into the Napoleonic saga. Another man who would one day be a marshal marched with the main body. He was Prince Poniatowski and it would have been difficult to convince him that this was not Poland's day of destiny. Watching the advance from a safe distance was an ex-marshal who was now a Crown Prince, for Bernadotte had found another fencepost, this time in Sweden. He was already sounding the Czar on the possibility of forming an alliance.

All through the month of July and the first half of August the army toiled eastwards. There was no big-scale battle, for the Russians were pursuing their time-honored custom of luring an enemy deeper and deeper into the vastness of the steppes and birch forests. Now and again the eager French van collided with the Russian rearguard but resultant clashes were usually short and indecisive.

The Russian, General Kutusov, knew his business. In spite of cries of dismay from the Russian nobility he and his colleagues refused to engage their main forces. Every day saw the French closer to the Russian capital.

Murat was the only marshal who enjoyed the long, dusty advance. All day and every day he pranced and curvetted in front of the astonished Cossacks, waving a gold-mounted cane and shouting school-boy insults in his Gascon accent. He had been correct in his surmise. The enemy was so impressed by this strange horseman that Murat's name became a legend before he had ridden as far as Smolensk. Ney, however, was far less impressed and raved that the antics of the "Emperor's plumed cock" did nothing but tire his infantry in their efforts to safeguard the cavalry. There were the usual recriminations and appeals to the Emperor but nothing could persuade Murat to forgo this unique opportunity to show off to such an impressionable audience.

There was a battle outside Smolensk, where Mortier was almost killed by a shell which scored a direct hit on his headquarters. The burly farmer's boy roared with laughter as the roof caved in and shouted to the Young Guard that the rascals had missed him again. Then the Russians abandoned the blazing town and there was talk of halting and establishing winter quarters at this point but after some hesitation Napoleon decided to push on and occupy Moscow. He was sure that the Czar would then sue for peace. The decision was to cost the Empire half a million lives.

. . .

St. Cyr, far out on the left flank, had found his fortune. Oudinot, as was customary, had been wounded in action and during his temporary absence in the hospital the supreme individualist took over the command. St. Cyr's freakish nature was already a standing jest in the ranks, where they called him "The Owl." Like an owl he perched himself silently outside Pultusk and when the Russians attacked him he beat them off and won a brilliant victory. Napoleon, delighted to learn that his flank was now safe, immediately sent St. Cyr his baton. "The Owl" had made it after all, in spite of his obstinacy, his oddities, and his unpredictability; in spite of refusing a seat at the Coronation.

Murat's theatrical displays with the advance guard were now irritating Davout more than they had infuriated Ney. Instead of raving and threatening, the Iron Marshal coolly reported Murat to the Emperor and Napoleon had to use all his famous diplomacy to prevent an open rupture in the field. In spite of the Imperial intervention in the quarrel the animosity between the two marshals became so acute that on one occasion they engaged in a shouting match in the face of the enemy. Astonished senior officers stood by helplessly, not knowing which marshal to obey. The incident would have resulted in a duel had it not been for the efforts of Murat's staff to restrain their chief's temper.

The much tried Davout then came into direct collision with one other member of the Imperial family, this time King Jerome, who had been given a command that he was totally unqualified to hold and soon proved as much by letting a cornered Russian general escape from a carefully prepared trap. This time Napoleon did not soothe and temporize. He promptly relieved his brother of his command and packed him home to Westphalia. Jerome at once joined the ranks of Davout's enemies but the marshal was unconcerned. As long as he was confident that he was doing his duty every Frenchman in the army could hate the sight of him and he would not lose a wink of sleep.

The huge army pushed forward into Russia like an impatient swimmer shedding clothes on his way to the beach. The force of half a million men was soon reduced to one hundred and thirty thousand by the detachment of garrisons, flank guards, and mobile supply companies. The heat was insufferable and the troops were choked with dust. Horses sickened and died through eating the unripe rye and Davout growled that if somebody did not do something to check the antics of that idiot Murat the Grand Army would soon be a mob of infantry advancing without a squadron of hussars to ride on the flanks. Victor, Oudinot, and St. Cyr were now far behind, guarding the interminable communications. Still with the main force a few days' march out of Moscow, were Murat, Ney, Mortier, Davout, Lefèbvre and Bessières. The presence of Bessières was to rob the French of their sole remaining chance of winning the war.

On September 7, after a fighting retreat that had lasted forty-two days, the Russian main forces made their stand near the village of Borodino. They occupied carefully prepared positions based on immense earthworks and pivoting upon an improvised fortification that was given the name of the Great Redoubt.

Notwithstanding the strong defenses Napoleon decided upon a frontal attack. He was far from being himself that day and it was soon obvious that he was a stranger to the man of Lodi and Jena, or even Wagram. All day long the columns of Davout and Ney assaulted the Russian positions and the slaughter on both sides was terrible. Nearly two thousand guns were in action, and in the cavalry charges against en-

trenched infantry Murat's men suffered huge losses. Ney, fighting under
the Great Redoubt, flew into one of his wild rages when the reserves
did not appear. Staff officers fought their way out of the mêlée and appealed directly to Napoleon, bearing messages from Ney begging for the
support of the Guard, which had been under arms since first light. Napoleon hesitated. Lassitude caused by nervous exhaustion, or by his recurrent
bladder trouble, had made him indecisive and his hesitancy increased as
the casualties piled up in front of the Great Redoubt, where Ney and
Mortier and Davout were trying to crush the defenders by sheer weight
of numbers. Each attack made limited progress but such progress was slow
and insanely expensive. Then another messenger arrived from the front
line, asking for the *coup de grâce* to be administered by the men in bearskins, long lines of veterans who had not fired a single shot throughout
the day. Napoleon glanced at them, and Bessières their commander looked
anxiously at his chief.

"Will you risk your last reserve this far from base?" he asked quietly.

Napoleon made his decision and the Guard remained inactive. The
battered regiments of the line, supported by further murderous cavalry
charges, at last ejected the enemy from the earthworks and saw the Russian
columns fall back in good order and trudge away to the east. As at Eylau
it was a victory that was almost a defeat.

Seventeen thousand French dead and maimed lay on the field. For
a mile on either side of the central redoubt the ground was littered with
dead men and horses, dismounted guns, and shattered equipment. Forty-
three French generals were dead or disabled, among the former the
bearded Montbrun, who had ridden all the way from Masséna's last field
in Spain to make the campaign. Ney, sickened by the slaughter, sulked
in his tent. "If he is too old for the business, why doesn't he go home
and leave the fighting to us?" he growled when they told him why Napoleon had refused to commit the Guard.

Murat remained in the field all night and all the next day. A sergeant
of the Guard saw him superintending the amputation of the legs of two
Russian gunners who were operated upon by the marshal's personal surgeon. When the bloody business was over he gave each man a glass of
wine and walked slowly over to the ravine where he and his cavalry had
made some of their most spectacular charges. The horrors of the subsequent retreat were not able to erase from the observer's memory the
recollection of Murat's cool and striking appearance in the midst of the

carnage. His gorgeous cloak floated in the wind and his Polish cap, sur-
mounted by a tall aigrette, made him a mark wherever he moved. The
sergeant who watched him carried this memory of the King of Naples
to his grave.

One other man lay dead under the redoubt, a brigadier general who
was totally undistinguished and whose death among so many went almost
unnoticed. Yet this man has a niche in history and it is an important
one, for without him there might never have been an Empire, a Russian
campaign, or a terrible battle under the walls of Moscow. His name was
Merda, and as an unknown gendarme eighteen years before, he had
stormed into the Hotel de Ville in the middle of the night and fired
a pistol at the terrorist Robespierre, ending the Rule of the Guillotine
with a single shot that shattered the tyrant's jaw. By doing this Merda
had arrested and changed the course of history, for that night the Convention was overthrown to make way for the Directory and the Directory
was succeeded by the Empire. Merda was buried on the field and nobody
remembered the vital role he had played in Thermidor, of the year III.

.   .   .

There was now nothing to prevent the French occupation of the Holy
Russian City. Dust-covered infantrymen paused on Mont de Salut and
stared down at the onion domes and acres of gilded roofs that glittered
beneath the heat haze and there burst from them at this moment a shout
of triumph and relief. They had marched into Vienna and Berlin and
Warsaw and Madrid and Lisbon and they had trudged a thousand miles
to look down on this city, the limit of their conquests, the climax of
all their trapesings that went back to the days when they had enrolled
as defenders of the Republic and gone out to fight Austrians and *émigrés*
in the Lowlands. For nearly all of them it was to be their final conquest,
the very last foreign city they would ransack for loot and women. But
that day, the day they looked down on Moscow, only a very few of them
thought of retreat. When the bandsmen appeared they polished their
equipment and swung across the Moskowa bridge with the bearing of
conquerors.

Just ahead of them, as always, was the Gascon innkeeper's son in
his plumes and furs but it was a strange and eerie triumph. In Prussia
the stolid Berliners had thronged the streets to see the men who had des-

troyed their army go by, and in Warsaw the Poles had cheered themselves hoarse. Even in Madrid Spaniards had gazed in awe at the colorful spectacle presented by the passage of Berthier's staff but here in Moscow there were no spectators at all. No cheers and no welcome of any sort. The only Muscovites who appeared to watch the entry of the Grand Army were convicts released from the jails by the retreating Russians, a few hundreds of filthy bedraggled wretches in leather smocks, with mad eyes and long, ragged beards. Some of the convicts tried a few shots at Murat's cavalry and when the troopers pursued them they ran and locked themselves in houses. Murat promptly blew in the doors with cannon and disposed of all he could catch but more and more emerged from cellars and from under bridges until special squads had to be recruited to hunt them down. One such convict, an elderly Muscovite with long white hair and beard, walked boldly up to the drum major of the Guard and aimed a blow at him with a three-pronged pitchfork. The drum major, indignant at this reception, picked him up and threw him in the river, but not all the members of this strange garrison were rounded up and it was soon obvious that they had been left behind for a very special reason. Within an hour of the French entry into the city smoke began to rise from public buildings and the tired troops were remustered as fire fighters.

Mortier, who had been appointed Governor of Moscow, was in charge of the fire-fighting teams and under his energetic direction the blaze would have been checked had it not been for a strong wind that carried the sparks into sections of the city not yet visited by the incendiaries. In the event no show of energy or vigilance could prevent fresh outbreaks and soon the area of the Kremlin was on fire and Napoleon had to evacuate. Berthier, anxious to see the extent of the blaze, mounted the ramparts but here the wind was so strong that he was nearly blown to his death. Within two days of the French entering the city a third of the houses were blazing. Within four days two-thirds of Moscow lay in ruins.

Ceaseless efforts to combat the flames did not prevent the veterans from indulging in the time-honored routine of looting. The blazing avenues were dotted with anxious little parties of soldiers weighed down with jeweled crucifixes, furs, bales of silk, and silver tableware. The men who had served under Masséna, Augereau, and Soult were experts at judging the value of such things. Mortier, a conscientious man, did what he could to check the pillage and ordered the men to concentrate on the collection of foodstuffs but the appeal was hopeless. Every bivouac soon took on the appearance of a Persian market, the ground about it strewn with carpets, crates of porcelain, pictures, and silver ikons. Scores of incendiaries were caught and bayoneted but still fresh fires broke out. In the end there was little left to burn and a systematic search of the cellars began in the hope of discovering more valuables. Such food as could be saved was collected in dumps and in a limited sense the army lived well, for there was a superabundance of sweetmeats, preserved fruits and Tokay wine. Very little solid food was discovered and the veterans quickly tired of the sickly fare and fought one another for scraps of bread and meat.

The Emperor was now faced with a vital decision. Was the army to remain in Moscow for the winter or was it to beat a retreat before the Russian winter made the march impossible? Once again he temporized, allowing six weeks to drift by while he waited for the Czar's reply to his overtures of peace. No reply was received and by the second week of October it was clear that there would be no reply. On October 18 retreat was decided upon and by the following morning word had got around that Moscow was to be evacuated, and the charred city was crowded with Jews and peasants eager to buy or exchange the portable pickings. That same afternoon the first of the troops moved out. Mortier, with ten thousand men, was left behind to blow up the Kremlin and destroy thousands of bottles of vodka in order to prevent the men of the Young Guard drinking themselves to death.

. . .

Long before the first snow fell on the retreating army the veterans of the Guard and the Gendarmes d'Elite, who had been withdrawn from Spain to serve in the Russian campaign, were regretting a transfer that had delighted them at the time. As the conditions of the retreat deteriorated every man must have thought longingly of the blue sky over Almeida and the orange-scented breezes of Valencia and Andalusia, but the battalions who were still fighting in Spain had troubles of their own and it would have been difficult to persuade them that they were lucky to have been left behind.

Nothing went right in Spain. A majority of Frenchmen serving there were by now convinced that nothing ever would go right in Spain. A curse of ineptitude and confusion seemed to alight on every marshal who went there, and while Napoleon and eight of the marshals were advancing across the steppes to the rendezvous with the enemy at Borodino, those who had remained in the Peninsula were nursing a grievance that seemed to them unwarranted, unbearable, and monstrously unjust.

Just before the Emperor headed east he altered his policy in the west. He had made brother Joseph the supreme commander of the French forces in Spain and sent old Jourdan to Madrid to act as Joseph's military adviser.

Jourdan was accustomed to carrying heavy burdens. In his younger days, it will be recalled, he had tramped from fair to fair with a pack of samples on his back but the burden he was now asked to carry was a good deal heavier than anything he had attempted in his youth. Answerable to him, by Imperial decree, was Suchet, who thought himself the cleverest soldier in Spain and probably was, Marmont, who thought the same and certainly was not, Soult who regarded himself as almost a king, and Joseph, who really was a king but prayed each night that he might cease to be one.

Jourdan was an honorable man and he did his very best. He soothed Joseph's fears and sent out streams of orders, all issued in the King's name, to his colleagues in Andalusia, Valencia, and Salamanca, but none of them took the slightest notice of the dispatches and edicts. Suchet went on administering Valencia and Catalonia in his own efficient way. Soult continued to comb Seville for old masters and church plate, and Marmont played hide-and-seek with the cautious Wellington in and around the valleys and gorges of the Portuguese frontier.

If Marmont had been as brilliant as he imagined himself to be, and had succeeded in driving the tenacious Irishman back to his labyrinth at Torres Vedras, there is no telling how long this curious situation might have lasted. But it did not last, for Wellington, although a cautious general, was an intelligent one. Soon every Frenchman in Spain received a severe jolt, for while the armies of Wellington and Marmont were marching parallel to one another in the vicinity of Salamanca, the long nosed Irishman saw his chance and pounced. In less than an hour the French were in full flight, and the ripples of Wellington's victory lapped into every corner of Spain. Marmont himself was wounded by a cannon shot early in the action and had it not been for the brilliant work of an obscure general called Clausel his defeat would have ended in a rout.

Soult heard the news and thought it was time to be moving. The border fortress of Badajoz had already fallen and he was in danger of being isolated. Hastily he packed his loot, commandeered a carriage for his Spanish mistress and her less fortunate sister left behind by Victor, and rumbled out of the province. All his life he was to think kindly of Andalusia, of its sun, its orange groves, its dark, bewitching women, and its innumerable works of art; especially of its works of art.

From now on the war ceased to be a struggle to dominate Spain. It became instead a hopeless endeavor to prevent the British, the Portuguese, and the Spanish partisans from exterminating every Frenchman in the Peninsula.

CHAPTER FIFTEEN

THE ROAD HOME

PROBABLY no army in history has presented such a bizarre spectacle as that of the Imperialist forces leaving Moscow. Casualties at Borodino, and others incurred during the occupation, had reduced the army to about one hundred and ten thousand men but it hoped to augment itself by numerous detachments on the way back to Germany. Its long columns were weighed down with every kind of loot and souvenir, and the march was slowed by thousands of carriages, handcarts, and even wheelbarrows, piled high with rugs, silks, furs, tapestries, gold and silver plate, and bronzes. Many of the soldiers wore looted clothing over their uniforms. Grenadiers of the Guard were seen striding along in green velvet mantles and plumed hats, chasseurs and lancers wore embroidered Chinese robes, and every knapsack in the army bulged with trinkets saved from the fire. Sergeant Bourgoyne, whose description of this retreat is among the best military memoirs of the period, turned aside one day's march out of Moscow and made a careful inventory of his luggage. He then threw away part of his uniform in order to make room for more negotiable objects.

Napoleon's original intention was to take the more southerly route home. It promised a more temperate climate and had not had to support the passage of armies during the advance. At Malo-Jaroslavitz, however, the Russians turned him back on the northern route and the army tramped across the battlefield of Borodino where thousands of half-buried corpses lay among the litter of that bloody contest.

One poor devil of a grenadier was said to have been found alive, with both legs broken, after having lived on putrid horseflesh for two months, but far more revolting rumors than this were circulating the ranks. Starving Russian prisoners were reported to be eating one another, and this only eleven days after the commencement of the retreat. All traces of discipline soon disappeared. If a cart carrying booty broke down, it was thrown off the road and there was a wild scramble for the contents. Tooled leather books were picked up, carried along for a distance, and then flung down again. Pictures, gilt candlesticks, and every variety of loot was kicked aside by the marching columns. The more farsighted of the men had put thoughts of gain behind and were concentrating on food and warm clothing.

Mortier, three days' march in the rear, blew up part of the Kremlin and hurried forward to rejoin the main body. When he overtook it his men were shocked at the changes in the ranks. The Grand Army had already degenerated into a disorderly, ravenous rabble, and stragglers, numbered by the thousands, were being snapped up by Cossacks hovering on the flanks. On November 2 all the seriously wounded were abandoned, their doctors and surgeons remaining with them to surrender to the Russians.

The retreat now became a frenzied scramble to reach the imagined security of Smolensk, where there were known to be large magazines and stores, but the first snow had begun to fall and the endless trudge through the forests and across the plain whittled away all but the toughest and most resolute. Horseflesh was the staple diet and those who had saved a few handfuls of meal, or a bottle of brandy, refused to share it with their closest friends.

Under the triple scourge of twenty degrees below freezing, semistarvation and Platoff's Cossacks, the spirit of camaraderie that had been the legacy of the Republican armies and the most striking feature of Napoleon's columns, all but disappeared. The march developed into a desperate fight for survival and when a posting station offered shelter for the night early arrivals fought off latecomers with the bayonet.

Yet some of the officers retained their professional pride and did all they could to maintain some sort of order among the half-savage contingents. Mortier showed a wry sense of humor and compassion for the private soldier. A survivor tells of him sitting in a hut over a miserable fire, while his supper of roasted horse liver and melted snow was being prepared. To this, being a marshal, he was able to add a little biscuit and a few mouthfuls of brandy. When he saw a sentry mounting guard at the door he asked the man why he was standing there. "You can't keep cold and hunger from coming in so move nearer the fire and sit down!" he said.

In the first stage of the retreat Davout took charge of the rearguard, but when conditions worsened and heavy snow began to fall, the Emperor detailed Ney's corps for the job. The red-headed marshal, whose fighting retreat from Portugal was already recognized as a great feat of arms, more than fulfilled the trust. From the first day he took up his post at Mojaisk his conduct was that of the real Michel Ney, a figure that dwarfs the petulant, backbiting, undisciplined bully of the Peninsula. He welcomed and accepted the challenge from the enemy and the elements. His very presence, musket in hand, braced the starving NCO's and men charged with the task of covering the army's withdrawal. As long as they could mutter through frozen beards "There goes *Le Rougeaud!*" they were confident that somehow, against all probability, Ney would lead them to safety, warmth, and regular rations.

On November 6 the real cold descended upon the stumbling columns. In the early hours of the morning men lying almost on top of their bivouac fires, exchanging gold rings and precious stones for horsesteaks and frozen potatoes, were struck with cold two degrees above zero. As the survivors staggered to their feet the Cossacks swept in, catching and stripping the stragglers, galloping in and out of the trees on their nimble little ponies, and hurrahing at the prospect of capturing or destroying every man in the Grand Army.

Their hopes were premature. They knew all about Murat, the dazzling horseman of the advance, with his bright yellow boots and leopardskin saddlecloth but they had not heard very much of Ney, the silent Alsatian in the marshal's cocked hat, who maneuvered the frost-bitten men of the rearguard like a trained sheepdog coaxing a flock to move off in a compact body. The boldest riders among them never had a chance to find out that the man within reach of his lance point was a famous marshal of France, for every now and again, pausing behind the most laggardly of his sheep, the man in the cocked hat took careful aim and dropped a Cossack in his saddle. He then reloaded and continued his unhurried march into the west.

Smolensk, when it was reached, proved a bitter disappointment. The weather had improved somewhat between the ninth and the fourteenth and about fifty thousand survivors staggered into the ruined city. The first few thousand found enough to sustain them. The remainder of the stores were trampled underfoot in the struggle that followed. The Guard received a few ounces of flour and an ounce or so of biscuit. The latecomers, which included the rearguard, nothing at all.

Victor's corps had been waiting in Smolensk for a month, and for once the talkative ex-sergeant was speechless as he gazed at the half-insane rabble pouring in and out of the ruined houses in search of food and firewood. Some kind of effort was made to reorganize the mob into an army. Battalions were reduced to companies and some companies to a few resolute men still marching with their eagle. The cavalry was almost non-existent. What remained of it was formed into the "Doomed Squadron" to protect the person of the Emperor. When news came that two Russian armies were converging on the River Beresina beyond Orcha, and that the implacable Kutusov was approaching from the rear, the position of the survivors seemed hopeless. Davout was detailed to hold on as long as possible and wait for Ney. The others continued their march westward, the Emperor, Murat, Mortier, and Berthier marching together and with them tough old Lefèbvre, bearing up better than most of the younger men and sometimes linking his arm to that of the man who had made him a duke.

Ney, with his valiant remnant, was ordered to remain behind and do what he could to hold off pursuit. Most men would have complained that it was surely someone else's turn to cover the rear but Ney made no such complaint. Quietly and methodically he collected about him his rabble of strays, lightly wounded, and the kind of individualists who can be found in any army, men who seem impervious to physical trials and survive by expert scrounging on their own behalf.

With these, about four thousand in all, he set off after the main body and marched straight into the Russian army that had just failed to catch Napoleon and later Davout, who had waited for him until it was almost too late.

The Russians were sixty thousand strong and there was a choice of three courses of action; attack, surrender en masse, or turn about and go back towards Smolensk. Ney did not hesitate. He ordered the drums to sound the *pas-de-charge* just as if he was at Jena with his entire corps at his back, but the attack failed and so did four succeeding attacks. When night fell a Russian officer came into Ney's camp with a proposal for honorable surrender. Ney stared at him in amazement. "Surrender? A marshal of France? Not me, my sword will get me out of this!" The man must have been dumbfounded. Ney himself looked like an ill-used brigand and his "army" was now reduced to about a thousand famished effectives with twice as many frostbitten wrecks lying in the wagons. Realizing that another attack would be his last, Ney ordered a retreat eastward and when some of the men protested at this outrageous order he said, "Very well, I'll go back to Smolensk alone!"

They got up and followed him, lighting a big cluster of bivouac fires to fool the enemy into believing they were still there. Ney's aim was to circle the Russians and find the Dnieper, and at last he located the river by breaking the ice of a stream and discovering which way the current flowed. At dawn the Russians stood to arms to receive the surrender of one of the most celebrated soldiers in Europe but as it grew light they rubbed their eyes in amazement. All they could see was a wide circle of embers. Ney and his forlorn band were nowhere in sight. Realizing that they could only have turned east the Russian commander shrugged and pushed on after the main body. The Cossacks would deal with them. The French rearguard was given up for lost.

But it was not lost. When the main river was reached it was not only half-frozen but they found a spot where there was an ice jam and scrambled across, jumping from floe to floe. The wagons containing the sick were abandoned and so were the guns but every man who could walk made the crossing and the rearguard pushed on towards Orcha.

For the most part they stuck to the woods but every now and again bodies of Cossacks attacked and they had to form a square. Ney had developed a technique to deal with these constant jabs. He kept his square moving and encouraged it with a ribald commentary on the appearance and timidity of the attackers. Joking and jeering he fired and reloaded until the Cossacks scattered in search of easier victims. In this way, three clear days after their failure to cut their way through, the rearguard came within sight of Orcha and Ney sent an officer to Napoleon to report that he was approaching.

The main body went wild with joy. Ney's uncertain temper had made him countless enemies but there was not a man in the army who did not throw up his hat when he heard that the rearguard was safe. "It was like a national celebration!" declares a man who was with the Imperial standard when the news was circulated. Napoleon, overjoyed, at once despatched Davout and Mortier to bring the heroes in, and still beating off attacks, the gallant remnant crossed the last few miles of slush and marched into the town. They numbered about nine hundred and every man among them was under arms.

The time had now come to make the supreme effort to cross the Beresina and push on for the Niemen and the safety of Prussia. Victor was told to hold off the attackers in the north in order to give the main body a chance to cross the river, but, after he had left, news came that another Russian army had burned the bridges at Borisov and was waiting on the far side. Escape seemed impossible, particularly as the weather had now turned almost mild and the Beresina, usually frozen hard at this time of the year, was free of ice.

Yet the main body did escape, partly through luck but more by its own strenuous efforts and Napoleon's intuitive genius. Victor managed to hold off the northern attack for a day or so and the French heard of a ford, below Borisov. When this was reached the engineers worked waist deep in water for hours, emerging half dead but with two practicable bridges built of felled trees and timber torn from houses. Oudinot, whose corps had now arrived to swell the depleted ranks, pinned down the Russian army around Borisov. While he was awaiting the arrival of some cuirassiers a bullet, fired from below, lodged itself in his body and he fell from his horse. The startled animal bolted and Oudinot, his foot caught in a stirrup, was dragged along the ground. The soft snow and an alert aide-de-camp saved his life. He was picked up and taken to a posting station which was being used as a first-aid post. A surgeon probed his wound but the bullet could not be traced. He carried it about for the rest of his life.

Even then Oudinot's adventures in Russia were not over. While he was awaiting a carriage seven hundred Cossacks and hussars swept down on the cabin, surrounding it and opening up with two light guns. There were nineteen men and one woman in the dressing station and all but the woman were wounded. Struggling up from his couch Oudinot borrowed the woman's pistols and fired repeatedly at the horsemen surging round the post. The defense was so resolute that the Russians broke off the attack and Oudinot was extricated by a French column coming up at the double. In the brief action the marshal had been wounded again.

The main body with the Emperor and such guns as were left crossed over on the twenty-ninth. Five times the bridges broke down under the strain and five times they were repaired. But although the fighting and the presence of the Emperor rallied a nucleus of the men. a kind of death wish had taken possession of the minds of thousands of stragglers, mostly frostbite victims and camp followers. They sat stolidly around fires on the east bank, making no effort to cross when they could have done so in safety. Old Lefèbvre was seen at the bridgehead, exhorting all to make one more effort and push on to Kovno. "Come on lads," he roared, "better big battalions than a mob of brigands and cowards!" He did not possess Ney's strange powers of persuasion. Only a few got up and stumbled across the bridge. The remainder waited until Victor's corps arrived with the Russians in close pursuit and then there was a fearful panic to reach the west bank. It was too late. The bridges collapsed and twenty thousand men and women died in the shallow waters of the Beresina.

During the fighting round Borisov Ney had been in the forefront once more, taking over when Oudinot was wounded. On the point of launching a forlorn attack, he paused to give philosophical advice to a hesitant officer. He told the man how Trappist monks were said to stand on the edge of their graves and say to one another, "One must die, brother!" The officer grinned. "One must die, brother!" he said to Ney and when the marshal had made the response they both went forward and drove the enemy from their positions. Then, when all who were capable of marching were across the Beresina, Ney fell into step as the rearguard commander and resumed the endless routine of fighting, joking and marching towards Prussia.

At one village he overtook Victor with several thousand of his corps, men who had been no further than Smolensk. Ney asked for help but Victor was not the man to volunteer for a forlorn hope. He marched on, taking his men with him.

Ney went back to his task. Even when there were no Cossacks in sight he ordered guns to be fired in the hope that it would make the laggards quicken their step and call in stragglers searching for food in the hamlets on either side of the route. A soldier remembers seeing him sitting over a fire on the road to Vilna, with no one at all between him and the Russian vanguard. Someone said to him it was time to be off before the Cossacks stormed into the village. Ney nodded to a group of about four veterans at an adjoining fire. "With men like that," he said, "I don't give a fig for all the Cossacks in Russia!"

The shattered remnants of the Grand Army, a few thousand men in formation, crossed the Niemen at Kovno and sought the safety of Prussian forests. Napoleon, learning of a bizarre conspiracy in Paris, had left the army at Smorgoni and rushed away by sledge, ignoring Berthier's pleas to be allowed to accompany him. Murat, the prancing horseman, was left in command but Murat's nerve failed him. He issued no orders and soon deserted, leaving the ghost command to Prince Eugene and making his way south to Naples. Murat had read the signs of the times and was wondering what insurance he could take out to preserve his throne.

There was one man who still did not hurry, whose nerve was unshaken in spite of the below zero temperature and the staggering losses of the last six weeks. That man was the Marshal Prince of Moskowa, Duke of Elchingen, and one-time hussar captain in the army of Sambre-et-Meuse. The very last man over the bridge of the Niemen into Prussia was Marshal Ney, commanding his fifth rearguard, now composed of a handful of Germans and about twenty French stragglers. The Germans threw down their muskets and ran as soon as the Russians attacked. Ney picked up their loaded weapons and emptied them, one by one, into the advancing Cossacks. Then, shouldering a weapon, he turned and strolled across the bridge where he set about collecting strays and directing them through the forests to the nearest garrison town.

On December 15 a ragged, blear-eyed desperado walked into a billet occupied by a staff officer at Gumbinnen. The startled officer asked who he was and what he wanted. Ney chuckled. "Don't you recognize me?" he said. "I'm Michel Ney!" and when the man stared at him in amazement he added: "I'm the rearguard. Have you any soup? I'm damned hungry!"

CHAPTER SIXTEEN

"A SET OF SCOUNDRELS GOING TO THE DEVIL"

"COME Berthier," said Napoleon, a few days after he had burst into the Tuileries in the middle of the night at the end of his record-breaking journey from Smorgoni to Paris, "come, my old friend, let us fight the campaign of Italy all over again!"

For although France was stunned, with half the country in mourning, the marshals sick to death of war and seventeen-year-old conscripts hiding out in barns and lofts all over France, Napoleon seemed undismayed by the disaster. Within a day or so of his return home he was bending all his tremendous energies to the task of raising a new army of a quarter of a million men, with five hundred newly-cast guns to replace those buried under the snow.

Perhaps he was not as confident as he appeared but was making every effort to inspire those about him. Every day couriers rode in with news from the capitals in Europe and every message pointed to the resurgence of hope on the part of browbeaten populations and humiliated governments.

Prussia was on her feet again, demonstrating a patriotism suspiciously like that of the Spanish guerrillas. Lutzow's night riders were out, poets were chanting, and here and there French soldiers were found with their throats cut. Austria. still nominally an ally, was plucking up courage for another try, and the long Russian columns were plodding west again, this time with captured battle flags. Britain, the implacable, was maintaining her everlasting blockade by sea and her steady pressure in the Peninsula. Sweden, Bernadotte's Sweden, was putting out feelers to the great Powers. And, finally, King Murat, down in Naples, was courting Metternich, the inscrutable Austrian chancellor, a man more deadly than any soldier in the field, who had sworn to achieve Napoleon's ruin.

The marshals did not share their commander-in-chief's optimism. Most of them were still loyal but every one of them wanted peace, wanted it most desperately, for their own sake, for the sake of their wives and children whose society they had never had time to enjoy, but above all for the sake of the France for which each one of them had shed blood over a period of more than twenty years.

France had now been at war for two decades, broken by one brief interval of peace, and no other country in the world would have given so freely of its manhood for the glory the Empire had brought them. Even a Frenchman, however, can have a surfeit of glory. Mothers with grown sons no longer thrilled to hear the salvoes of cannon announcing another victory, and the prosperous bourgeoisie, to whom the years of national triumph had brought wealth and rich investment, began to ask what would happen to their savings if the Cossacks and Prussians crossed the frontiers and the redcoats and kilted Highlanders came over the Pyrenees into the southwest.

Napoleon would not even consider such a calamity. "I will meet and defeat them on the Elbe!" he thundered and it was towards the Elbe that he marched with his mixed force of two hundred thousand veterans and half-grown youths and his hastily assembled cavalry reserve, a mere fifteen thousand for a campaign to be waged in the ideal cavalry country of Saxony.

Berthier was with him, sleeping upright in the now world-famous coach, and at the head of the young conscripts was Ney, hero of the terrible retreat, of whom men were saying: "He not only saved all he could of the army, he saved its honor!" Ney seemed physically indestructible. He had just marched five hundred miles and fought every step of the way, a feat that crowned twenty years of almost continuous marching and fighting. If Napoleon needed a leader to inspire the raw lads from the recruiting depots he could not have picked a better man. From the rank of colonel downwards Michel Ney was a soldier's idol.

With Ney went that other indestructible, Nicholas Oudinot, with three more scars in his leathery hide, and beside Oudinot were the *émigré's* son, Macdonald, and Marmont, the Emperor's oldest friend, and Victor, who had marched away in the snow and left Ney to stay the Russians with a handful of invalids. Bessières was there with the Guard, to whom this was just one more war, and within call were the new marshal St. Cyr and the Pole Poniatowski, soon to receive the twenty-fifth baton. Lastly, and lagging somewhat, came King Murat, once again dragged from his throne room in Naples and cursing the terrible man in Paris. He was now almost certain that the game was up and had not yet been able to clinch his deal with the Austrians.

Had Murat been a little more of a laggard, or had the summons that brought him to Dresden been a little less imperious, he might not have reported at all. Metternich, the Austrian fox, had already persuaded his master Francis to promise Murat his Neapolitan throne if he betrayed the man from whose hands he had received it. Napoleon was not fooled by Murat's belated appearance to command the makeshift cavalry. A month or so before he had written, "I presume you are not among those who believe the lion is dead . . . if you make this calculation you are completely deceived!" Murat choked with rage when he read this letter but it did not anger him nearly so much as had a notice in the *Moniteur,* the official newspaper, which began: "The King of Naples, being indisposed, has been obliged to resign his command of the army, which he has transferred to the Prince Viceroy [Eugéne]. *The latter is more accustomed to the management of important trusts. . . ."*

One other marshal, and one ex-marshal, watched each other very attentively during the early months of 1813. Up in Hamburg Davout had one eye on the restive Germans and the other on his former colleague, Bernadotte, Crown Prince of Sweden. For Europe was about to witness a most astonishing feat, something for which Royalists, Jacobins, Imperialists, British, Austrians, Russians, Italians, and Spaniards had been waiting for nearly twenty-five years. It was the descent of Charles Jean Bernadotte from the fence on which he had been squatting since he was old enough to shave. When this incredible occurrence took place Davout wanted a front seat, if only for the chance of planting a powerful kick in the royal posterior if Bernadotte landed off balance. There was an extremely wide range of likes and dislikes among the marshals of Napoleon but none surpassed in intensity the implacable hatred Davout felt for the Crown Prince of Sweden. He would have bartered wealth and rank and even honor for the chance to grind the Gascon's face in the mud.

.   .   .

Three marshals (in addition to the long-retired Pérignon, Moncey, and Sérurier) were not present in Saxony that summer. Two others were still campaigning in Spain and the last, André Masséna, had achieved his fondest ambition and retired to count his enormous wealth and cosset his pretty mistresses. Masséna does not emerge on stage again as a warrior but he appears from time to time in the wings. His single eye was still watching developments very closely although some offered an opinion that he did not give a franc piece who won the war in Germany.

Suchet was still holding down Catalonia and Valencia and achieving far more than any of his colleagues had ever achieved against the British. Poor old Jourdan was still stuck with the thankless task of military adviser to brother Joseph, the king who had been convinced from the very beginning of the Spanish adventure that it was all a dreadful mistake.

Wellington, Prime Minister of Caution, had certainly taken his time exploiting his success in the Peninsula. There had been occasions when an energetic commander who was prepared to run a small risk could have chased the French clean out of Spain but Wellington was no gambler. He only backed certainties and certainties were hard to find in Spain.

By the summer of 1813, however, the odds against his opponents were piling up every hour and at last the British army had advanced so far into Spain that a battle between the two main forces was inevitable. It came at Vittoria, on the longest day of the year, and the decision to stand and fight was, surprisingly enough, King Joseph's and not that of his war-weary chief adviser who could see but one outcome from a fight. Jourdan's view was proved correct. The French were outmaneuvred and outfought in a couple of hours and were soon in flight towards the Pyrenees.

Not for a long time had a French army bolted with such precipitation. The booty captured by the redcoats was immense, including as it did a hundred and fifty guns, about a million pounds sterling, and all the loot including some pretty señoritas) that French officers had accumulated during their long stay in Spain. Some of the spoils of that day can be seen at the Wellington Museum, Hyde Park Corner London. They include many paintings and King Joseph's Sèvres breakfast set. Jourdan was rather pleased that his prophecy had proved accurate. It is recorded that as they galloped over the mountains he said to Joseph: "Well Sir, you had your battle and it seems to have been a defeat."

The news of Vittoria frightened Napoleon. Swiftly he recalled Jourdan and sent for Soult, who had left Spain and was now in Saxony. To the former Viceroy of Andalusia the Emperor said: "Go to Spain in an hour! All is lost through the strangest mismanagement!" Soult left

Saxony at once and showed more energy and initiative than at any time since he had launched his attack on the Pratzen Heights, at Austerlitz, eight years before. Like his colleague Ney he salvaged his reputation from the welter of retreat.

. . .

The campaign in Saxony opened with tragedy. For the second time since the foundation of the Empire a marshal was to meet his death in action. On May 1, the very first day of the new war, Bessières, the former Royalist and the close personal friend of his Emperor, laid down his life for France.

The early fighting was directed against the Russian advance guard that had now pushed beyond the Elbe and was posted in the defiles of Poserna. At Rippach they held strong positions, crowned with artillery, and it was necessary for the French to carry the defile by storm. Bessières went forward with the Tirailleurs of the Guard, and when the battle was won he lay dead, his chest shattered by a cannon ball. They covered him with his cloak in case his body was recognized and the men who loved him lost heart, but Ney was fetched and looked down at his colleague's corpse with a thoughtful air. "It was a good death, our kind of death!" was his epitaph.

The death of Bessières deepened the gloom among the officers at Imperial headquarters. Unlike Masséna, or Bernadotte, or Ney, this son of a Languedoc surgeon had made few enemies. Lannes had hated him but Lannes was dead, and Masséna had never forgiven him for his gratuitous advice and niggardly help in Spain, but Masséna had withdrawn from the struggle and was skulking in retirement. The rest of the army sincerely regretted Bessières, forgetting his fatal advice to Napoleon regarding the employment of the Guard at Borodino and remembering only his gallantry and unfailing courtesy and complete lack of "side." Bessières had always behaved with dignity and had loved the common soldier and gone out of his way to safeguard his interests. He was not a very talented man but he was popular and Napoleon thought of him as a devoted personal friend. When he was told of the death the Emperor put aside his work and wrote a moving letter to the marshal's widow.

The next day the French drove the Russians back and the day after that, on the Lutzen plain where the Swedish hero Gustavus Adolphus had died in 1632, they won what might have proved a great victory had they possessed adequate cavalry to press the pursuit. Ney was the hero of this fight, standing beside his boys all day under a plunging artillery fire and subsequently reporting to Napoleon that the conscripts' behavior was magnificent. The strategical effects of this battle were not impressive but its impact upon the allies was considerable. It was plain that the staggering losses in Russia and Spain had not yet undermined the confidence of the French in their captains or in their own prowess as warriors.

Unluckily the French shortage of cavalry prevented them from profiting by victories, for at Bautzen the same thing happened again. Ney, with sixty thousand infantry, held his ground while Napoleon half encircled the enemy, but there were always vast Russian and Prussian reserves, and Sweden was on the brink of declaring war, and Austria was wobbling, and the British were battering at the backdoor into France, so what availed a dozen victories like Lutzen and Bautzen? After the latter Napoleon exclaimed: "Not a gun or a prisoner for all this slaughter? These people don't leave me a nail!" The position, although not yet desperate, was full of anxiety for men who knew the facts. One such man was Berthier, the chief-of-staff, who now took his courage in both hands and counseled Napoleon to accept the moderate terms offered by the Coalition.

It was no use. Berthier was snubbed and after him bluff, plain-speaking Oudinot who, when told by Napoleon that the allied terms for peace were unacceptable, replied as Lannes might have done: "Then we continue the war? Otherwise a bad thing!" Napoleon, who had expected the kind of yesmanship he was getting from Victor, was so annoyed by the remark that he ordered Oudinot to withdraw from his presence. Oudinot did so unperturbed and an hour later was discovered by his friends playing with some children. "You have done yourself great harm with the Emperor!" said someone. "Nonsense!" laughed Oudinot. "He needs me and I'll be forgiven tomorrow." He was right. This was no time for sacrificing old friends. Too many new ones were mumbling excuses and leaving early.

The allies were now pursuing the policy of withdrawing wherever Napoleon was known to be and attacking his isolated lieutenants. It was a method that hurt the pride of old Blücher and Wittgenstein, the Russian general who had succeeded Kutusov, but it paid good dividends. By early June Napoleon had agreed to a six weeks' cessation of hostilities, a fatal decision as it proved, for although it gave him time to summon Eugéne's army from Italy it gave his enemies a chance to resolve their own differences and double the Coalition's forces in the field.

Down in Spain Soult was putting new confidence into the survivors of Vittoria and had actually taken the offensive in the famous pass of Roncevalles but the very best he could do with the men and material available was to fight a holding action and hope for better news from central Europe.

It did not come. Stubbornly, foolishly, the Emperor rejected the terms of men who still feared him. They offered him Italy, Switzerland, Flanders, the left bank of the Rhine and the protectorate of the German Confederation. Berthier begged him to accept but he refused, categorically. "Restore the Pope and give up Poland, Spain, and Holland?" he shouted. "That would be one vast capitulation!" In August the Austrians joined the allies and the Crown Prince Bernadotte made his spectacular leap from the fence in the company of another renegade Frenchman, the old Republican General Moreau, under whom Bernadotte had fought in the glorious days in the Revolution.

Davout, still holding on to the north, was not granted his wish to march against his old enemy. The first French marshal to try conclusions with the traitor was bullheaded Oudinot, who made up his mind that he was going to capture Berlin and sent his army in driblets against superior forces of Swedes, Russians, and Prussians. Bernadotte was a rascal but he was a far better strategist than Oudinot, whose notions of war were confined to advancing sword in hand and blasting the opposition from its position. He was defeated and thrown back and in late August the same thing happened to the unlucky Macdonald in a passage of arms with Blücher, at the Katzbach.

Macdonald was probably the unluckiest of all the marshals. He had never forgotten the drubbing the Russians had given him when Napoleon was in Egypt and although his plans were usually precise and intelligently worked out he had no flexibility of mind and was utterly unable to adapt himself to a sudden change of conditions. This is what happened at the Katzbach. Instead of waiting for Blücher to attack him he crossed the river and ascended to the plateau. A tremendous storm of rain then flooded the stream and rendered his position critical. The Prussian infantry formed square and although the rain had made their firearms useless they resisted the efforts of Macdonald's chasseurs to break up their formations. For some time cavalry and infantry glared at one another over a hedge of bayonets, the Prussians unable to fire a shot, the chasseurs unable to reach the infantry with their sabers. Presently Macdonald sent in the lancers, whose longer weapons broke gaps in the squares and enabled the chasseurs to cut away at their leisure but Macdonald had overlooked two important factors, the vast superiority of the enemy cavalry reserves and the swollen torrent at his back. When the Prussians counterattacked the French were pushed off the field and Macdonald had to take refuge in the ranks of the chasseurs. Somehow, leaving the bridges to the infantry, they got over the river to safety but they left behind most of their guns and thousands of prisoners. It was the most heartening victory the allies had won so far.

Ney was sulking again. Before Bautzen Napoleon, knowing that he was not temperamentally equipped to handle large masses of men in the field, had sent him the clever Swiss theorist Jomini as his chief-of-staff and Ney regarded his arrival as an insult. There had been a time when he had listened very carefully to everything Jomini had to say. When the Grand Army was in training on the coasts of the Channel Jomini had been his trusted confidant. But a great deal had happened since the summer of 1804 and Ney, who had since quarreled with the Swiss soldier of fortune, now resented his presence as military chaperon. Indignantly he offered to resign but Napoleon was accustomed to Ney's spurts of temper and ignored the threat. He was aware that as an independent general Ney was of small value, that as Corps Commander he was fair, and as a divisional commander he had few equals. As a rallier of half-hearted men, however, Michel Ney was better than any other soldier in the world and Napoleon was prepared to make full use of the material to hand. Ney's reputation alone was worth two divisions in the field.

Augereau, now fifty-six years of age, played no distinguished part in this confused campaign. All that summer he was looking over his shoulder at his old friend Masséna, safely out of it all, and hoping to be forgotten by everyone. During the fighting Augereau remained with the reserves and his opinion of the Emperor would not have been printed in the *Moniteur,* or in any other newspaper. For the time being, however, he kept his counsel. Gone were the days of Castiglione when he hammered the table and shouted: "Advance with every man and gun within call!"

St. Cyr had crossed swords with the Swedish renegade but St. Cyr was Bernadotte's military equal and held out in Dresden until the Emperor arrived. Poniatowski was also distinguishing himself and the dogged loyalty of the Prince and his men must have made Napoleon regret that he never kept his promise to make Poland an independent country. Every other ally had to be watched and the treachery of Bavaria and Saxony were soon to bring the French army to the brink of disaster.

One more great victory was in the cards. At Dresden, soon after

the resumption of hostilities, the allies forgot their resolution and attacked
the Grand Army while it was under the personal command of its Chief.
In a few hours the Russians, Prussians, Austrians, and Swedes were pouring back in confusion and for a day or so it looked as though all their
intrigues and marches and counter marches had been in vain, and that
they never would defeat this astonishing nation while Napoleon was in
command. But the chance was lost. As at Borodino Napoleon's mind was
sluggish and unable to rise to the opportunity. Vandamme, the swaggering
Augereau-type soldier, who boasted that he feared neither God nor devil,
was sent in pursuit but was trapped when the allies turned and hit back
at him. Vandamme and all his men were taken prisoners. The Frenchman's
bearing when confronted by Czar Alexander proved that Republican embers still smoldered in the Grand Army, for Vandamme, charged with
excesses in Germany, retorted: "At least I didn't kill my own father!"

More than defiance was needed to win this war. Ney was beaten
by Blücher at Dennewitz and wrote to Napoleon: "The spirit of generals
and officers is shattered and our foreign allies will desert at the first opportunity!" The conscripts were brave enough in action but they could not
stand the rigors of war like the old moustaches and died in hundreds
from exhaustion and pneumonia.

On October 3 the allies crossed the Elbe and the French fell back
on Leipsic. On October 7, at the other end of the long front, Wellington
crossed the Bidassoa and began knocking on the back door. Only Soult
was there to bolt it.

.   .   .

In mid-October the scene was set for one of the most murderous
battles in history, an engagement that was to be known in history as The
Battle of the Nations.

The Grand Army was at Leipsic and every outlying village of the
city had been fortified and garrisoned. Round this vast semi-circle lay the
allies—Russians, Prussians, Austrians, Swedes, and even a small party of
British trying-out an experimental rocket-firing battery. The odds against
the French were about three to one, and every private soldier in the French
army knew that the outcome could only be a fierce defence and an ultimate
withdrawal over the rivers of the Pleisse and Elster that ran between
Leipsic and the road to the Rhine.

It was almost the final rally of the fighting marshals. Berthier was chief-of-staff, and defending the ring of villages were Murat, Ney, Mortier, Marmont, Oudinot, Victor, Macdonald, and Augereau, perhaps the most formidable team of captains ever assembled under one banner on one battlefield. They were under no illusions as to what would be the cost of defeat. Failure to hold the villages could result in a rout as bad or worse than that which overtook the Prussians after Jena. There was a good bridge over the river Pleisse and the road back to the French frontiers was open but one bridge was hopelessly inadequate for an army of this size, engaged in a desperate rearguard action, and orders were supposed to have been issued for the building of two further pontoon bridges. The orders were never given and Berthier later claimed that Napoleon had not instructed that they should be built. Whether he did or did not, this is a poor excuse. As chief-of-staff Berthier should have regarded the provision of adequate escape routes a priority.

Fighting began on the morning of the sixteenth, with the allies closing in on the villages. The hand-to-hand combats of the sixteenth and seventeenth were among the most sanguinary in the history of the long war and we have the testimony of an Englishman who was present that the French fought valiantly for every yard and earned the grudging respect of their opponents. Nowhere in that ring of embattled village streets was there hesitancy or cowardice among the French. With their allies, notably the Saxons, it was a very different story.

On the first day the attackers were everywhere repulsed. Victor mauled the Russians at Jossa, Poniatowski threw back every assault upon the approaches of the river Pleisse, and when he was hard-pressed Oudinot, in command of the central reserve of the Old and Young Guard, sent him help and the Austrians were flung back to their own lines. Ney, furiously attacked by Blücher's Prussians, yielded up Mokern but he held on to the suburb of Halle. Nearby Macdonald beat back the Russians at Holzhausen.

But as fresh assaults piled up against the loopholed cottages and garden walls of the villages, treachery punched a gap in the lines that no amount of battering could produce. In the midst of the fighting, when Blücher had almost ordered his new ally Bernadotte to attack Mockau now defended by Ney, the Saxons advanced against the Swedes and Prussians and suddenly wheeled about, turning their guns and muskets on their allies. The betrayal was shameless. Had it been made earlier some excuse could have been put forward on behalf of the Saxons, who could argue that this quarrel was not theirs and that their first loyalty was to Germans. It was the timing of the betrayal that maddened the French. At one point of the line a Saxon sergeant major rushed into the open shouting "To Paris! To Paris!" "To Dresden, you swine!" shouted a French veteran, and shot him dead. But the same thing was happening all along Ney's front. Every Saxon unit that was in a position to desert did so and the French went down in hundreds under the concentrated fire of the Crown Prince of Sweden, advancing into the gap. "It was a Frenchman, for whom the blood of Frenchmen had earned a crown, that dealt us this finishing stroke!" comments Marbot, bitterly. His own regiment lost thirty men at this part of the line.

Meanwhile Macdonald's men had been facing a curious form of attack. Twenty thousand Cossacks and Bashkirs advanced on them and the Bashkirs, screaming like Dervishes, assailed the French cavalry with bows and arrows! The volley did little harm, for the Bashkirs were unable to fire horizontally for fear of killing one another and shot their arrows parabolically into the air. A countercharge of chasseurs soon dispersed the bowmen.

In another part of the line Marmont, who had more than his share of injuries during the wars, was wounded in the hand and had to leave the field. Another casualty was Ney, unhorsed and wounded in a furious counter-attack upon the village of Schonfeld. Both marshals had their wounds dressed and returned to duty. When night fell each army occupied the position it had held when fighting commenced.

Yet the situation of the French was now hopeless. They had lost forty thousand men to the enemy's sixty thousand but the allies could afford the loss and the French could not. In the three-day battle of Leipsic the French artillery fired just under a quarter of a million rounds and by the evening of the eighteenth its reserves were reduced to less than twenty thousand rounds. On the seventeenth and eighteenth the allies made limited inroads into the French positions but in the main their attacks had been held. In spite of this Napoleon realised a retreat was obligatory and the orders were issued to move out under cover of darkness.

One new marshal was present at that evening's conference. On October 17, in the middle of the battle, Napoleon had conferred upon Prince Poniatowski an honor he had earned by nearly eight years' service to the Grand Army. He had been the first to welcome the Emperor as liberator when Napoleon rode into Warsaw on New Year's Day, 1807, and he had used all his powers to persuade the lovely Countess Walewska to become Napoleon's mistress and thus to insure the reestablishment of the ancient kingdom of Poland. Since then, however, he had given all he had to the service of France and he and his men had taken part in every war. His lancers were reckoned to be the best-trained and most aggressive unit in the Grand Army's cavalry. Now, when it was too late, Napoleon promised to free Poland and meant it and to prove his intentions he made Poland's hero a marshal. The Prince was to enjoy the honor for just over forty hours.

The fighting retreat commenced on the night of the eighteenth. Murat had led a charge to give the exhausted infantry a chance to break off the combat and fall back. The King of Naples' heart was not in this struggle but when he sniffed powder and looked over the vast chaos of the battle, his cavalryman's instinct was too strong for him and the charge was as brilliant as his advance across the snow at Eylau. No one who saw it would have realized that he was witnessing the end of an epoch. There were plenty of cavalry charges at Ligny and Waterloo but they were nothing like Murat's stupendous efforts.

To Macdonald and to the new marshal, Poniatowski, fell the honor of covering the withdrawal but as usual Michel Ney joined the rearguard. Victor, brave enough in advance, was never a laggard in retreat. He was one of the first across the bridge and with him went Augereau, who had had one eye on the escape route since first light. Augereau was utterly disenchanted with the Empire. The fire in his heart had died and he wanted peace at any price.

Ney and Marmont held the inner suburbs while Macdonald and Poniatowski established themselves in houses in and around the ancient battlements. The Leipsic magistrates had petitioned the allies for an armistice in order to spare the city the horrors of street-fighting but it was peremptorily refused. In spite of this Napoleon rejected the suggestion of firing the town to cover his retreat at the expense of civilians. Instead he withdrew, after asking Ney, Macdonald, and Poniatowski to try and hold on for twenty-four hours and give the main body a head start.

The clansman and the prince did their best but the odds were too great. Soon they found themselves struggling in the center of the town. Poniatowski's Poles made a forlorn charge and the remnants of the two divisions fell back towards the bridge. At that moment occurred the greatest tragedy of the campaign. The explosive charges under the bridge blew up with a roar that was heard far beyond the embattled city. Twenty thousand men and over two hundred guns were isolated on the wrong side of the river, within pistol shot of an enemy who now outnumbered them by something like twenty to one.

Ney got across but Macdonald and Poniatowski were still in the town. There was no thought of surrender. Poniatowski had only held a baton for two days but the example of Ney in Russia had become a tradition. Rallying what men they could find the two marshals urged their horses into the water while enemy skirmishers, emerging from the houses, took pot shots at the swimmers. Junior officers and men followed their leaders' example, the infantry holding on to the tails of the cavalry horses.

Poniatowski, already wounded, received a second wound but he crossed the Pleisse and reached the bank of the Elster. Here, however, the exhausted man failed to climb out and horse and man slipped back into the current. He was too badly wounded to swim and went under at once. His body was washed downstream and was found the next morning in a garden alongside the river. He had served Napoleon eight years and Poland all his life. It was the kind of death he would have chosen.

Macdonald saved himself by his exceptional strength and agility. His horse was drowned but he managed to struggle ashore near the bridgehead. He had shed most of his uniform and was practically naked. His command was reduced to two thousand bedraggled survivors and across the river he could hear the roar of battle as the enemy hunted survivors in and out of houses where they had taken refuge. In the first fury of the assault on the barricaded buildings no quarter was given and thirteen thousand Frenchmen were butchered. Seated on a horse in the town square, surrounded by Russian, Prussian and Austrian staff officers, the Crown Prince of Sweden watched his countrymen being cut to pieces.

They found Macdonald some dry clothes and he hurried along the river bank to make his report to the Emperor. For the shivering wretches he left behind there was no respite. Drunken Prussians, laying planks across the section of the bridge where it was blown, crossed over and began to bayonet unarmed men. As on the road from Moscow, however, there were plenty of Frenchmen on hand whose nerve was equal to any kind of trial. A group of chasseurs charged back along the river and exterminated every Prussian who had crossed the bridge. Then, in a strange silence, the eighty thousand survivors of the army of three hundred and fifty thousand strong that Napoleon had led in the field in April began to move back along the road to the Rhine frontier. For the second time in twelve months a Grand Army had melted away.

Macdonald met Augereau that night and found him in the foulest of tempers, cursing the Emperor in the argot of the Paris slums. "Does the bugger know what he is doing?" he roared, as the stream of fugitives poured past. There was some excuse for Augereau's rage. In killed, wounded, and prisoners the French had lost seventy thousand, and two hundred guns, in three days' fighting, and there was still a hostile army athwart their escape route.

At Hanau, beyond Erfurt, the Bavarians challenged their progress but it was a rash act on the part of the enemy. Savagely, almost contemptuously, the French cut their way through and pushed on to Frankfurt. "We marched on over their bodies," says one of the survivors of Leipsic. This battle was won by five thousand infantrymen and a small force of cavalry, the remnants of Victor's Corps and Macdonald's swimmers. During these depressing days Macdonald was beginning to emulate Ney in his refusal to accept defeat, or to be cast down by hopeless situations. In Hanau forest he reined in his borrowed horse to listen with approval to an educated bugler quoting Virgil in praise of the fine beech trees. "Well, at least there's one chap whose memory isn't disturbed by his surroundings!" he chuckled.

Murat's mercurial temperament did not enable him to show a bold face to adversity. At Erfurt he had mumbled something about it being his duty to return to Naples and Napoleon let him go, knowing full well that he would imitate Bernadotte at the first opportunity and that Caroline, his wife, would not value family loyalty above the throne she had received from her brother's hands. His misgivings were fully justified on January 19 of the new year, when King Joachim tried his hand at a proclamation designed to enlist his men against Napoleon. It was a remarkable effort for a man more accustomed to a farrier's tool than to a pen. "Soldiers," it read, "there are but two banners in Europe. On the one are inscribed 'Religion, Morality, Justice, Law, Peace, Happiness'; on the other 'Persecution, Falsehood, Violence, Tumult, War, and the Mourning of all the nations!'" Murat had very keen eyesight and it seems strange that he should have ridden behind Napoleon's banners since 1796 and only just read what was inscribed on them.

Napoleon crossed the Rhine in early November and the pitiable condition of his army frightened the burghers out of their wits. Typhus was rife, particularly among the young conscripts, of whom Napoleon said sourly: "They fill the hospitals and clutter up the roads with their bodies!" Thus far had he degenerated from the days when a genuine interest in the welfare of his men made him loved and respected throughout the ranks.

Yet there were still Frenchmen willing to die for him and his fading dream of a federalized Europe centered on Paris. France had subscribed two and a half million men for his armies in a period of fourteen years but was not yet ready to accept a return to the Bourbons. For the third time in two years orders went out to the towns and villages to comb the countryside for conscripts. This time their task was not to conquer and occupy foreign lands. It was to defend the soil of France.

. . .

St. Cyr had been left behind in Dresden with twenty thousand men. The individualist had already make up his mind what he would do when he was presented with the ultimate choice of loyalties. He sternly forbade looting and requisitioning. He did not want to face angry citizens when the time came to surrender.

It was otherwise with Davout, shut up in Hamburg with another large garrison. Davout had been Napoleon's man, body and soul, since the Egyptian campaign and he was incapable of switching his allegiance. He held on to Hamburg with a grip of steel, and the flatteries, threats, and promises of a stream of allied emissaries made absolutely no impression upon his cold, crusty conception of the word "Duty!"

Suchet was still holding down Valencia and Catalonia. The British advance across Spain had by-passed him and his area was now an island of French influence. Notwithstanding that, it was efficiently administered, for Suchet had the ability to get on with the job in hand and ignore what was taking place beyond his control. In some ways it was a pity he had not gone into the silk business. Lyons, the center of the trade, boomed under the Empire and he would have been a great success as a merchant.

Soult was fighting the battle of his life in the northern Pyrenees. Step by step, displaying courage and dexterity, the old looter who might have been a village notary, or a village baker, or Nicholas the First of

Northern Lusitania, fell back into southwest France and in early December he had his back to Bayonne. With him was Clausel, the man who had saved the army after Marmont's blunder at Salamanca, and although mainly on the defensive, the French were always ready for a quick pounce on the cautious British and not above employing a *ruse de guerre* when they caught them off guard. At one point, where the pickets were very close to one another, Soult's men pretended to be engaged in a sportive rough-and-tumble while the tolerant redcoats looked on. Suddenly the game stopped, the French fell into line, and rushed down on the British positions, taking them by storm.

Wellington had so many things to think about in this final advance that he was guilty of an unpardonable military error. Crossing a river to rejoin his pickets one night he forgot the password and an efficient Irish sentry was on the point of shooting him. With his finger on the trigger the Irishman recognized the commander-in-chief.

"God bless your long nose!" he shouted. "I'd sooner see you than a rigment o' sodjers!"

As the long campaign dragged on the two armies developed a great respect for one another's fighting qualities. The savagery of the Peninsula fighting was now a thing of the past. Whenever the French and British met they fought stoutly but entirely without rancor, and Soult became a kind of mascot with Wellington's men, particularly among the men of the Light Division. He was judged by them a gallant opponent and a clean fighter, and this opinion was to stand him in good stead in his old age. Of all Napoleon's fighting men Soult alone was to capture the imagination of the British public. Perhaps the most curious feature of the fighting down here was the emergence of Soult as a strategist fit to rank with Masséna and Napoleon himself. He lost every battle and was constantly falling back but with each fight his reputation as a general rose a point. When the war ended he found himself a hero.

There was no such sporting atmosphere about the war further north. Renewed terms of peace were made to Napoleon but each time he temporized until they were withdrawn. In mid-November they offered him Belgium, Savoy, and the Rhine, but he could never convince himself that some extraordinary stroke of luck, or a quarrel among the allies, would not be the means of restoring his fortunes. The marshals grumbled and sometimes protested, but all of them, with the exception of Murat, remained loyal. Finally, in the last days of the old year, the Coalition stopped offering terms. Old Blücher, hero of a hundred fights, and at the age of seventy-two still capable of leading a cavalry charge, summed up the general opinion when he said: "This man has visited every capital in Europe. It is only polite that we should now return the call. Let us advance on Paris!"

On December 31 the allies crossed the Rhine. They were two hundred and sixty-five thousand strong and against them Napoleon had the wreck of the Leipsic army and the scrapings of the national barrel, veterans who had been put on half-pay owing to age or wounds and a few thousand half-grown boys in sabots and smocks, many of whom had never been taught how to load a musket. With the Emperor at this time were Berthier, Ney, Mortier, Oudinot, Victor, Macdonald and Marmont. Down at Lyons with the reserve was Augéreau and he was determined to stay there as long as possible. Davout was holding out in Hamburg. Soult was doing the impossible in the Toulouse area. Suchet was in Catalonia. Murat was going over to the allies. Old Moncey and Lefèbvre were in Paris. Lannes, Bessières, and Poniatowski were dead and the retired group were too old to be of any use. There is still one unaccounted for, Bernadotte.

Bernadotte was not there because he had promised to support the Czar, the Hapsburgs, and the Hohenzollerns. He too had seen a vision and it was a splendid one, beginning with the arrival of a respectful deputation asking the Crown Prince of Sweden to accept the Imperial throne of France as soon as Napoleon had been killed or exiled. The Gascon said little about this vision, not even to his wife or his closest friends, but he remained hopeful. He was an optimist by nature and it did not occur to him that Frenchmen would be unlikely to shout *'Vive l'Empereur!'* to a man who had watched their comrades butchered in Leipsic.

Napoleon, the great psychologist, may have divined what was going on inside the handsome head of the Crown Prince of Sweden and this, together with whispers of betrayal in Paris, and a disturbing half-heartedness among the other marshals, may have prompted him to growl that winter's day: "They are all a set of scoundrels, going to the devil!"

CHAPTER SEVENTEEN

"HE IS DEAF TO OUR CALAMITIES"

THERE were men among the allies advancing into France during the first week of the new year who were convinced that Napoleon was not the man he had been in the days when he had defeated them severally and in alliance with one another. These men, Blücher among them, were soon to be disillusioned for never at any time in his astonishing career as a soldier did the Emperor display more genius in the art of handling an army in the field. The campaign of France, which lasted from January 1 until the abdication in mid-April, saw Napoleon at the very top of his form. With fifty-thousand ill-found men he defied a splendidly equipped force of just under half a million. It was not only a tribute to his talents and personality, it was also astonishing evidence of a middle-aged man's physical stamina.

It was a confused, whirlwind campaign, a story of darting attacks and miraculous withdrawals,.of isolated columns of Russians, Austrians, and Prussians being surprised and beaten in detail, when and where they least expected it. Europe looked on anxiously while this David and Goliath duel was fought out in the pleasant country of Champagne, over ground that a century later was to witness the terrible struggles of World War I—Château Thierry, Montmirail, Chattilon-sur-Marne, Vauchamp, Craonne, Laon, Arcis, all battles fought against considerable odds and often won against all probability.

Eleven times during February and March the tiny army pounced on the invaders and mauled them so savagely that the allied high command began to lose heart and its isolated leaders forgot everything in a desire to get out of range of this half-caged tiger. "He has beaten every one

of us in detail!" complained one allied officer, bewailing the fact that a
conquest promising to be so easy was turning into an exhibition of
allied incompetence. But isolated victories could not stop the advance
of three hundred thousand men, smarting under two decades of failure.
The slow tide of Uhlans, grenadiers, Cossacks, hussars, and Croat infantry
edged forward into France, and in Paris, behind the lines, men like Talleyrand began to prepare for a return of the Bourbons. Brother Joseph, feeling even more insecure as Governor of Paris than he had felt as King of
Spain, ordered a mass exodus over the Loire.

Macdonald, Ney, Victor, and Oudinot were in the front line week
after week. Victor was wounded and Oudinot almost starved within a
day's march of his home. Fearing for his wife's safety he sent a staff
officer to conduct her into the camp. The Maréchale, who adored her husband, was preparing for the journey when the officer suggested that it
might be an excellent idea to load some provisions into the carriage. "Your
husband hasn't eaten a square meal in days!" he told her. The good lady,
amazed at this information, threw out trunks to make space for supplies
of food and her arrival in the camp was a welcome event for the staff.
Pies, hams, and chickens were unloaded and passed among the half-starved
men, but in the midst of the feast the good-natured Oudinot exclaimed:
"Here what am I doing? I must send for my neighbor before it is
all gone!"

His "neighbor" was Macdonald, whose appetite did full justice to
the windfall. Then Oudinot's wife went on to Paris and the two marshals
attacked again.

In mid-March, having beaten the enemy wherever he came to grips
with them but failed to check the advance on Paris, Napoleon adopted
the simple and reckless plan of marching directly east. "Whenever I threw
a few hussars across their communications in the past they always came
pelting back," he said, but this time the bluff was called. A letter giving
details of the daring plan was captured on its way to Marie Louise and
the allies left their communications to look after themselves and closed
in on Paris, defended by Mortier and Marmont. Happily the Russian gunners selected sites for their batteries. "The time has come for Father Paris
to pay Mother Moscow!" they said.

But Paris was not Saragossa or Genoa and its defenders were not
bigots and fanatics but tired, hungry soldiers with a cynic in command.
Mortier stood aside, his honest nature quite bewildered by all this to-ing

and fro-ing, and it was Marmont who made the first move. On March 31 Paris surrendered and the marshals and their garrison marched out under the terms of the capitulation. Talleyrand at once issued a proclamation calling the Emperor a despot. "He is deaf to our calamities!" it began.

He was not deaf to reports that the allies were concentrating on his capital. The night that Marmont surrendered Napoleon came bustling up from Troyes and when they stopped him and told him the news he refused to believe it and would have driven straight into enemy positions. At last they convinced him and, dazed with shock, he fell back on Fontainebleau. The scene was set for what Europe hoped was the final act of tragedy.

Nobody told him, for no other marshal knew at this stage that the situation was even worse than it appeared to be and that Marmont, anxious to be among the first to preserve his rank, title, and wealth, had already notified his divisional officers that Napoleon was abdicating and that the army would not march to its death under the walls of its own capital. Just to make sure Marmont had written a friendly letter to the Czar, thus taking upon himself the responsibility of expressing the opinion of the armed forces as a whole.

There was still a slim chance that help would come from the south and Napoleon sent piteous appeals to Augereau at Lyons, ordering him to march north with his twenty-five thousand reserves. The old soldier-of-fortune made no move. He had no intention of committing himself or his men to a cause so obviously lost. Civilians in his area were already wearing the white cockade of the Bourbons and Napoleon wrote again, telling the marshal to shoot and hang these traitors, but Pierre Augereau shot no one and hanged no one. In times gone by an order of this kind would have decorated every available tree with a corpse, but that was in Spain or Italy or Germany or Poland, and Augereau was now in his native land where he had every intention of spending the rest of his life. He wrote saying that his troops were unreliable and untrained, that he was short of supplies and ammunition, that he could not risk a march into the combat area. He made all manner of excuses, some spurious, some genuine, but he did not join the six marshals still with the Emperor at the Palace of Fontainebleau. One other marshal did, however, old Moncey, who had not fired a shot in years but was urged by his sense of honor to march out with a column of civilian soldiers and range himself alongside the few men whose loyalty was not in doubt. The gesture was

typical of the sixty-year-old veteran and it was understood and appreciated
by all. Soon the group of anxious, indecisive men was joined by another,
gallant old Lefèbvre. Lefèbvre had never quite lost his admiration for
the man who had presented him with that magnificent Mameluke saber
on the eve of the great coup, in 1800. Even after all these years he did
not realize that the gift had been a bribe.

The eight marshals discussed the situation among themselves but only
seven contributed to the discussion. The eighth, Berthier, withdrew without indicating what course he would advise if the Emperor persisted in
his crazy notion of marching on Paris, or the equally crazy one of carrying
on the war beyond the Loire. When Napoleon had broached the suggestion to Oudinot a little earlier, the latter had rejected it out of hand.
"That would mean we cease to be soldiers and become partisans!" he
protested and turned on his heel.

Yet a decision had to be made, here and now, without another moment's delay, and when Ney suggested that they should form themselves
into a deputation and approach the Emperor, someone, no one is sure
who, expressed the fear that Napoleon would regard them as mutineers
and have them all shot. Macdonald laughed aloud at this. "Rubbish!"
he snorted. "Those days are gone! He wouldn't dare!" He then approved
Ney's tentative suggestion that two or three of them should approach the
Emperor and speak for the marshals as a whole.

Ney volunteered as spokesman and the two old veterans, Lefèbvre
and Moncey, agreed to second him. The three of them went into the palace
leaving the others to await the outcome on the terrace.

Berthier was alone with Napoleon when the deputation tramped into
the audience chamber. They made a strange group, one Emperor, two
Princes, and two Dukes, all five owing nothing whatever to birth and background. Two were the sons of lawyers, one the son of an architect, and
the remaining pair, Lefèbvre and Ney, the sons of a miller and a cooper.
Yet these five men, and a million like them, had overthrown half a dozen
dynasties in the last twenty years and had stormed into capitals as widely
separated as Moscow and Madrid. Now they were back at starting point
and only one of them refused to face the fact.

Ney made a short speech, pointing out that the time had come to
make terms with the allies and end the war. He had probably been expect-
ing a violent outburst and was fully prepared for it, looking to Berthier
to support him if necessary, but there was no outburst. Napoleon listened

to him patiently and then countered by pointing out a series of master-strokes he had in mind. He spoke of Augereau's reserves in the south and of a national uprising that would destroy the invaders.

As the four men listened in complete silence the door opened and Oudinot walked in to report the arrival of his men. Oudinot had probably had a word with Macdonald on the terrace, for Macdonald was at his heels and ranged himself alongside Ney, Moncey, and Lefèbvre. When Napoleon had stopped speaking Macdonald said quietly: "We have decided to make an end of this!" Napoleon began to talk again but this time Ney interrupted him. "The army will not march!" he said flatly and when Napoleon, his excitement mounting, retorted that the men outside the Palace grounds would obey their Emperor, Ney interrupted again. "They will not," he said, doggedly, "they will obey their generals!"

No more was said. The deputation turned and walked out. During the whole of the interview Berthier had said nothing at all. Outside, Lefèbvre made an attempt at self-justification. "It's his fault really," he mumbled, "he took the packs off our backs too soon!" It is curious how this comment matches Napoleon's own remark on the conduct of his marshals during the crisis. "I should have retired them all earlier and carried on with junior officers who had their way to make!" he observed shrewdly.

That same evening, Napoleon decided to abdicate in favor of his four-year-old son, the King of Rome, with his wife, Marie Louise, as Regent. He appointed Ney and Macdonald to take the document to the czar and instructed them to pick up Marmont en route. They rode off with relief, glad that so much had been accomplished without a violent scene and determined to do everything in their power to secure Napoleon's dynasty.

Marmont received the two marshals with embarrassment, which increased as soon as he learned that he was expected to join the deputation. He said nothing of the instructions he had already issued to his divisional generals and nothing of his letter to the czar, or a conversation he had recently had with Schwartzenburg, the Austrian leader. When they got to Paris, however, he made an excuse and left his colleagues, promising to rejoin them later. They must have thought his conduct strange but neither Ney nor Macdonald commented upon it. Instead, they went straight in to the czar and stated their case, Ney pleading eloquently for the continuation of the dynasty.

The czar received them very courteously. Napoleon could not have chosen a better man than Michel Ney for a mission of this sort. Alexander's chivalry responded to a spokesman whose conduct in Russia had rung round the world and he was inclined to support the plea. "Who are these Bourbons?" he had remarked, when it had been suggested that the gouty Louis XVIII should take Napoleon's place. "I know nothing of them!" During the second interview, however, his attitude changed. A staff officer came in and whispered something to him and at once he turned to Ney and said: "You assured me that the army as a whole is still loyal to the Emperor?" Ney said that this was the case. "Then how is it that Marmont's corps has just marched into our lines?" asked the czar.

Ney was struck dumb by this intelligence, the gist of the staff officer's whispered conversation. He did not know what to say and neither did Macdonald. They stood there looking at one another and the audience was over. As soon as they were dismissed Ney made furious inquiries and soon established beyond doubt that the czar's information was correct. At that very moment Marmont's men were marching through the invaders' lines to Versailles and only their generals knew where they were going and why. When given the order to march the men thought they were advancing against the enemy, but it was soon clear that the Prussians and Russians were not going to attack. As soon as the column arrived at Versailles the NCO's and rankers realized what had happened. They personally had provided Marmont's insurance and their first reaction was one of impotent rage. So angry were they that there was talk of lynching the marshal and when Marmont appeared to harangue them they called him traitor and shouted him down. The damage, however, was done and gradually their tempers cooled. They were in the heart of the enemy's camp and nothing more could be done to get them out again. Moreover, their very presence there snapped the slender thread by which the Napoleonic dynasty was hanging. There would be no Regency now and no Imperial throne waiting for the King of Rome when he came of age. Marmont had seen to that and made certain of his own titles and estates.

Of all the twenty-six marshals of the Empire Marmont had known Napoleon the longest. Even before the famous incident under the walls of Toulon, when artilleryman Bonaparte had worked out the best method of taking the city, Marmont had been the Corsican's intimate friend, the man whom he had invited home when they were both junior officers at Auxerre, the man whose friendship for the Emperor antedated that of Victor, also at Toulon, or Murat, who had made possible the whiff of grapeshot, or Berthier, who had lived cheek by jowl with Napoleon since 1796. It was Marmont, the old comrade-in-arms, who had done more than any Frenchman to restore the Bourbons. Of all the blows rained upon Napoleon's spirit that spring this left the largest bruise.

.   .   .

There was no swift means of letting Soult know what had happened in Fontainebleau and Paris. Days passed before a courier came in with news of Napoleon's abdication, of his failure to preserve the throne for his son, of Marmont's treachery, and the Emperor's unsuccessful attempt to commit suicide with poison that had lost its lethal qualities over the years.

In any case Soult had been too heavily engaged to pay any attention to what was happening elsewhere. He was now entrenched outside Toulouse, the largest city of the southwest, and he was displaying the cunning and tenacity of a netted lynx.

Days after the game was up in Fontainebleau, Soult fought the last pitched battle of the Peninsular war and deserved to win it, so clever were his dispositions, so gallant the behavior of his men. He did not win it, however, but had to fall back after losing three thousand men and five generals. The sacrifice, together with that of the British and Spanish amounting to nearly five thousand casualties, was cruel and pointless. Immediately after the battle Wellington received news of the abdication and at once sent the information to his opponent under a flag of truce. Soult was suspicious and awaited confirmation. Presently confirmation came and on April 18, twelve days after Napoleon had renounced the throne, a convention was arranged for the suspension of hostilities.

The war in the Peninsula was over. It had lasted without pause for more than six years and the British forces alone claimed a total of two hundred thousand Frenchmen killed, wounded, or prisoners. Forty thousand British dead left their bones in the Peninsula and the cost to the British Treasury had been one hundred million pounds. It was Napier, the British military historian who fought under Wellington, who paid a soldierly tribute to his opponents. In writing of the French troops in this theater he says: "To them summer and winter were alike. They endured terrible privations and for their daring and resource a single fact will suffice. Strong places were captured without any provision of bullets save those fired on them by their enemies!"

Yet only Soult and Suchet added to their reputation in Spain, the one by his magnificently stubborn rearguard campaign, the other by his first-class administration and defense of Valencia and Catalonia. The others, Masséna, Ney, Jourdan, Victor, Augereau, Bessières, Lefèbvre, Murat, Mortier, and Marmont, had all botched their work in one way or another and had retired, or been withdrawn as failures. From first to last the war had been a hideous muddle and a fatal drain upon the Empire's resources, and in the end Napoleon recognized as much. "The Spanish ulcer destroyed me!" he said at St. Helena, and it was a plain statement of fact.

Almost the last thing Soult saw when he led his war-weary battalions through Toulouse was a crowd of several hundred civilians pulling on a long rope, one end of which was attached to the neck of Napoleon's statue in the town. As the troops passed the statue crashed to the ground. Some of the soldiers must have given a thought to their comrades who had passsed down this road on their way into Spain during the last six years, men who were now rotting in British prison hulks or in the new jail on Dartmoor, or the less fortunate ones whose bones were lying in rocky passes and under parched plains all the way from Bidassoa to the Tagus. They might have asked themselves what had been gained by such blood-letting, for this, more than any other Napoleonic campaign, had been a war waged for personal ambition, a war against a people rather than a dynasty or government. It was over at last, however, and the author himself was traveling south from Paris, heading for the tiny island of Elba in the Mediterranean, a kingdom he had just exchanged for the sovereignty of half Europe. He traveled down the old Route Napoleon and only one Peninsular veteran crossed his path. In the little town of Valence, where sixteen-year-old sub-lieutenant Bonaparte had served before the mob stormed the Bastille, Augereau waited beside the road as the cavalcade approached.

When Napoleon saw the tall figure of the marshal he stopped the carriage and got out, embracing him and chiding him gently for not marching north in response to repeated appeals. Augereau received the ex-Emperor very coldly. "Your own insatiable ambition brought you to this!" said the old soldier, and as a gesture of defiance kept his cocked hat on his head after Napoleon had removed his own. Did he remember that impressive little scene in Nice eighteen years ago, when Napoleon, physically dwarfed by his new generals of division, had imposed his authority on them from the start by removing his hat and replacing it immediately?

Napoleon felt the snub keenly but he was getting used to them. Shortly before all the preliminaries of the abdication had been arranged, Berthier, the shock-headed chief-of-staff known as "The Emperor's Wife," had made an excuse to go to Paris "to look for papers" and had slipped away without a word of farewell. "You will be back, Berthier?" Napoleon had asked as he left the room, and when Berthier stuttered that he would, Napoleon had smiled, grimly, "We shan't see him again!" he said and he was right. They never met again but Berthier's name was one of those on Napoleon's lips when he lay dying seven years later.

One marshal's loyalty stood out like a rock. Cut off in Hamburg, Davout refused to believe envoys who told him further resistance was useless, and that his chief was already on his way into exile. Coldly and stiffly the man who had defied the Prussian army at Auerstadt showed his visitors the door. It took an official dispatch from the French War Ministry to convince Davout that events had left him behind and when he finally handed over the city and returned to Paris he found himself not only in disgrace but under the threat of persecution. Loyalty was a dangerous sentiment in the Paris of 1814. Those who flaunted it were likely to see the inside of a jail.

In early May Napoleon embarked for his island kingdom. Not one of the marshals who had marched and fought beside him since the first victories in Italy, accompanied him into exile. Each, according to his temperament and record, was doing what he could to adjust himself to a strange new world where a man who possessed a title need not have earned it by charging through a crossfire of grapeshot or escalading heavily defended ramparts sword in hand. They did their best to get used to this curious state of affairs but gaffes were frequent and sometimes tempers ran dangerously high.

Within a week or two of Louis's arrival in the Tuilleries where, on looking round, he remarked: "He was a good tenant, this Napoleon!" the sons of masons and the daughters of small tradesmen were beginning to wonder whether the ex-Emperor had been such a scoundrel after all. At least he only rewarded people whose recommendation was a willingness to shed blood that was red. He did not heap blazing stars on those who reached out for them because their blood was said to be blue.

CHAPTER EIGHTEEN

"SEND NO MORE MEN: I HAVE ENOUGH!"

EVERY dynasty in Europe made costly mistakes in its dealings with Imperial France but not Romanoff, Hapsburg, Hohenzollern or Hanoverian committed errors on the scale committed by France's own kings, the Bourbons, on returning home after twenty-two years' exile, in the spring of 1814.

They had everything in their favor. The country, sick of war, was ready to welcome the fat, gouty stranger, restored to them by foreign bayonets, and when Napoleon rode into exile mobs reviled him, surrounding his carriage, burning his effigy, and calling him tyrant. The white cockade of the ancient kings of France was displayed by every class in the community, and had Louis and his train of arrogant followers possessed a spark of tact, humility, or even common sense, there is no doubt but that bourgeoisie and working classes would have suffered them gladly.

Unfortunately the Bourbons were not renowned for common sense. One of their first public acts was to parade the statue of the Virgin Mary through the streets with a group of ex-Republican marshals as candle-bearers! Luckily Lannes was dead or the ceremony might have been enlivened by a broadside of oaths.

Another attempt to wipe out the past was Louis's decision to pretend that the Revolution and Empire had never existed at all, and to date his reign from the death of the Dauphin in the Temple Prison, so that he mounted the throne in the twenty-second year of his reign and dated documents accordingly. Under Napoleon honors had to be won. Now they were for sale. The coveted ribbon of the Legion of Honor, which veterans had preferred above promotion and gratuities, could be bought for the equivalent of about twenty pounds, and in the period between August and December, 1814, the Bourbons made more Legionnaires than Napoleon had made in the twelve years of his reign!

Within six months of the restoration the popularity of the exile in Elba was increasing at a rate that thoroughly alarmed men like Talleyrand and patriots like Ney and Oudinot. Inconceivable errors of judgment stemmed from the new government. Injured pride and a spirit of malice dictated its every gesture, for the returning exiles had come home determined to exact revenge for twenty years' penury and obscurity in Britain and elsewhere. They wanted more than obedience. They demanded groveling subservience.

These vain and rather pitiful men and women cared nothing for the glory won by French arms against successive coalitions. They only remembered that they had been bundled out of their homeland by the uprising of a rabble they considered less than human and forced thereafter to live on charity, or on their wits in foreign lands. Here, for the first time in their lives, they had had to earn their bread and watch their country march to triumph after triumph under the man they had once hoped would restore the privileges they and their kind had enjoyed under Louis XIV and XV. Their outlook was still entirely feudal and they tried by every means in their power to re-rivet feudal fetters upon a people to whom Napoleon had given cohesion and boundless opportunity. It would have been better for France and for Europe if every one of them had died in exile or perished during the Terror. In the new century of scientific advancement there would soon be no place for them but they meant to enjoy the Indian summer purchased for them by the valor of Wellington and Blücher and by the power of English guineas.

Louis also made the grievous mistake of supposing that by honoring the marshals he was automatically enlisting the support of the army. He had no conception of the warm relationship that had been shared by senior officers, junior officers, NCO's and men during twenty years in the field. To him and his intimates an officer was a professional brute, and the men under him were dumb, patient serfs, ready to be flogged into obedience as the Prussian armies were driven on by the whirling canes of their drill sergeants. To be on the safe side, however, the marshals were ennobled. Their juniors were put on half-pay and their rank and file, among them thousands of veterans who came limping back from the captured fortresses and prison hulks, were treated like unlicensed beggers. It never seemed to occur to anyone of the new régime that these men had given their blood for a cause they identified as that of their motherland, or that they took pride in their fabulous achievements since the far-off days when Jourdan had led them to victory at Fleurus. They were demobilized and told to stay out of trouble. Within weeks of their return they began to growl.

Any government less arrogant than that recently installed in Paris would have regarded the mere presence of these men as a menace to good order and would have done something, anything, to propitiate them and win them over. The Bourbons reacted in quite another way. They slapped the noisiest grumblers in jail, discharged the rest without full arrears of pay, and then set to work to build up an officer class among their own kind. Very few of these handsomely accoutered gentlemen had ever fired a musket. Time was to show how few of them had any desire to learn.

Then, within a matter of weeks, the *émigrés* made an even graver mistake. They began to ruffle the feelings of the marshals and more particularly the marshals' wives, by sneering references to their ancestry. Barbed innuendoes were unable to penetrate the tough skin of Lefèbvre's charlady Duchess, who still began conversations with: "When I was scrubbing for Madame So-and-so . . .," but they crushed sensitive little women like Aglaé Ney, of whom the frigid Duchess of Angoulême, niece of the king, was once heard to ask: "What is the niece of Mme. Campan, the baker's daughter, doing at court?"

Ney, who considered that he had done more than anyone to persuade Napoleon to abdicate and make way for the Bourbons, flew into one of his famous rages when this sneer was reported to him and stormed out of Paris with a complexion as red as his hair. His blood pressure rose even higher when he heard that the Emperor of Austria was talking of removing the bronze column made of Austrian guns. "So?" he roared, in his terrible voice. "Does he want us to capture enough to make a second column?"

Of the twenty-two surviving marshals all but one submitted to the monarchy. Davout was the only exception and went into exile. He could have made his peace with the Bourbons, even after his obstinate refusal to surrender Hamburg, but he preferred to turn his back on them. It was a quarter of a century since he had led the abortive mutiny in the officers' mess but he had not lost his hatred of unmerited privilege. The others, every single one of them, were absorbed into the new France and each set about the task of adapting himself to the changes as best he could. Some were more adaptable than others. It was a matter of background, temperament, and character.

Ney, Marmont, Oudinot, Mortier, Moncey, Macdonald, Lefèbvre, Kellerman, and Berthier all went to Compiègne to welcome the gross-bellied king when he arrived in France. Victor was not present at the welcoming party but he soon became the most enthusiastic royalist in the country and as a reward they made him commander of the Household troops. Unlike the stern Davout he seemed to have forgotten all about his ride into Paris the summer the Bastille fell. Soult followed suit and after a short spell in Brittany returned to Paris as Minister for War. Even his enemies, and he had made a great number, were pleased about this, for Soult replaced the despised Dupont, the man who had surrendered to a pack of Spaniards in 1808 and helped to fan the flames of Spanish patriotism into war. Already, it will be seen, the French were becoming very touchy about their military traditions.

Augereau, after his gruff passage with Napoleon at Valence, announced that in his opinion the Emperor ought to have gone out in a blaze of glory and found a spectacular death on the field by charging a battery sword in hand. He was so convinced of the rightness of this finale that he wrote a proclamation about it. It won him new friends and he joined Ney and Macdonald on the Council of War.

Suchet submitted with dignity and Oudinot, always a genuine patriot, went over after a private wrestle with his conscience and never went back on the decision. What may have helped him make up his mind was a startling letter he later received from Ney, in which the former devotee of the Emperor exhorted him to "unite against the common enemy!" Ney's behavior was now embarrassing his friends. He was so critical in his judgments of Napoleon, and the causes of his downfall, that he might even have been mistaken for the champion of the Bourbons had he not criticized them just as outspokenly. He had never begun to understand the ways of politicians but his erratic behavior was probably the result of twenty-two years' warfare, capped by two campaigns that would have put a less robust man in hospital with nervous exhaustion. Americans of World War II would have classified him as a victim of battle fatigue. The British of World War I would have said he was shell-shocked. He mooched about

Paris and the provinces muttering and grumbling, sometimes inveighing against Napoleon and sometimes comparing the Emperor with his successor to the latter's disadvantage. Louis, the old king, trusted him completely, but the *émigrés* did not and began to go out of their way to rile him. Knowing how terribly sensitive he was of the honor he felt due to all the marshals, one of the courtiers threw him into a violent temper by pretending not to recognize one of Ney's famous colleagues and remarking, after a puzzled stare, "Now who *is* that fellow over there?" Wherever he went Ney's touchiness was the target of the court wit and the scandalmonger.

Murat was still a king but was hanging on to his Neopolitan throne by his fingertips. It had been granted to him as the price of his treachery earlier in the year but nobody really trusted him and he knew that one false move might be fatal to his survival. His wife, sister Caroline, did her best to insure the continuance of allied patronage. She went so far as to share a bed with Metternich, the Austrian Chancellor, who was renowned all over Europe for his success with the ladies and once boasted that he maintained half a dozen mistresses at once.

Berthier, also loyal to the new régime, was yet feeling conscience-stricken over his abrupt desertion of his old friend at Fontainebleau. He went along to Malmaison, where the ex-Empress Josephine was receiving all the crowned heads of Europe, in order to explain to her just why he had slipped away when the Empire was tottering. He did what he could to justify himself but he was a born worrier and this year, his last on earth, was a troubled and unhappy period for him. Of all the men who now wore the king's coat Berthier had been the closest to the exile in Elba. Their intimacy had been the focal point of his life and when they parted company he was less than half a man and could never get his bearings. He said very little and kept as clear of public life as was possible. Ever since childhood he had indulged in the habit of biting his nails. By midsummer 1814 they were down to the quick.

For the older men, Kellerman, Jourdan, Moncey, Lefèbvre and Sérurier, the transition was much easier. Kellerman and Sérurier had originated from wealthy families and were at ease in the new society. Moncey, Jourdan, and Lefèbvre were honest, plodding fellows who had no difficulty in convincing themselves that the welfare of France was best served by a return to its ancient traditions. They made no trouble and they performed such administrative tasks as they were given competently and unremarkably. The principal occupation of Pérignon and Lefèbvre at this time was the care of old soldiers at the Invalides. These five men might have lacked the dash and glitter of a Murat or a Bernadotte but their records, viewed across the years, make better reading.

Brune, he who had once been the friend of the man who claimed a king's head as a gauge of battle, also made his peace with royalty. Little is heard of Brune during the first restoration but he makes a tragic reappearance in the crisis immediately ahead.

Masséna emerged from retirement to enlist under the banner of the fleur-de-lis. He came out into the open rather like an old tortoise after the tumult and tramp of armies had passed him by. He was accepted and given command of the south of France, his old territory during his fruit-selling and smuggling days, but he had no need to return to the smuggling now. He was fabulously rich and could have told anybody exactly how much he was worth at any time of the day or night. He kept quiet and they left him alone with his boxes of gold and jewels and his pretty mistresses. He wrote no memoirs and aired no grudges. He had got what he wanted from life and all the devils in hell were not going to deprive him of it at the age of fifty-eight.

Bernadotte, the tall, handsome Crown Prince of Sweden, did not stay very long among the conquerors of Paris. Even the romantic Czar realized that it would be fatal to let him play an important part in the reconstruction, for every Frenchman alive regarded Bernadotte as a traitor and a scoundrel.

The Gascon had always possessed great personal charm and was an extremely persuasive talker at conferences and salons but even he was unable to talk himself out of the charge of leading an army of foreigners into his own capital and then waiting around to be chosen successor to Napoleon. His wife Desirée loved him dearly but she also loved Paris and was very happy to be back after her long spell in the gloomy Swedish capital, where the shops were uninviting and nobody gossiped. But very soon a somewhat chastened Bernadotte slipped away never to return. Perhaps he was speeded on his way by Lefèbvre's wife, who called him a traitor to his face.

So the months slipped by and the distracted country showed no signs of settling down under the gouty Louis. Instead, it raised its voice in protest against every new edict that emerged from the Tuileries, and never more loudly than when Soult, as Minister of War, tried to put into effect a decree banishing certain Imperial officers from Paris. One of them, a famous cavalry blade named Exelmans, called the bluff and refused to go. He was put on trial but his acquittal, in January, 1815, was received with shouts of joy all over France and the new government dropped another rung down the ladder of public esteem.

The train was laid and the powder magazine was waiting. All it needed was the spark and on March of that year the spark was struck. The resultant explosion was heard as far away as the ruins of Moscow and the Scottish Highlands, where veteran officers of Wellington's Light Brigade were enjoying their first spring of peace since they were lads at school. For on that day, with about a thousand of his Guard, Napoleon landed on the Riviera coast and began his amazing march on Paris.

· · ·

It had been the maddest, most reckless adventure of all and had almost ended before it was well begun. A few days' sail out of Porto Ferrajo the brig, crammed with eight hundred old moustaches and three hundred desperate Imperialists, was challenged by a French sloop of war. When its captain hailed the vessel and discovered that it was from Elba, he asked: "How is the Emperor?" The guardsmen lay flat on the deck and Napoleon answered himself, *"Il se porte à merveille!"* he shouted and the sloop bore off, leaving the brig to continue its voyage.

In the first six days of his march inland Napoleon recruited four peasants. The people as a whole were indifferent and neither cheered nor opposed the little column marching by but the appearance of the first troops, part of the Grenoble garrison, gave a great showman a chance to impress. Opening his greatcoat to display his star of the Legion of Honor, he walked unescorted up to the advance guard. "If there is a man there who wishes to kill his Emperor, let him do it!" he said quietly and as the men wavered he took another step and cried: "Do you know me, comrades?"

As one man the battalion threw down its weapons and rushed to embrace him. Not a single shot was fired in defense of the king who claimed to have ruled France for twenty-three years.

After that it was the same story with every detachment sent to bar his progress. Generals, captains, NCO's, privates, drummers, they all joined him, until his tentative advance was converted into triumphant progress. A day or so later a placard appeared on the railings of the Vendôme column, purporting to be a letter from Napoleon to Louis. It ran: "Dear Brother, don't send me any more troops. I have enough!"

Enough troops, enough junior officers perhaps, but had he enough experienced, high-grade leaders accustomed to handling an army corps in the field? Every marshal with the exception of Davout had pledged himself to the Bourbons and some were already in the march to arrest him.

The first was old Masséna, sunning himself down in Marseilles where he commanded all the troops in the Riviera area. Probably Masséna was the only man in France other than Talleyrand who could have avoided impaling himself on one or other of the two prongs but Masséna managed it. He let Napoleon get a good start and then sent troops in pursuit, knowing they had no chance whatever of barring the road to Paris. He then settled down in Nice to see what would happen. Either way he was well insured. If Napoleon won he had not opposed him. If Louis won Masséna could always shake his head and mutter: "Ah sire, these lads of mine don't march as fast as their fathers!"

The return from Elba and the period known as The Hundred Days was the most severe test of character to which the marshals of Napoleon had been subjected, not only as soldiers and patriots but as individuals. Every one of them owed their exalted position to the invader and while some, like Masséna and Ney, also owed a great deal to their own talents and courage, there were plenty of others, such as Victor and Mortier, who would never have risen so high in their profession without Imperial tuition and patronage. It is interesting to discover how each marshal reacted to the situation and to find, within that reaction, the character of each one of them. For an accurate estimate of each marshal's personal worth one does not have to study records from the Revolution onwards; one has only to concentrate on that page of the record covering the period March–April, 1814.

Masséna, as we have seen, produced the almost perfect alibi but the others, who did not enjoy the old smuggler's geographical advantage, discovered that alibis were not easily manufactured. Some did not even seek one and perhaps the best example of an honorable man in this dilemma is that of ex-grenadier Oudinot, the scarred, front-line fighter, whose forthright character most nearly resembles that of the dead Lannes.

Oudinot was in charge of the Metz area when he learned of Napoleon's return. Up to the last moment of the abdication period he had fought bravely and well. Now he was too straightforward to go back on his oath and assembled his men to defend the Bourbon cause. But even Oudinot's personal popularity could not compete with the magic of Napoleon's name. At Toul, where he called his officers together and outlined his plan for marching against the invader, a young captain stepped forward and saluted.

"We feel it only right to tell you, sir, that tomorrow on parade when you shout 'Long live the King' we shall reply by shouting 'Long live the Emperor!' " he said respectfully.

It was an honorable ultimatum and Oudinot accepted it. He dismissed the officer and left his command. He had made up his own mind but he was not going to persuade others. He went back to his country estate and took no part at all in The Hundred Days. Davout, the only marshal who could report to Napoleon with clean hands, wrote him a moving letter, asking him to return to his old allegiance but Oudinot, who had been Davout's only true friend in the marshalate, was not to be won over. He wrote back explaining his motives and the friendship between the two men ended.

Oudinot was not alone in his adherence to the new king. Victor, once a fire-eating revolutionary sergeant, noisily declared in favor of the race of kings. With Victor it was not a matter of oaths and duty but one of self-interest and the strong streak of snobbery often found in radicals. By this time Victor had forgotten that his real name was Perrin but he had never digested his title, Duke of Belluno, until a real live king made him commander of the Household Troops. Napoleon had never reposed that much trust in him and he was not going to risk his all to serve another self-made man.

Macdonald, from more honest motives, remained loyal to Louis and at least made a sincere effort to stop the usurper. He posted down to Lyons as soon as the alarm was raised and joined forces with the Court of Artois but it was soon clear to count and marshal that the men they led were totally unreliable. "Shout for the King!" one subaltern was ordered, when the Royalist troops were about to make contact with Napoleon's ever-increasing army. "Not me, my shout is going to be *'Vive l'Empereur!'* " said the young man calmly and when the rival patrols met on the bridge of La Guillotiere the Bourbon infantry echoed the officer's shout. Within seconds the opposing sides were fraternizing.

The Court of Artois bolted. All over France the aristocrats bolted.

They had kept body and soul together abroad in the past, and they could do it again; it was better than being marched over by the man in the gray coat. Sadly, and without loss of dignity, the son of the clansman followed them. Napoleon had never trusted him within sound of the bag-pipes but he might have done so with safety. Macdonald, so long out of favor with the Emperor, was an honorable man and like Oudinot he refused to go back on an oath.

Macdonald arrived back in Paris just in time to join the great exodus from the Tuileries. For a man who had been occupying a throne for twenty-three years Louis did not waste much time making up his mind to vacate it. King, court, and hangers-on galloped pell-mell for the Bel-gian frontier and with them, somewhat embarrassed by the haste, went Macdonald, Marmont, Mortier, and Berthier, the staff-wizard they once called "The Emperor's Wife."

Berthier's fingernails must have been gnawed during the journey northeast. The former chief-of-staff, the man who had sat beside Napoleon for twenty years and helped to direct the onslaughts at Marengo, Auster-litz, Jena, and countless other battles, was now in an agony of indecision and more wretched than he had ever been in his life, even when he had been torn from his beautiful mistress to go into Egypt. Berthier was cap-tain of the Royal Bodyguard and was therefore obliged to conduct his sovereign as far as Ghent, but at the frontier, Macdonald, feeling that he had done his duty, turned back and followed the example of Oudinot by retiring to his estates. Mortier, who had never been very happy under the Bourbons, was far more of a gambler. With a booming laugh he stopped running and threw in his lot with the man his troops were already cheering. Marmont, handicapped by the memory that it was he who had ruined the chances of Napoleon's dynasty, did not care to return to Paris and ask for pardon. Instead, he pushed on to Ghent and when they reached there Berthier left the king and went to Bamberg to join his family. He was careful to explain to anyone who would listen that he wasn't flying from Napoleon like Marmont, but was merely making cer-tain domestic arrangements. But the fear that he might be mistaken for a coward became an obsession and when he got to Bamberg he was still undecided which course to pursue. Could he persuade himself that France needed Napoleon and return to his old position like Mortier? Should he adhere to his oath like Oudinot? Or should he try to face both ways like Masséna? He had never been any good at making a decision unless Napoleon was at hand to make up his mind, and now the claims of personal loyalty and patriotism were tearing him to pieces and his soul was in torment. The agony lasted ten weeks. On the first of June he was in an upper chamber of his lodging when he heard the tramp of armed men under window. It was a column of Russians, marching west to meet Napoleon. He looked down on the column and then, some say, he stood on a chair in order to get a better view. A moment later the Prince of Neufchatel and Wagram, the magician who could have told you at any hour of the day or night where the Imperial divisions were located, and what part they were expected to play in a campaign, crashed to his death in the street below. Was it an accident or suicide? The question has never been satisfactorily answered but Berthier lay dead on the flagstones and when they brought the news to Napoleon he wept.

Five marshals were too old for hysterics. They had lived too long and seen too much to show surprise at the latest turn of events. The average age of Lefèbvre, Moncey, Kellerman of Valmy, stiff old Pérignon, and solid old Sérurier was now sixty-seven. Kellerman, senior among them, was eighty. Of this group only Pérignon, the ex-aristocrat, made any demonstration of loyalty to Louis. The others shrugged their shoulders and let events take their course.

Brune, now fifty-two, had never been an enthusiastic Royalist. He had been too intimate with giants like Danton and others who had turned Paris upside down in the wild days of '93 and '94. He did not need much persuasion to return to the man who had brought order out of the Revolution.

St. Cyr had never admired Napoleon. He had never admired or trusted anyone very much and when his troops mutinied at Orleans he sneered and slipped away to join the Royalists. The ex-actor had had a hard job getting to the top of the bill. Like his friend Victor he was not going to risk becoming involved in a resounding flop.

Bernadotte heard the news in his capital in far off Sweden and could do nothing to oppose the man he had betrayed. It was noticed, however, that he made no move at all to help the stunned victors, who had already spent eleven months double-crossing one another at the Conference of Vienna. Perhaps his reticence was due to the fact that his wife, Desirée, once courted by the man marching up from Lyons, was shopping in Paris at the time and he did not wish to compromise her. Some said Desirée was there to spy but anyone who knew the soap-boiler's daughter dismissed this as unlikely rubbish. When he arrived on March 19 Napoleon did not even place her under house arrest.

Jourdan, the old haberdasher-pedler, surprised everybody by deciding that this was one more fair he must attend. He damned the Bourbons and rejoined the Emperor. Murat occasioned no surprise by marching his Neapolitans against his new friends the Austrians on behalf of the man he had betrayed fifteen months before but the dashing innkeeper's son made a fatal miscalculation. He took it for granted that everybody in Naples liked him and badly wanted him to remain King. It never occurred to him that the average Neapolitan did not give a plate of spaghetti who ruled in Naples, or that one and all of the male population were horrified at the prospect of donning a uniform and marching to the sound of the guns. Manfully, and with all his legendary glitter, the Gascon King of Naples advanced against the foe on the line of the River Po. Many times in years gone by Murat had scattered Austrian battalions in this part of the world but those days were past and everyone but Murat was aware of it. He might be the most famous cavalryman in Europe but even he could not win a war single-handed. At the first discharge of musketry his entire army fled. The Italian attitude towards war may not be heroic but it is both sane and logical. To the average Italian an ounce of glory is not worth a pint of blood and nobody has ever been able to convince him that it is. Murat joined the stampede and escaped from Italy in disguise.

On March 20, only a few hours after Napoleon's triumphant arrival at the Tuileries, Davout arrived to offer his services and his appearance was a triumph for the excited Bonapartists. Not one man in all Paris could point to the Marshal Prince of Eckmuhl and Duke of Auerstadt and say: "There goes a renegade!" Davout had never made his bow to a Bourbon and never would, not if he was present at fifty restorations. He came in quietly and unemotionally and Napoleon flung out his arms and embraced the cold, unsmiling man. He was the one man in all that cheering mob who could never be bribed, threatened, cajoled, or bullied into switching his allegiance. Among a million timeservers and sycophants he stood quite alone.

Soult, as Minister of War in Paris, had timed his quarrel with the Bourbons very accurately. He was dismissed from his post a few days before Napoleon arrived. Suchet, the last marshal but one to surrender the previous year, returned to Napoleon at once, almost as though he had been waiting around for something like this to happen. Augereau lay low and supported nobody. Napoleon might have forgiven him his plain-speaking on the road to Elba the previous year but the old swashbuckler did not seek forgiveness. Coldly he ignored the entire upheaval and remained in retirement.

Of the twenty-five marshals three were dead, four had openly adhered to the Bourbons, seven more had gone into retreat; Masséna, pleading illness, was hurriedly transferring his money bags overseas, Murat was in flight, Bernadotte was no longer a Frenchman, and a handful had declared for Napoleon.

There remained one, the most famous marshal of all.

. . .

Michel Ney, Prince of the Moskowa, was playing cards at his country home when a courier arrived with orders from Soult, Minister of War, to go down to Besançon and take over the command of the Sixth Corps. Ney had no idea why he was ordered south and was puzzled. He had just returned home from one of his periodical sulks and all he wanted at that moment was to be left alone to brood on his real and imaginary wrongs. Sighing, he got up, ordered his carriage and went to Paris where his notary told him the stupendous news. Napoleon had escaped and was marching north, calling upon every Frenchman to support him.

Ney's uncertain temper could not withstand a shock like this and he exploded. They calmed him down and advised him to see Soult and demand an interview with the king. Soult told him that the king was ill and could not see him but Ney was not prepared to be snubbed by his old rival in Spain and bellowed that he insisted upon an interview at once. He got his way and stamped into the Presence, boasting that he, Michel Ney, would soon put a stop to this outrageous nonsense. He would not only march against Napoleon but bring the criminal to Paris in an iron cage! Louis was startled by the marshal's ravings. "An iron cage?" he remarked, the moment Ney had left. "What a canary!" The courtiers tittered and settled back with relief. If Ney was heading south in this mood they had little to fear from the Ogre.

Unfortunately for them, for Louis, and for Ney himself, the ranting mood did not last. Arrived at Besançon and hearing the news of Macdonald's failure at Lyons, Ney became doubtful of the loyalty of his own men. Along with these doubts came depression and mental confusion resulting in fits of irrational irritability and unreasoning outbursts, now directed against Napoleon, now against the feebleness of the Bourbons. Slowly it became clear to him that he alone stood between Napoleon and the bloodless reconquest of France. The awful responsibility of the crisis terrified him. Royalists looked to him to stay the advance of Napoleon, Bonaparte looked to him to open the road to Paris, the ordinary people wanted him to save France from civil war and from a second foreign invasion. Alone and without a single friend to turn to for comfort or advice, Ney's iron nerve began to crack. This was a far more testing challenge than that he had faced so magnificently in Russia. Ney was a man of action and his mind was as unsubtle as a child's.

When two guardsmen called on him at the Inn of the Golden Apple, in Lons-le-Saulnier, he read Napoleon's proclamation with emotion. "Nobody can write like that nowadays," he said sadly, "this is the way to move soldiers' hearts!" And to an anxious Royalist he added: "The king ought to come down here and inspire the men, even if he appeared on a stretcher!"

On March 13, less than a fortnight after Napoleon's landing, Ney was still writing of "this man's crazy enterprise," but shortly afterwards, aware that every soldier under his command was waiting for him to hoist the tricolor, he was grumbling: "Can I stop the movement of the sea with my hands?"

The next day he abandoned the attempt and read a proclamation to his assembled troops, declaring that France had accepted Napoleon back and concluding with the shout *"Vive l'Empereur!"* Most of his officers slipped away but the men threw their shakos in the air.

Five days later, at Auxerre, Napoleon received the marshal with friendship. When Ney began to make excuses for his curious conduct over the past year, the Emperor cut him short. "There's no need for excuses," he said, "I never doubted your true feelings!" He had doubted them and still did. He had no illusions at all about his former marshals. A superb judge of men he had learned almost all there was to know about human conduct during his abdication and exile and he understood those around him so well that there was no room in his heart for anger or contempt. He knew that they would only remain loyal so long as the army as a whole supported him and he accepted this as sobering, inescapable fact. He could read Ney's mind like the bold print of a proclamation.

Thus, protesting his unswerving loyalty, voicing his idiotic excuses, and damning his recent masters with oaths and insults that were as colorful as the curses of Augereau and the dead Lannes, Michel Ney was swept into the adventure he had called "a crazy enterprise." So explosive and unpredictable had he become that even his old friends began to avoid him. He realized as much and drifted away, wretchedly and despondently, more unsure of himself and his duty than at any time in his adventurous life.

Weeks passed before he was summoned to the Imperial headquarters and in those weeks he learned of the death of the other muddle-headed waverer, Berthier. Ney was more of a fighter than Berthier, however, and when Napoleon marched northeast towards Ligny, Quatre Bras, and Waterloo, he shook off his self-doubts and hurried up to the front. He had never understood politics and intrigues but he knew better than anyone in France how to storm enemy lines. For a while, a very little while, Michel Ney was himself again.

CHAPTER NINETEEN

"WE SHALL BE HANGED IF WE
LIVE THROUGH THIS!"

ON June 12 the Grand Army moved up the road to Charleroi towards
its nearest enemies, Blücher's Prussians and Wellington's mixed force of
British, Dutch, Belgians, and Hanoverians who were quartered in a
ninety-mile arc covering Brussels.

For many of the veterans it was a familiar stamping ground. Here-
abouts in the great days of '93 and '94, they had shown the world what
civilian volunteers could do against pressed men and caste-ridden officers.
It was full circle for those who had served in the immortal Sambre-et-
Meuse army, and the columns of the last Napoleonic army contained a
very large proportion of veteran soldiers. The former conscripts of Lutzen
and Leipsic were now battle-hardened soldiers and with them were men
from the British hulks, the Austrian fortresses, and the Russian prisoner-
of-war depots, men with old scores to settle and more confidence in themselves than any army that has ever marched to war. Four marshals accompanied them, four of the seven who had declared for Napoleon, and
of these four one had never gone into battle carrying a baton although
he had marched with the Grand Army for more than twenty years.

The new man was Emmanuel Grouchy, the aristocrat who had gone
over to the Revolutionaries when the mob was dragging cannon to the
gate of the Bastille and had since fought as a heavy cavalryman in every
Imperial theater of war. He was an honest, unimaginative soldier, with
the kind of face one would be more likely to find behind a counting-house
desk.

Grouchy brought the tally of Imperial marshals up to twenty-six but by the time he received the coveted baton the company was sadly thinned. Lannes, Bessières, and Poniatowski were already dead and Berthier was to die almost at once. Bernadotte was nearly a king and Murat, after trying for so long to stay royal, was a fugitive. Masséna, Augereau, Oudinot, and Macdonald were on their estates and so were most of the old Republicans. Jourdan was too old and too much of a failure to march and Brune was commanding in the south. Suchet was with the Army of the Alps and Davout, as the one man in France whom Napoleon could trust, had to remain behind and watch doubtful friends in Paris. The others, like Victor and Marmont, were enemies and the new marshal began the march with two colleagues, Soult and Mortier, neither in charge of corps. For Soult had been given the job of chief-of-staff and Mortier had to drop out almost at once when crippling sciatica prevented him from sitting a horse. A customer for his stable was at hand. Ney, still without a command, turned up in civilian dress and bought two of Mortier's chargers and when Napoleon saw him ride up he gave him First and Second Army Corps, a total of fifty thousand men.

So Grouchy rode on in the company of at least two famous men and as he approached the Lowland plain he must have remembered the days when he was twenty-eight and had just returned from the abortive and slightly absurd naval expedition to Ireland, where he had been tempted to throw the French Admiral over the side of his own flagship. It had been a long, hard road for the marquis, a road that had led to and fro across central Europe in the vanguard of the Grand Army and then down into hateful Spain, then back across the Russian plains and finally across Saxony to France and surrender to the Bourbons. Now it had all ended in a marshalate and Grouchy probably wondered if there was still time to win as much glory as Ney or Masséna or the heroic Lannes. If he could have read the future he might have resigned his command on the spot. There was no speck of glory ahead for Emmanuel Grouchy, only an undeserved reputation for being a hopeless bungler.

．　　．　　．

Napoleon's plan was bold and simple. Behind the British and Prussians were countless reserves, armies of the Russians and Austrians already on the move from distant bases. Behind Napoleon were a distracted France and very few reserves. His only hope was to shatter his nearest enemies and strike such terror into their hearts that a negotiated peace became possible. Already he was outnumbered. He had with him about one hundred and ten thousand men. Wellington and Blücher between them could muster half as many again. To defeat them he would have to attack each in detail and the fact that he was able to do so, and come very close to achieving a shattering double victory, is proof that both Wellington and his Prussian ally grossly underestimated the man's genius and the marching powers of his men.

On June 16, only four days after the campaign had opened, the French flung themselves on Blücher at Ligny and fought him to a standstill. The Prussians resisted desperately but they were driven from the field. Their leader, seventy-three years of age, was unhorsed in a cavalry charge and ridden over but he was rescued, badly bruised but otherwise unhurt. It took more than a tumble from a charging horse to daunt the man whose nickname was "General Vorwarts."

In the meantime, Ney had engaged the British at Quatre Bras, on the French left. The two battlefields were separated by about sixteen miles. Ney had probably been told to fight a holding action which accounts for the uncharacteristic hesitancy of his attack. The British held on, fed by a flow of reinforcements, and when the battle reached its climax Ney had to send for Count d'Erlon's reserve army of twenty thousand. D'Erlon (better known as the veteran General Drouet) was in great demand that day. Napoleon, edging the Prussians from the field at Ligny, sent an equally urgent order to him to march his corps across the flank of the retreating Prussians. He was on his way to achieve this when Ney's furious appeal reached him. D'Erlon obeyed his immediate superior and marched back, arriving too late to fire a single shot.

The consequences of Ney's counter-command were tragic for the French. At either battle d'Erlon's corps would have turned the scale. As it was the Prussians got off with a mauling and Wellington was able to withdraw to Waterloo and establish himself along the gentle slope of Mont St. Jean, athwart the Brussels road.

When it was clear to Ney what had caused d'Erlon's late appearance on the field the marshal flew into one of his crazy rages and cursed the Emperor for ruining his chances of smashing the British. Napoleon probably felt equally enraged at seeing the half-beaten Prussians escape but he retained Ney in his command. Who was there to replace him?

After a needless delay, for which no one but the Emperor was to blame, Grouchy was given thirty thousand men to follow the Prussians and accordingly headed away to the east. Careful reconnaissance might have established the fact that the battered old Prussian was withdrawing *northward* but Grouchy was a heavy cavalryman, more familiar with the battering-ram tactics of cuirassiers than the scouting duties of hussars. He disappeared in the direction of Gembloux, riding out of the smoke of battle and into the fog of historical controversy. Nobody has ever been quite sure what Emmanuel Grouchy did with the next forty-eight hours but in that wink of time the history of the nineteenth-century was resolved.

•   .   •

Only one Napoleonic marshal plays a dramatic role in the most famous battle of all time. Of the four marshals involved in this thunderbolt of a campaign Soult was inactive (and very incompetent) as chief-of-staff, a role he should never have been given, for he was not by any means ideal staff material, Mortier was prostrated by sciatica along the road to Paris and Grouchy marched his thirty thousand off the map. Only Ney, the hero of the Great Retreat, was to be remembered by French and British alike for his fanatical solo performance at Waterloo. It was a fitting curtain for the personal drama of a man who had been fighting almost nonstop for twenty-three years.

When Napoleon saw the British bivouac fires twinkling along the crest of Mont St. Jean he planned to deliver a sledgehammer blow that would carry him into Brussels by nightfall. Soult was not so sanguine. He had fought the British yard by yard across the length of Spain and had experienced on numerous occasions their devastatingly accurate small-arms fire. He urged a flanking movement. "Because Wellington has beaten you you think him a good general!" Napoleon remarked acidly, and Soult, who had acquired Masséna's armor against insulting words, respectfully held his tongue. What happened that day may have afforded the wily art-collector a gleam of satisfaction. Thus it was Ney who gave the order to attack and Ney who led his men into action. As usual he did it in person, as at Jena, Friedland, and Borodino.

At 1:00 P.M. on the eighteenth the artillery duel ceased and the hero of a hundred fights advanced against the British-held farmhouse of La Haye Sainte. After murderous hand-to-hand fighting the orchards were captured but not the buildings. On their right the British hung on to their other strongpoint, the Château of Hougomont. Attack succeeded attack, cavalry charge followed cavalry charge, until the shallow depression between the two armies was strewn with dead and wounded men, dead and maimed horses, and scattered equipment, and the earth was furrowed like carelessly ploughed fields by the ricocheting balls of opposing batteries. Still the British line held, although panic-stricken Nassau troops broke and poured back into Brussels with news of another Napoleonic triumph. Among those who heard their tale of woe was Marmont, waiting uneasily for news that would determine his next move.

Ney fought like a madman, always in advance of the shock battalions, ordering a third horse after two were shot under him, but untouched, miraculously so, by bullet, bayonet, or blade. Yet those who had seen him organizing the tiny rearguards on the road to Smolensk and Orcha and Kovno noticed a curious change in his bearing. During the long fighting retreat he had been calm, quiet, and restrained. When he did not speak it was in level and half-ironical tones, a grim jest to encourage the weak and drive despair from the dying. There were no jests or encouraging words from Ney at Waterloo. He cursed and swore and hacked at his enemies but he did not jest. He raved and ranted and exhorted but such encouragement as he gave his men lay in his example, not in his words. At Quatre Bras, two days earlier, he had been heard to growl: "If only an English bullet would kill me!" Now, on the slopes of Mont St. Jean, he seemed to many to be deliberately seeking death. Was it the result of a tortured conscience or the death wish a man might develop after a life dedicated to war?

By late afternoon the buildings of La Haye Sainte were in French hands and the garrison were bayoneted to a man. But beyond the farmhouse the British line still held and all hell was loose round the shattered gate at Hougomont. It was then that Ney committed the worst blunder of a campaign that bristles with tactical errors on both sides. He ordered up the heavy cavalry and taking his place at their head charged the unbroken British squares beyond the lip of the plateau.

Never again in a century that was to see the introduction of automatic firepower was anyone to witness a spectacle such as this. It was the final rally of old-style warfare and the death of a tradition that went all the way back to the charge of Hannibal's elephants against the Roman phalanx, or further still to the defence of Themopylae. After Waterloo the order: "Form square and prepare to receive cavalry!" was rarely given to infantry. The tradition died hard and was practised as late as Omdurman, but never again was it to be performed on this scale or to impress those who witnessed it as it impressed at Waterloo.

Cuirassiers, dragoons, chasseurs, lancers, hussars, gendarmes d'elite, swept forward at the trot and crossed the Valley of Death to the plateau and here the exhausted British infantry received the mass of horsemen in triple rows, kneeling, crouching, and standing upright and repulsing each attack by a rolling volley fire. Orderly squadrons melted away under this fusillade and the flower of the Grand Army's cavalry was converted into a milling mass of impotent horsemen, thrusting and slashing at the hedge of bayonets, tumbling down one upon the other or retiring to the valley to re-form and come on again and again and again, until each of the nine squares was ringed by a rampart of dead and dying. "It is too early for that!" said Napoleon, watching from the elevation of Belle-Alliance but he could do nothing to stop it and when he saw his splendid cavalry being ruined he sent in Kellerman's reserve in the vain hope that more squadrons would break through and push the squares from the field.

Ney was in the forefront of every attack and when he saw how things were going he sent a strident demand for reinforcements. The shadow of failure was already crossing Napoleon's face. "Reinforcements?" he murmured. "And where the devil does he imagine I can find them?" Yet still he left all the fighting to Ney. Sitting his horse in constant pain (he had been suffering from bleeding piles ever since landing in France) he watched the last squadrons of the Grand Army dash themselves to pieces on the shrunken squares and it was not until early evening that eleven battalions of the Guard moved forward in one last, heroic effort to drive the British from the plateau.

A long column of men was closing in on the French right and a German prisoner said it was the Prussian advance guard. "Rubbish!" said Napoleon. "It is Grouchy! At last!"

But it was not Grouchy. It was indeed the Prussians, keeping Blücher's promise to Wellington, and desperately needed battalions of the Young Guard had to be sent to hold them in check while the French made their supreme effort to win before darkness fell.

Ney the tireless, led the attack, this time on foot. By now five horses had died under him and an eye-witness describes him as he went forward up the slope, his face blackened with powder, an epaulette shot away, his uniform torn and smeared with mud. Someone raised the old cry:

"There goes *Le Rougeaud,*" and even the wounded got up and followed the Guard. The greatest showman on earth could not have designed a more impressive tableau for the final hour of the Napoleonic saga.

It closed as Ney knew it would close, in death, dispersal and utter disaster. Caught in the flank by artillery fire and mowed down by close-range musketry in front, the Guard melted away and when the stragglers, the exhausted cavalry and the infantry of the line saw bearskins falter a vast wave of panic engulfed the last Napoleonic army and it turned and fled down the road to Charleroi.

Yet one man did not panic. In the whole course of his life Michel Ney, Prince of the Moskowa, Duke of Elchingen, and barrel-cooper's son of Saar-Louis, had never turned his back on an enemy for longer than it took to rally stragglers and load a musket and he was not going to violate his code on his final field. With a sword snapped short by a British bayonet the cursing Alsatian barged his way into an unbroken square and retreated step by step, as from the barren wilderness outside Lisbon, as from the Cossacks of the Czar. "Come and see how a marshal of France can die!" he shouted as men streamed by; and, half to himself: "We shall be hanged if we live through this!"

When the square broke he found another group and when this dispersed, and darkness began to fall, he found a corporal. Together they climbed a bank, Ney waving his stump of a sword and screaming at the fugitives to rally and hold back the advance. Even in an extremity of terror there were a few French soldiers who retained their respect for the red-headed marshal. "Long live Ney!" they cried as they swept past. It was not an expression of irony but recognition of a superman.

The British came on, limbering up what remained of the artillery and raking the broken squares with grape. The Prussian hussars broke through on the flank and gave no quarter, sabering right and left as the mob of weaponless men surged down the road and across the trampled cornfields. Only when it was too dark to fight did Ney limp away, leaning on the shoulder of the stray corporal and in the chaos behind Belle-Alliance somebody found him a horse. He mounted and rode away slowly towards the Sambre, the last senior officer to leave the field.

CHAPTER TWENTY

"VIVE LE PLUS FORT!"

WHEN, at the head of the pursuit, a British officer entered the capital, he heard a man welcome him with a shout of *"Vive le plus fort."* Struck by this he went across and spoke to him. The man laughed and showed him a two-sided cockade. On one side was the tricolor, on the other the white emblem of the Bourbons. That Parisian typified the French outlook during the summer of Waterloo.

Nothing had ever happened slowly to Napoleon Bonaparte. He was world-famous at twenty-six, master of France at thirty, virtual Emperor of Europe at forty, a fugitive flying for his life at forty-five, and dead at fifty-one. The higher he rose the faster turned the wheel of fate. It never spun faster than in the days between June 15 and July 15, 1815; by the latter date he was a voluntary prisoner aboard the British warship *Bellerophon.* The week that followed Waterloo had been sufficient to tumble him from his throne for the second time.

Napoleon is sometimes quoted as an example of a man who refused to acknowledge defeat, but he recognized it easily enough now. Whatever chance there might have been of bluffing and glossing over the disaster that had overtaken him on the slopes of Mont St. Jean, was lost by Ney. For Ney, who had struggled into Paris three days ahead of the Prussian light cavalry, now tried his hand at politics again. In reply to Carnot's attempt at extenuation he shouted: "It is false! You are deceiving the Chamber! Wellington is advancing, Blücher has not been defeated, there is nothing left but the corps of Grouchy and the enemy will be at the gates of Paris in a week!"

There was no gainsaying the word of a man who had been the last to leave the field. Napoleon at once withdrew to Malmaison, the country

214

home of the rejected Josephine who had died before her husband's return, and a day or so later he was at Rochefort on the coast, turning over various extravagant projects for an escape to America. It is only fair to record that brother Joseph, who had been such a failure as a king, now made the gesture of a lifetime. He offered to change places with his brother and give Napoleon his passport. Rejecting this generous offer and another idea of escaping in a barrel, Napoleon saved his life by surrendering to the British. If Blücher had caught him the victors of World War II would have had their precedent for Nuremberg Trials. He would have been put on trial and shot.

Louis and his courtiers were already back in the Tuileries. They were somewhat short of breath but trying not to show it. To distract attention from their embarrassment they began a witch-hunt and the balm they most needed to soothe their smarting pride was the blood of Ney, the man who had promised them a Corsican canary in an iron cage.

Paris was in a turmoil. The politicians awoke from their Hundred-Day trance and asked one another what on earth could have possessed them to have accepted Napoleon a second time. In the wild scramble for personal reinsurance he was almost forgotten. The waverers crept out wearing the white cockade and the Royalists, once again reinstated by foreign bayonets, went about the task of eagle-spotting with the single-mindedness of men who have been made to look utterly ridiculous by an eagle.

Only one obstacle prevented them from arresting, banishing, or shooting every prominent man who had fought for Napoleon at Ligny, Quatre Bras, or Waterloo, but it was a formidable one. When the allies advanced up to the gates of Paris they came face to face with Davout and even the Bourbons would have found it difficult to put the Iron Marshal on trial, for he alone had never pledged allegiance to them. Davout held a strong hand. He sat in his office at the Ministry of War and played it with skill and patience. Either the allies undertook to grant a blanket amnesty to all who had taken part in the restoration of Napoleon or he, Louis Nicholas Davout, would march the army over the Loire and carry on the war indefinitely. They might take it or leave it, those were his terms. The allies chose another marshal to parley and Macdonald went in to treat with the stubborn man. Macdonald advised acceptance and terms were signed. Then, and only then, were the British and the Prussians allowed to march in, King Louis returning twenty-one days after Waterloo.

In Louis's train came the Bourbon marshals, Victor, Marmont, St. Cyr, and Pérignon. With rather more dignity Oudinot emerged from retirement and old Masséna, who had gone to a great deal of unnecessary trouble transferring capital abroad, appeared in Paris and vetoed a feeble attempt to establish a Regency in favor of Napoleon's infant son, now under close guard in Vienna.

St. Cyr took over from Davout as Minister of War but it was left to ex-sergeant Victor, the garrulous Republican of the Bastille days, to lead the witch-hunt and list his old friends as traitors. Victor had not made a great show as an independent commander in the field but he excelled himself as a police agent and was ably seconded by his friend Marmont, Duke of Ragusa, whose name became synonymous with the practice of betrayal. Just as in World War II, the name of the Norwegian creature Quisling came to have a special meaning in Hitler's Europe, so did the word "Ragusa" win similar odium among the men who had ridden with Marmont down the years from 1793 to 1814.

St. Cyr, still an individualist but as anti-Bonaparte as either of them, was more generous to his enemies. When Ney was finally persuaded to flee (he had been mooching about Paris unaware of his danger) it was St. Cyr who signed his passport and advised him to make himself scarce. Davout added his signature and Ney disappeared, hiding in the house of an old friend on the edge of Cantal, near Aurillac. Here, for a time, he was safe and his loyal wife Aglaé kept in close touch with him pending a proposed flight to Switzerland.

Soult had slipped away and headed for Albi, in the valley of the Tarn, where there were plenty of old friends to protect him. During the panic that followed Waterloo Soult had behaved admirably, not only doing everything in his power to rally the fugitives but achieving singular distinction by locating the missing Grouchy. His luck held. He got down into his own country and was warned just in time that his name was on the proscribed list and that if caught he was liable to be shot. The warning came from a sporting British officer (all the Peninsular veterans had a warm respect for their opponents of the Pyrenees) and Soult enlisted the aid of a friend who owned a post chaise and made a dash for the territory of Berg. He got away and spent the next four years in exile.

The summer wore on and it proved a dismal season for the Imperial marshals. On August 1 Brune was caught and killed. On August 2 Ney was recognized and arrested. In October Murat reappeared in the south and was promptly stood against a wall and shot. Two months later Ney was dead, the victim of a ruthless persecution by men who were unfit to polish his boots.

. . .

Perhaps Brune's fate was the cruellest of all. He died under the feet of a hysterical mob in Avignon and the manner of his death was as vile as the accusation that prompted it. For the mob that tore the friend of Danton from his carriage and lynched him were under the impression that Brune had been one of the instigators of the murder of the Princesse de Lambelle during the Terror, twenty-three years before. The princesse had been a victim of the horrible September Massacres and her head had been paraded on a pike under the windows of the queen. This was a libel on the name of Brune, who had admittedly served as military escort to Terrorists in '92 but had done everything in his power to save the victims of their purges. He had never been a Terrorist in the proper sense of the word but a bloodthirsty mob did not stop to sift evidence. Brune was practically torn to pieces and his mutilated body was flung into the river Rhone. He is said to have muttered, as he died, "Good God! To survive a hundred fields and die like this . . ."

Ney was exceptionally unlucky to fall into the Bourbon net. Learning that his refuge was to be surrounded by gendarmes a local man who admired the marshal grabbed a horse and dashed off to warn him, but the gallant fellow suffered a heavy fall during the night ride across country and lay unconscious until morning.

Ney received the police agents calmly. The gendarmes had orders to convey him to Paris in manacles but Ney gave his parole and the handcuffs were thrown aside. A friendly gendarme offered to connive at his escape but Ney refused the offer. "If I were free I would have you shot for suggesting such a thing!" he said quietly, "I have given my parole!" Nearer Paris the cavalryman Exelmans made the same proposition but again Ney refused. He had given his word of honor and there the matter ended. On arrival in the capital he was lodged in the *Conciergerie,* the prison that had had the worst reputation during the Terror. Here had come Charlotte Corday, the girl who stabbed Marat, and Marie Antoinette to be lodged in an airless cell and many another distinguished prisoner. It had been many years, however, since the *Conciergerie* had received an inmate as famous as Ney. The Bourbons ordered a court-martial and Louis, who was not a vindictive man, wrung his hands when he learned that Ney had bungled his escape.

"Why did he let himself be caught? We gave him every chance to get away!" he wailed.

Frenchmen who had been observing Ney's conduct over the last few weeks concluded that the marshal would now allow himself to be condemned without submitting a defense but they were wrong. The mere suggestion that he had tarnished his honor put him on his mettle and he at once challenged his enemies' right to try him by court-martial and demanded to be tried by his peers. Davout, desperately anxious to save him and furious at this flagrant violation of the armistice, did everything in his power to get Ney's decision reversed and St. Cyr convened a special Court with no fewer than four of Ney's fellow marshals as judges. The men selected were Moncey, named as chairman, Augereau, Masséna, and Mortier.

It is very curious that Mortier was included. Ney had ridden to Waterloo on horses purchased from Mortier and had the farmer's son not been laid up with sciatica he would have been standing alongside the prisoner in the dock. From the first, however, there was a natural reluctance among the veterans to judge the man whose exploits in Russia were already legendary. Mortier said he would sooner be cashiered, Masséna pleaded a personal quarrel with Ney, and Augereau took to his bed. Moncey's course was more honorable. He wrote to the king, categorically refusing to sit in judgment over a man he revered and his letter is one of the most moving documents in the history of the period. "Where were those who accuse Ney while he was on the field of battle?" he asked. "At the Beresina it was Ney who saved the remnants of the army. I myself had relatives, friends, soldiers there who loved their leaders and it is I who am called upon to condemn to death a man to whom so many Frenchmen owe their lives, so many families their sons, husbands, fathers! No Sire . . . if I am not to be allowed to save either my country or my own life, I will at any rate save my honor!" Moncey concluded: "Forgive Sire, the frankness of an old soldier, who has always avoided intrigue and has only concerned himself with his profession and his country."

This letter enraged the courtiers and after being dismissed from the army the gallant old fellow was hustled into the Castle of Ham and sentenced to three months' imprisonment. It is fortunate, perhaps, that his family had given up trying to make Moncey a lawyer all those years ago. He was obviously unsuited to the legal profession. His place was taken by Jourdan, who had also deserted the Bourbons for Napoleon the previous March. These little adjustments having been made the trial got under way.

While these sensational events were happening in Paris an episode of minor importance took place in far away Calabria, in the toe of Italy. Joachim Murat, innkeeper's son, ex-King of Naples, and the most celebrated cavalryman in the world, was making his last ripple in the sea of Italian politics.

Murat had been greatly impressed by the theatricality of Napoleon's landing from Elba and by his splendid gesture in approaching within lunging range of the men sent to arrest him and opening his coat to reveal the Legion of Honor. It was the kind of gesture that made an immediate appeal to Murat. He had been doing things like that ever since he was a boy at his father's posting station in Cahors. Since the failure of his bid to regain the throne of Naples in May he had been skulking in Corsica and elsewhere, but now, so bad was his sense of timing of everything but a cavalry charge, he judged it the moment to make an exactly similar appeal and be swept back to Naples on the tide of popular approval.

Unfortunately for his chances of success he not only misjudged the timing but two other factors—the Neapolitan character and his own popularity. He got ashore with a handful of followers, was arrested, taken to the castle yard at Pizzo, and shot.

It all happened as quickly as one of Murat's charges but the Gascon died as bravely as any man. All his life had been a posture and he postured to the very end. When they offered him a bandage for his eyes he rejected it in the best tradition of firing-party conduct. Then he said: "Spare the face, straight to the heart!" It was the final flicker of the fire by which he had warmed himself for forty-eight years.

Caroline, the scheming, sensuous woman to whom Murat owed so many of his failures, soon found another husband and shrugged off the memory of the gallant ass who had sent hussars galloping to her school to guard her during the touch-and-go hours of the Great Coup in 1799, but France did not forget him so readily. Silly, untrustworthy, and vain as a peacock, he was also the most dashing horseman a nation of soldiers has ever produced. When we think of him now it is not as a bombastic, overdressed egoist, strutting among his yes-men at Naples but as a gay young hussar with bulging thigh muscles, dashing across the snow at the head of eighty squadrons of cavalry and waving a gold wand instead of a saber.

.   .   .

On November 9 the legal farce designed to eliminate the bravest man in France commenced in the Palais de Justice. Ney faced a remarkable assembly of judges. In the chair was Jourdan, under whom he had fought at Fleurus. Beside Jourdan was the embarrassed Mortier, who had eventually allowed himself to sit rather than follow Moncey's example and be cashiered. We are not told whether Mortier was still suffering from twinges of his sciatica but his conscience must have been giving him considerable discomfort. Beside Mortier was Masséna, who had allowed Napoleon to march on Paris unchecked, and the quartet of marshals was made up by Augereau, who had been talked out of bed and was feeling just as shamefaced as Mortier. The verdict lay with these four old comrades and three other high-ranking soldiers.

Davout, who went on insisting that Ney's future would be far safer in the hands of a court-martial than a court of peers, protested that no one could condemn such a man. "Not even Ragusa!" he added optimistically, and at first it looked as if Davout was right, for the attitude of the judges towards their prisoner was most respectful. Ney stuck to his claim that the court was not competent to try him and after a good deal of legal wrangling the judges agreed with him, "We were cowards," said Augereau, afterwards. "We ought to have insisted upon our right in order to save him from himself!" By five votes to two the judges decided that Ney's claim should be upheld and the sitting closed. Jourdan, Mortier, Augereau, and Masséna gasped with relief.

The government was furious at this check but preparations were immediately made for a new trial. Aglaé Ney spent the interval in fruitless appeals to people in high places. Among those she called upon was Wellington, who was a party to Davout's protective clause in the capitulation treaty, but the victor of Waterloo did not possess the kind of courage needed to face this kind of crisis. He told Aglaé that Britain could not intervene in the affairs of France. From a man who had spent the last seven years hammering French armies, and had twice played a major role in deposing Napoleon and reinstating the Bourbons, this is a somewhat lame excuse. Aglaé, desperate by now, turned to the Duc de Berry but she found even less sympathy here and was told that the King's throne was unsafe "so long as one of those soldiers was left alive!" She moved on to the Czar, whom she approached through Jomini, the Swiss soldier with whom Ney had associated when the Grand Army was training to invade England, but the Czar returned the same answer as Wellington. So it went on, appeals, excuses, more appeals, more excuses, an orgy of handwashing by every Pilate who might have saved the life of France's bravest soldier. The Bourbons (with the exception of Louis himself) grew impatient at the delay and events were hustled forward to the new trial on December 4.

The verdict was a foregone conclusion but even so there were times when the prosecution was in difficulties. The principal accusation lay in a charge that Ney had not merely gone over to Napoleon at Lons-le-Saunier, but had done so in pursuance of a pre-arranged plan made while Napoleon was still in Elba. This, of course, was nonsense. Ney claimed that he had abandoned the Bourbons only after it was clear that his troops would not fight for them, and that he was protected by Davout's amnesty clause. At the trial he conducted himself with great dignity. When General Bourmont, who had been with Ney when the proclamation in favor of Napoleon had been read to the troops, said that the only way he could have stopped the marshal would have been to kill him, the prisoner exclaimed: "You would have done me a great service! Perhaps it was your duty!"

Sympathy was now building up for Ney all over France and the prosecutors had to work fast. Their masterstroke was to rule out of order the clause regarding the amnesty. After that, employing one legal trick and another, they made headway, the kind of headway a steamroller makes when it rolls forward crushing everything in its path.

By the early hours of December 7 the second trial was over and the peers retired to record their votes. By one hundred and seven votes to forty-seven Ney was found guilty of receiving Napoleon's emissaries at Lons-le-Saunier; by unanimous vote (with one abstention) guilty of reading the proclamation to his troops, inciting them to mutiny and himself re-enlisting under Napoleon. One hundred and nine voted for death, seventeen for deportation, and five abstained. Among those who voted for the death penalty were Marmont, Victor, Kellerman, Pérignon, and Sérurier, five men who had fought beside Ney since the campaign of Italy.

Two other names stand out among the one hundred and nine moral cowards who voted for Ney's death. They are Generals Dupont and Maison. Dupont was the man who surrendered when his army was surrounded by Spaniards in 1808 and by his incompetence and cowardice set the Peninsula aflame. Maison was one of the few men who had marched through the snow with the rearguard from Smolensk to Kovno and on at least one occasion during the retreat Michel Ney had saved his life.

The prisoner was taken back to the Luxembourg and seen by his devoted wife and four children. Aglaé had exhausted herself traveling from place to place seeking a reprieve but even now she had not abandoned hope. Ney knew there was no hope and was as calm and relaxed as when they roused him from beside a bivouac fire in Russia and told him that it was time to march.

On the morning of December 7, in a thin, miserable drizzle, they drove him to a spot near the Observatory in the Luxembourg Gardens, the place where today his statue stands in the Carrefour de l'Observatoire. Twelve veterans were waiting under the command of a Piedmontese captain. The captain showed the condemned man where to stand and Ney walked over, turning and taking off his hat. The command was given and one soldier aimed deliberately at the top of the wall but eleven other balls found their mark and the marshal fell dead. His body was taken to the *Hospice de la Maternité* and the curious came to look at it, among them a group of Englishmen. A Frenchman, observing them, said quietly: "You did not look at him so calmly at Waterloo!"

CHAPTER TWENTY-ONE

TO VALHALLA

OF the twenty-six paladins seven were now dead and all seven had died
by violence. Lannes and Bessières, dyer's apprentice and barber, had died
in action and so had Poniatowski, son of a prince. Berthier had fallen,
or had thrown himself from a high window, and Brune had been lynched.
Murat and Ney had died facing firing squads. Now, after many wounds
and half a lifetime of war and rough living, ill-health began to steal down
upon some of the company, for all were physically exhausted and some
were old in years. Everyone of them had scars to show and in winter,
with the frosts and rains, the wounds of Rivoli and the Pyramids chafed
and ached and the rheumatism accumulated in their bones throughout
years of campaigning slowed them down. The wars were over, really over.
Not for more than half a century was Europe to see the movement of
armies on the scale seen in the last two decades. There were to be scuffles
and bickerings enough but they were trival affairs and men who had taken
part in the sweeping advance upon Ulm, or the long trek to Moscow,
could hardly regard them as wars. The surviving nineteen marshals settled
back to enjoy hard-won comfort and ease. From now on their wars were
fought on paper or round the fireside when old comrades came in for
a chat and a glass of wine.

Victor, Oudinot, Marmont, and Macdonald were high in favor with
the Bourbons. Davout was still hated by them but this did not cost him
an hour's repose. St. Cyr became Minister of War and refused Davout's
generous offer to stand trial for a group of proscribed officers. Macdonald occupied himself warning prospective victims and giving them
ample time to slip away and lie low until Bourbon passions cooled. Victor
pursued a different course. He caught and handed over every Bonapartist

he could hunt down. St. Cyr continued to take the individualistic line. If he disagreed with anyone, Bourbon or Bonapartist, he said so in clipped, icy tones and slammed the door on them. No one ever emerged victor from a verbal duel with St. Cyr but nobody ever grew to like him.

Exactly a year after the débâcle at Waterloo the marshalate lost its first member through natural causes. Augereau, swashbuckling hero of so many adventures, died quietly in bed at the age of fifty-nine. Considering his record it was a ripe old age. He had forgotten how many times he had missed death by inches. He had been present at more engagements than any of them, battles that went right back into pre-Revolution days when he was a soldier-of-fortune with the Russians and was paid to kill Turks. He died at his château, a rich man, and was buried, like most of the marshals, in the famous cemetery of Pére Lachaise, where Ney lay in an unmarked grave.

Time's next victim was a very old friend of Augereau and a like spirit. In early April, 1817, Masséna relinquished his grasp upon his cash boxes and went looting elsewhere. His claim that he had been unfit to lead the army down into Portugal seven years before had not been so frivolous. He was an old, old man at sixty-one. Before he died he had the dubious pleasure of meeting his great rival Wellington in Paris and the two master strategists exchanged reminiscences about the days when they had faced one another over the redoubts of Torres Vedras. "You turned every hair in my head white!" said the stooping Prince of Essling. "We were pretty even!" said Wellington magnanimously.

Eleven months later public attention was drawn to another marshal. Bernadotte ascended the throne of Sweden. He had been a popular crown prince and was to make an excellent king. The Swedish soldiers who had broadcast his charms so diligently after their capture at Lübeck in 1806, had no reason to regret their choice. One of Bernadotte's more generous actions after the wars had been to offer Ney's oldest son a commission in his army, but the former Marshal-Prince of Ponte Corvo never returned to his native land and his wife, Desirée, had to console herself with Swedish shops and Swedish gossip.

That same year, in December, 1818, the sixty-four-year-old Pérignon died and was buried at Père Lachaise. So was Sérurier, who died a year later, aged seventy-seven. The records of these two men went back to the days when French soldiers marched into battle wearing powdered hair queues. Both had witnessed scores of riots, a Revolution, and two Restorations, but the national convulsions had done little to alter their characters. They began and ended as stiff, pedantic warriors of the dead century. France would have remembered them more affectionately had they acted like the other old trooper, Moncey, when asked to condemn a comrade to death.

After Sérurier's death the Bourbons called off the witch-hunt and a general amnesty was announced. Tough and embittered Bonapartists began to drift back into France, where they found they were at last able to discuss the great days in tones above a whisper. Unpredictable St. Cyr put in a word for Soult and the man who had once dreamed of being a village baker, and later a King of Northern Lusitania, came back without apologies to breathe his native air once more. Luck had already played a great part in the life of Nicholas Soult but it still had benefits to bestow. As the years rolled away Soult was destined to become the most famous veteran of all.

In September the oldest marshal answered the recall. Kellerman of Valmy, aged eighty-five, died two days before his old comrade Lefèbvre. It was getting on for thirty years since Kellerman had confounded every military expert in Europe by standing still when the Prussian army advanced on Valmy mill and watching it turn about and expose the Continent to another twenty years of war. The marshal was set in his ways when the mob had advanced to the Bastille but he was still young enough to embrace the new order and to build himself into one of the legendary figures of the Revolution. In his old age he became just as ardent a Royalist, sufficiently so to join Pérignon and Sérurier in helping to send Ney to his death. All three had found no difficulty in eliminating the words "fraternity" and "equality" from the Republican battle cry. The same cannot be said of Lefèbvre, who, with his lovable charlady duchess, devoted his old age to caring for old soldiers. Thirty years had elapsed since Lefèbvre had marched beside a fugitive king and queen, and held off the rabble during the return from Varennes but to the end of his days the old sergeant major stood firm for fair play and decent behavior.

Reaction was setting in all round and one of the signs that old hatreds were disappearing was Ney's rehabilitation in the hearts and minds of Frenchmen. Before he had been in his grave five years accounts of the disastrous Russian campaign began to appear in print and Ney, as they would say today, "stole the notices." He emerged as a hero and like all heroes he engendered a legend, the legend that attaches itself to all giant killers and mystic knights. By 1819 people were saying that Michel Ney was not dead, that his execution had been an elaborate farce, and that he was now living in America. In that year a man calling himself Peter Stuart Ney appeared in North Carolina, a silent, badly scarred man who taught in a village school but was known to be an expert swordsman, horseman, and shot. For more than twenty years this enigmatic figure teased the imagination of his neighbours and, when he died in 1846, everyone declared that he had admitted to being Marshal Ney. Doubts regarding his true identity persist down to this day but investigations proved that, whoever Peter Stuart Ney was, he was not the Prince of the Moskowa. That Ney died under the wall of the Luxembourg in December, 1815, there is not the faintest possible doubt.

Among those who deeply regretted his shameful death was the Duchess of Angoulême, the sole survivor of the pitiful family who were imprisoned in the Temple during the Terror. Her father, mother, and brother had died during the Revolution and she was understandably frigid towards Bonapartists. When they gave her a copy of Ségur's account of the Russian campaign and she read of Ney's example to the rearguard, she put down the book with tears in her eyes. "If only we had known!" she exclaimed.

*   *   *

In May, 1821, couriers galloped into every capital in Europe with the news from St. Helena. The man of the island, whom some called the Usurper, some General Bonaparte, and others the Emperor, had died after six years of captivity. Details of his last hours were eagerly sought after by enemies and friends throughout the length and breadth of France. Soon it was learned that in his final moments Napoleon's thoughts had returned to his trade and that his last words were *"tête d'armée."* Someone else told of a few words overheard at his bedside during a delirium and those words included the names of dead comrades—Lannes, Bessières, Murat, Berthier, and Ney among others. His spirit, it would seem, was already inhabiting the only kind of paradise Napoleon was capable of imagining, a kind of Valhalla where the ghosts of dead warriors fought their battles over again. The surviving marshals, Soult among them, must have chuckled when they learned that British soldiers, in relays of twelve, had carried the Emperor's corpse to the grave and had fired volleys over the coffin. Napoleon had devoted the greater part of his life to the hopeless task of overthrowing the British and here they were acting as his pallbearers.

Two years later, in 1823, the Iron Marshal followed the man he had served faithfully and well for so many years. Davout's contempt for the Bourbons and his loyalty for Napoleon persisted to the very end. He returned to France under the amnesty but he did not unbend. He held onto his old hatreds and his old loyalties as tenaciously as he had held his positions at Auerstadt. Nobody loved Davout but every man who had served in the Imperial armies respected him and he too was laid to rest at Père Lachaise.

Three years later, in 1826, Suchet died. He was sixty-two and had played a modest part in public life since the Hundred Days. The polite, unobstrusive man who had made such a success of his missions in Spain was the only marshal to leave the Peninsula with a Spanish title. He was a long way from being the most spectacular of the band but he shared with Davout the distinction of being the most efficient, both as a soldier and an administrator.

But now France grew restless again and in 1830 a new revolution broke out in Paris and Charles X, successor to Louis, was swept away to make way for the Citizen King, Louis-Philippe, of the Orléans branch. Paving-stones were up again and after a lull of forty-one years Parisians rushed to the familiar barricades. There, to try conclusions with them, was Ragusa, or Marmont as some preferred to call him, for Marmont was now Governor of Paris and was expected to disperse the mob and save the government. His counterrevolution was a failure. Too many years had passed since the gunner-cadet had come to grips with this kind of situation and there was no Bonaparte to plant the cannon, and no Murat to fetch them. The popular movement swept Charles, the Court, and then Marmont out of Paris, and old Soult was summoned to the Ministry of War by the new King. It was in this same eventful year of 1830 that St. Cyr died at Hyeres.

Soult came gladly, sixty-one years of age but delighted to stand in the limelight again. Soult must have hugged himself all the way to the capital for now the tables were turned at last and it was Marmont who was flying for his life in a borrowed carriage.

The man who had toppled the Napoleonic dynasty and voted for the death of a fellow marshal began a strange, Orestes-like pilgrimage that was to continue for the remainder of his life. Never again could he return to France, where he was hated by everyone. From now on he drifted to and fro across the scenes of his youth in a kind of nostalgic trance and few men could have endured a lonelier old age. London, Vienna, Rome, Venice, he visited them all and found no peace anywhere. In Vienna, however, on the New Year's Day following his flight from France, he was given a pleasing assignment. The Hapsburgs persuaded him to "educate" the twenty-year-old Duke of Reichstadt, once King of Rome, and the most famous baby in the world when one hundred cannon shots had saluted his birth as Napoleon's heir in 1811.

Marmont's instructions were to point out to the youth how wicked his father had been and how mischievously he had turned the world upside down. The boy had been a prisoner at his grandfather's court ever since his mother had taken him there, after the first abdication. He was a somber, intelligent child and grew into a pensive and frustrated young man.

The first meeting between Napoleon's only legitimate child and Napoleon's oldest friend was a disappointment. "He is suspicious but will get friendly," commented Marmont optimistically. The marshal persevered and there were many interviews spread over three months. Marmont described all Napoleon's campaigns in detail and the youth listened patiently. He must have thought it odd to find himself lectured by the man who had destroyed whatever chance he ever had of becoming Emperor of the French. After a time, however, Marmont's charm won him over and the Duke presented the marshal with his portrait.

When the lessons were finished Marmont packed up and left, drifting down to Italy and crossing all the old battlefields. Nearly forty years had passed since Marmont, full of youthful enthusiasm for the young Napoleon, had written: "What promise he holds out for us all!" He visited Lodi and Castiglione and Arcola, where General Bonaparte had led the attack across the bridge. He was constantly finding bivouacs he remembered and looking over his shoulder for his lost youth. He was much given to this kind of thing. A few years previous to his Italian tour he had paid his first visit to Russia to attend the coronation of the new czar and on that occasion had traveled out to inspect the field of Borodino. He found the spot where Ney and Murat had stormed the Great Redoubt at such a terrible cost and the place where Bessières had warned Napoleon not to risk his last reserve.

This same year old Moncey, now nearly eighty, made a quiet re-entry into public life, succeeding Jourdan as Governor of the Invalides. Jourdan died at the age of seventy-three, almost the last link with the invincible sansculottes of '93 and '94. Jourdan could recall battles even before that, muddled, sniping affairs, played out in the woods and creeks three thousand miles away when he had gone with Major Berthier to help the American colonists trounce King George's redcoats. All things considered he had ridden out the storms fairly well and one wonders if, in his age, he ever regretted having turned his back on the haberdashery trade.

There were not many of them left now. Marmont was a lonely outcast and Bernadotte was seated on a throne. The other seven, Moncey, Macdonald, Mortier, Oudinot, Soult, Victor, and Grouchy, were honored among Frenchmen and beginning to be so among their former enemies, notably the British, who are famous for overpraising vanquished foes. Nine out of twenty-six were still alive but soon this total was reduced to eight and by a means familiar to battle-hardened men. In the summer of 1835 sixty-seven-year-old Edouard Mortier was struck down, not by illness or the drag of old wounds, but by an assassin's bomb thrown at the King.

Of all the marshals easy-going Mortier had made the least enemies. The British Peninsular veterans had always thought of him as a gentleman and somehow, either by luck or by sheer amiability, he had managed to avoid incurring the odium of any sect or faction. Assassination by bomb was just becoming popular among terrorist troups and Fieschi's bad aim deprived France of a man whom the veterans of Spain and Russia remembered with affection. A bomb had almost killed Mortier when it crashed through his headquarters at Smolensk but this one had not even been intended for him. Soult was very upset by the incident and so was Bernadotte, in far-off Sweden.

Two impressive ceremonies enlivened the life of Soult in 1838 and 1840. One was a coronation and the other a funeral procession. In June, 1838, on a lovely, cloudless day, the nineteen-year-old Victoria rode to her coronation between cheering rows of Cockneys. Notabilities from all over the civilized world were in the procession. There were kings, queens, princes, and ambassadors by the coachload and every foreign power was represented. Storms of applause greeted the hook-nosed Iron Duke, the most celebrated soldier in the world, but there were plenty left for his old opponent, Nicholas Soult, representing his sovereign, Louis-Philippe.

The old veteran had decked himself out in all his orders and stars and decorations and London gave him a wonderful welcome. Thirty-eight years before he had sat in his pavilion on the cliffs at Boulogne and dreamed of capturing London. Now, after half a lifetime, he had at last succeeded in doing so but without bayonets and siege artillery. It was one of the happiest days of his life.

In December two years later he experienced a vastly different but equally satisfying emotion. Shortly before Christmas, in a flurry of snow, the Emperor came home to his splendid tomb of red granite in the Invalides, granite hewn from the quarries of Russians who had almost destroyed him in 1812. Bitterness had distilled itself into tolerance between the traditional enemies of France and Britain. Nearly twenty years after the Emperor had been laid in his tomb on St. Helena, and the British Governor had sternly forbidden any inscription other than his name to be engraved on the coffin, the islanders yielded up his remains to be honored by a nation he had led to victory on fifty battlefields. It was an impressive ceremony and despite bitter weather every Bonapartist in Paris attended. Four marshals were present, Soult, Moncey, Oudinot, and Grouchy, their average age seventy-six. Victor, showing more sense of fitness than usual, declined to attend.

It would be interesting to know the thoughts of these four men as the coffin of Napoleon was drawn through the snow to the Invalides. Did Moncey recall the occasion when he had joined Ney and Lefèbvre and marched into Napoleon's study at Fontainebleau to demand his abdication? Did Soult recall his bitter disappointment at not being made Duke of Austerlitz? Did Oudinot think of the moment when this man had presented him with his baton among the dead and dying at Wagram, or Grouchy of his part in the disaster of Waterloo? Perhaps not. They were all getting old and feeble and could regard triumphs and disasters with equal detachment.

Macdonald, son of the clansman, had died that year and went to his grave honored by all as a man who had done his duty and gone out of his way to heal the country's wounds. If he was admitted to Valhalla he must have been welcomed by his father, follower of Bonnie Prince Charlie, for by his life and service Macdonald Junior had forged another link in the long chain of friendship between France and Scotland that went back to the days when the Scots rode over the border the moment the English king disembarked his knights and archers on the Continent. Nobody thought of playing the bagpipes at Macdonald's funeral but it is to be hoped there was a pipe on the far side of the ferry.

Victor, ex-Republican sergeant, fervent Royalist and Chief Witch-hunter of Bonapartists, died the following year. Perhaps somebody mourned him but if they did it does not seem to be recorded anywhere.

Moncey died the following year, the final link with the victories of the civilian armies of the Republic. Moncey's gallant behavior in the matter of judging Marshal Ney had not cost him so much after all, for now Ney was a hero and Frenchmen remembered with pride Moncey's nobility at the time of the trial. In 1815 he had written "Excuse the frankness of an old soldier," but he was a great deal older now, getting on for ninety. He left behind no great reputation as a soldier but his honor, on which he set so great a store, was intact.

Two years later, in March, 1844, Bernadotte died in Sweden, the only paladin of Napoleon who had managed to die a king. All of them had dreamed of thrones, and two of them had actually sat on one, but alone among the twenty-six the tall, handsome Gascon had succeeded in founding an hereditary line of princes. In his time Bernadotte had been a hypocrite, a trimmer, and a traitor, but to some extent he had atoned by proving a moderate and accomplished sovereign, a better king in every way than his fellow Gascon Murat and, if judged by permanent results, a far better one than Napoleon Bonaparte.

Three years later, in 1847, when the new century was almost half-way through, Grenadier Oudinot died in his eighty-second year. Bullets were still traveling around his scarred old body. He could have peeled off his shirt and pointed to thirty-four scars, the results of musket balls, lance points, grapeshot, bayonet thrusts and saber strokes. Yet not one of these wounds had incapacitated him for long. His hide was tougher even than Lannes' and the standards he set himself were always as honorable as Moncey's and as inflexible as Davout's. The men he led had loved him as they had loved Ney and Lannes because he was their type of commander but he carried into his public life a steadiness of vision that neither Ney nor Lannes possessed.

Grouchy died the same year, having spent a vast amount of his time over the last thirty-two years explaining where he was on June 18, 1815. Facts were, indeed, beginning to emerge that went far to excuse his non-appearance at Waterloo and his failure to keep track of Blücher but history has dealt mercilessly with Grouchy. There is such a thing as a "lucky" general. Wellington was one and so was Cromwell. In our own day Montgomery was one and men will always follow a leader with this reputation.

Emmanuel Grouchy was unlucky and has had to bear the consequences down to this day.

Only two survived, Soult and Marmont, one the most honored veteran in France, the other a wanderer living in the past.

Soult, now rising eighty, had enjoyed a splendid old age. Unlike brother Joseph, sometime King of Spain, he had managed to retain the better part of his Spanish loot. When King Joseph's carriage was rifled after Vittoria a total of one hundred and sixty-five Spanish pictures were found. They had been lifted from their frames and cut from their stretchers. Wellington had them stored, pending their return to King Ferdinand, but the Spanish king made the duke a present of this magnificent collection. In 1814 he wrote: "Touched by your delicacy His Majesty does not wish to deprive you of what has come into your possession by means as just as they are honorable." The duke agreed and kept the collection and they can still be seen in Apsley House, with other spoils of the battle. Soult had fewer scruples than Wellington. His country home was crammed with souvenirs of his long stay in Andalusia. The only prize he seems to have lost during the long retreat was the pretty Spanish señorita, one of the two sisters he shared with Victor.

Soult was attached to the area where he had spent his boyhood and had no wish to lie beside the other marshals in a crowded Paris cemetery. He prepared his tomb in his native village and in November, 1851, he took possession of it, mourned by every old soldier in France and by many beyond its borders. Among the twenty-four marshals who had gone before, Masséna would be the first to welcome him. Although they had not been the best of friends in life, they were, in most respects, as alike as two peas. In all the Grand Army there was not one man who could hold a candle to either of them as carefully discriminate looters or as masters of defensive warfare. Yet in one respect Soult was Masséna's superior. He had lived over forty years to enjoy his loot and in the process had gathered not only the financial interest but also universal admiration! It was a good thing he had thought twice about the bakery trade. His kind of career cannot be built with flour.

One marshal remained, Auguste Frédéric Marmont, Duke of Ragusa, and even now he was not invited back to France. Still alone, still looking for his lost youth, Marmont wandered back to Italy, the drums of '96 beating a rhythm in his brain, the faces of dead friends appearing on battlefields of which he had written: "It is a splendid thing we are doing . . . !"

Down here, in the sunlit valleys under the Alps, the last of the splendid young men who had conquered Europe remembered so many things that must have seemed as far away as the Golden Age. He remembered Murat's thundering charges, Augereau's roar of victory, Desaix and Muiron falling under a hail of Austrian fire, and shockheaded Berthier crouched over his maps and transmitting the General's orders to bring up the guns. But more insistent than any of these tugs on the memory was one of walking with young Bonaparte in the gardens at Montebello and watching the visionary weave his dreams. For it was here that the two gunners had first realized that if they believed in themselves everyone else would believe in them and a splendid future would take shape under their blades.

It was this memory which drew Auguste Marmont, the oldest friend of Napoleon, back to Italy and it was here, at the age of seventy-eight, that the last marshal of the Empire died.

He had survived his oldest colleague by one year. He had survived the young man who spun dreams by thirty-one years. To Marmont, dying in Venice, the dreams must have seemed more tangible than reality.

THE SOURCES OF THIS BOOK

EVERY fact in this book has been taken from some other book. An avalanche of memoirs followed the cessation of the Napoleonic wars. Almost everyone who held an important position with the Imperial Court wrote down his impressions and many of the old soldiers wrote books on the military aspects of the period. Some of these memoirs are absorbing, some accurate but dull, some lively but unreliable. Authors tried to justify their own behavior and almost every one of them had an axe to grind. I have been reading Napoleonic memoirs for over thirty years and it would be impossible to set down a comprehensive list of all the books and pamphlets I have used as a basis for this book. Such lists give the impression that the author is a scholarly fellow but they are of little interest to the general reader and mine would be incomplete. The best I can do, therefore, is to recommend a few of the sources to anyone who would like to know more of these remarkable men. Junot's wife, the Duchess d' Abrantes, wrote a witty and extremely interesting two-volume account of her life, and Bourienne, for a long time Napoleon's secretary, wrote a much longer account of the period as he saw it. Oudinot's wife wrote a faithful account and Marmont compiled his own justification. Among the first-class military material available the memoirs of Baron de Marbot is preeminent. Marbot was a staff officer of seven marshals and served in every campaign from 1800 to Waterloo. His book is an honest, exciting, and fascinating record of the wars. Equally enjoyable (although it covers only the Russian campaign) is that of Bourgoyne, a Sergeant of the Imperial Guard, and Ségur also wrote brilliantly of the Great Retreat. These books, and others, can be read in English. For the rest, there are literally hundreds of more modern books, many of them excellent reading, dealing with the period between 1789 and 1815. I have read a vast number of them and learned something from each. There is still, however, as much again to be learned and when he has been reading all his life the most diligent student will realize that he has only scratched the surface of the period 1789–1815.

INDEX